WHAT PEOPLE ARE SAYING

Rickardo has written a classic masterpiece. Clearly one of the most relevant, bold, thought-provoking, self-searching, self-discovering, soul-searching, well written, personally and professionally impactful, and highly researched leadership transformational books I have ever come across. Use it as a manual for life, and for for-profit and non-profit organizations. Get it and recommend it to others.

REV. SAMUEL RODRIGUEZ
Presidential Advisor
Pastor, New Season Church
President of the National Hispanic
Christian Leadership Conference

Superb leadership book!

MAJOR GENERAL VITO E. ADDABBO
United States Air Force

End the Reign of Pain: Identifying and Treating Toxic Leadership is a frank, straight-shooting, and comprehensive resource that hits a uniquely important issue facing too many churches today: toxic leadership. But the problem of toxic leadership in Christian communities and ministries is one that is complex, with many factors at play, including not just the leaders themselves, but also the system surrounding the leader that looks for such leaders.

Too many Christians today (for reasons both spiritual as well as psychological) are vulnerable to toxic leadership. Rickardo offers a clear, thorough, Scripture-grounded guide to identify many forms of toxic leadership, challenging many unhealthy belief patterns such as toxic masculinity along the way and encouraging leaders to develop skills and traits that are not only great for leadership, but also supportive of our spiritual maturity as well—traits such as empathy, character, self-awareness, and even physical health.

I especially appreciated his encouragement for leaders to consider counseling or psychotherapy if needed. Overall, a very practical and challenging resource.

DAVID C. WANG, TH.M., PH.D.
Cliff and Joyce Penner Chair for the Formation
of Emotionally Healthy Leaders
Fuller Theological Seminary
Editor, *Journal of Psychology and Theology*

Rickardo Bodden has written an important book with a goal of educating and inspiring people to create healthy workplace cultures. Since everything rises and falls on leadership, it behooves churches and organizations to identify and rid themselves of toxic leadership styles. This book can help!

DR. JOSEPH MATTERA
Presiding Bishop of Christ Covenant Coalition

Dr. Bodden takes readers on a provocative journey into the very real but darker side of leadership and humanity. As the book unfolds, self-examination will allow leaders at all stages of their careers to truly see themselves, ask tough questions, and make any needed adjustments to improve their lives and the impact of their leadership.

This book also offers readers a unique lens into accurately seeing toxic traits in the leaders around them. This view will allow readers the opportunity to pray for these leaders and avoid some of the toxicity. Readers can also identify the traits that support and empower these toxic leaders.

At the end of this revolutionary book, readers will find self-help lists. If readers take the time and do the work, they will find that this tool will improve all areas of their life. Being a healthy person (mentally, physically, and emotionally), allows each of us to become better leaders and followers.

DR. STACEY L. DUKE
Dean of Adult, Graduate, and Online Studies
Belhaven University

In this book, Dr. Rickardo Bodden addresses his concern relative to the toxic leadership environment that is plaguing our country. It is a serious concern that requires introspection, truthful and honest self-analysis, and a new and bold way forward. This book provides a roadmap for a surgical introspection for not only leaders but for those who desire to look deeper into their souls and ascertain who and what they really are. "What is your trajectory?" he asks. What is your fundamental reasoning that influences the basis of your decision-making process? Simply stated, what is at your core?

Dr. Bodden discusses major pitfalls that befall leaders these days. Hubris comes to mind and gives sway to the age-old adage that "Power and greed blinds the vision of men and drives sweet eyed Wisdom from Her Sacred Throne."

He offers the reader questions. And if answered honestly, you will come away with a good idea where you stand not only at work but also in your personal life. His intent in this book is to assess the whole man or woman and provide a path that will most assuredly produce a better fruit.

Dr. Bodden assesses the managerial ecosystem that involves both leaders and followers, emphasizing the importance of the social aspect of this ecosystem. One cannot survive or thrive without the other. He also dissects types of followers by assessing their level of engagement and the consequent impact they have on an organization.

Dr. Bodden also discusses the importance of critical thinking, and how it enhances one's understanding of the leadership phenomena.

I would recommend this book be included in any seminar, class, or discussion group that is concerned with leadership.

BILL PEGUES
Program Director (Retired)
Raytheon Technologies

The title and framing for Rickardo Bodden's book is provocative, indeed. Its design helps leaders and aspiring leaders understand the elements of bad leadership in ways that make it clear that such behavior is not so much a product of bad people, but most often reasonably well-intentioned, yet flawed, people with "blind spots." Fortunately, the good news is that by revealing areas that challenge leaders and as a result, those that they lead, people can be more equipped to build trusting, more resilient relationships based on the spiritual principles of love, compassion, empathy, and understanding made manifest. In an increasingly disrupted world where people are looking—often desperately—for answers from the most amplified voices or those with the most followers, the principles laid out by Bodden provide a roadmap to navigate these murky times to be the leader you want to—and that the world needs you—to be.

J. Johnson
Sr. Business Executive
Former Military Officer

Dr. Rickardo Bodden's book, *End the Reign of Pain: Identifying and Treating Toxic Leadership*, is in your face from the title to the conclusion. From chapter-to-chapter, Dr. Bodden challenges his readers to take a hard look at themselves. While dealing with the important topic of effective leadership from a biblical worldview, he considers our values and vices. We all have blind spots, and Dr. Bodden asks his readers to take a journey with him: a journey of self-reflection. I encourage you to read this book and invest in your personal development.

Dr. Joshua Henson
Associate Professor of Leadership
Southeastern University

Dr. Rickardo Bodden has boldly addressed the elephant in the room in our culture. An anxious world like ours is largely leaderless. We face crisis after crisis—environmental destruction, global pandemics, economic downturns, political polarization, and racial division—and we do so without leaders who focus on the common good. Instead, the leadership void is often filled by the power-hungry for whom self-interest dominates. They promise quick fixes to our problems to gain support, but they cannot deliver.

Instead, they use our anxieties to gain trust and advance their self-serving agenda. Bodden calls these people "toxic leaders." They are found in government, industry, the private sector, and churches. They poison and pollute their environment with their abusive leadership style. He draws a clear picture of such leaders, warns of their dangers, and offers a biblical-based pathway for those who choose to avoid following their example. This is a book that speaks to our times.

R. ROBERT CREECH, PH.D.
Director of Pastoral Ministries
Baylor University
George W. Truett Theological Seminary

The very title of this book immediately grabbed my attention and struck my curiosity. Yet, while delving further into the pages and content my curiosity turned into a deeper thought-provoking process. I have to say that there are numerous books written and published on leadership. In fact, I've written and taught on it over the years. Rickardo Bodden has a list of credentials from being a former military officer, to having earned degrees on leadership, as well as being an author, and much more. Yet, what is refreshing to me is that this book is not written by some ivory tower theorist, but from one who has the personal experience and insights to go with it.

Rickardo has truly taken on the challenge to address some very important and difficult aspects of what leadership is not and what leadership is or should be. If approached with an open heart it can be liberating to those who are willing to take a candid and honest read through the intensely thought-provoking pages. Of the many statements that caught my attention, this particular quote resonated: "Leadership is a social enterprise that involves other people. Leadership is not all about you as the leader." So true. Too often we think leadership is a title or some sort of hierarchal position of power. I appreciate how Rickardo confronts this, and redirects us to what leadership should actually be.

I'm also encouraged by how he is unafraid to utilize timeless and proven examples in scripture to give us a plumb line for what true leadership should be. In the volatile world in which we live, when too many are swayed by every societal pendulum swing, we are in great need for unwavering stability and groundedness. I doubt that most leaders set out to willfully fail, yet life has many unexpected detours and challenges that can cause us to get off course. I encourage you to take time to read through this book, take some honest reflection, and recognize where we may have become untethered from our moorings.

DR. DOUG STRINGER
Founder / President
Somebody Cares America
Somebody Cares Int'l.
Houston, Texas

Finally, a book that addresses the question, "As a leader, do I conduct myself in a manner that is destructive to those I lead, those I influence, and even myself?" In *End the Reign of Pain: Identifying and Treating Toxic Leadership,* Dr. Bodden powerfully explores the truth of why some leaders continue to inflict harm on their followers, families, and friends, even more so in these times of great temptations. Knowing oneself is critical to being an effective leader. This book takes the leader on a journey of spiritual and pragmatic self-reflection. After reading this book, the reader will clearly understand how to confront their inner darkness and understand what it means to lead people with dignity, respect, and honor and unlock one's true potential as a leader.

DR. DENNIS M. REILLY
Doctor of Strategic Leadership
MBA Program Director
College of Business
Castleton University

Rickardo Bodden is immersed in the world of leadership formation, and is profoundly adept in mentoring and coaching emerging leaders. His graduate work in Leadership Studies has provided him the opportunity to explore leadership in depth, and help us all to navigate the current turbulent waters that leaders find themselves having to sail in. His observations, insights, and concerns about the current crisis in leadership and the state of leadership are clear, concise, and compelling. In this book he endeavors to make us aware of the ways in which toxicity is ever a challenge for leaders in an age of transition and chaos. He painstakingly takes us as readers through a process to invite us both to self-awareness and self-examination, so that from a deep place of self-reflection, we might, with sobriety, approach the nature of and sources of toxicity, so that we can place needed boundaries in our lives to cause us to lead from a circumspect place of integrity and honor.

BISHOP MARK J. CHIRONNA
D.Min., Post-Graduate Researcher
Church On The Living Edge
Mark Chironna Ministries
Longwood, Florida

Dr. Rickardo Bodden brilliantly captures everything on leadership for personal, professional, and spiritual development. It is a great deal of information which will serve as the perfect guide as you encounter leadership challenges throughout life. This book really hit home for me. As I strive to become a better leader and help my team reach their own personal leadership goals, Dr. Bodden has given me practical steps to inspire and challenge myself and others to become effective leaders. Read this book, put this wisdom into practice, and you will be transformed into a genuine leader of people and self.

ANN-MARIE N. PADGETT
Regional President - Asia Pacific
Bechtel

This book is about more than just toxic leadership. The author's goal is to inspire reflection and develop self-awareness so that we can recognize and combat toxicity in every area of our lives—from parenting to our male/femaleness, even to our very souls and worldviews. His core idea is that the unaddressed inner life leads to toxicity; that we are all wounded and in need of healing. Of course, the stakes are higher the more influence you have, so it makes sense that leaders, even more than most people, should be working hard to combat toxicity at every level.

Warning: you are entering into challenging territory and this book will definitely challenge you. I felt like Dr. Bodden had his finger in my chest for most of our journey together. When one is in crisis mode, there's no time to be gentle. Seeing how rampant toxicity is in leadership these days, and how painful the consequences are for us as individuals and as a society, his tone is warranted!

There is a lot that this book has to offer as he draws from a wide variety of sources. The best part of the book, I think, is in chapter 5 where he describes how to grow in self-awareness. In this chapter, he also talks about why people continue to follow toxic leaders. Great stuff. Also, one of the best outcomes of Dr. Bodden's work is where he equips us to consider what we as followers and organizations might be doing to enable toxic leaders to continue in their toxic ways. Some of his best insights are in both chapter 5 and chapter 12 where he covers the topic of followership in some detail.

Overall, there's a lot here to recommend. This book is a worthy contribution to the leadership community! It should be read slowly, with a humble openness to being challenged, and reflecting deeply on one's life and leadership. Dr. Bodden is passionate, pointed, and very informative in his efforts to combat the toxic leadership that seems to be around every corner these days. Bring it!

JAY MOWCHENKO, D.MIN.
Paul E. Magnus Chair of Leadership and Management Studies
Briercrest Seminary

We have all known that toxic leader—you know the one who looked out for themselves and found everyone else expendable, and maybe they were so good at it you did not even notice the toxicity. Whether we were aware of it or not, we learned from them—how to lead or how not to lead. And at times we looked in the mirror and saw that it was us. These leaders damage others even if they are highly productive, even efficient, even rewarded and awarded. And yet they often leave a path of destruction. Dr. Bodden walks us through toxic leadership from a biblical perspective, guiding us to look introspectively and completely at who we are and who we ought to be. We all have opportunities to turn from—to grow—to be better. And even if you think you are a great—or even a good—leader, take this journey into toxic leadership. You will find conviction, confirmation, and maybe even some healing on your own path.

KATHLEEN PATTERSON, PH.D.
Professor
Director, Doctorate of Strategic Leadership Program
President, Regent Faculty Senate
Regent University School of Business & Leadership

Absolutely excellent! In his new leadership book, Dr. Rickardo Bodden speaks to the issues of failed leadership. He is calling those who lead to reflect a biblical standard of service and sacrifice in leading. This book is a candid, honest reflection of leadership flaws that need attention in our leadership service. It is both a call and a reminder to step up in our leadership efforts.

TOM LANE
Executive Leadership Institute
Gateway Church
Southlake, Texas

Healthy, godly leadership is needed now more than ever! Dr. Bodden exposes the multifaceted faces of toxic leadership while skillfully integrating how healthy leadership with a biblical approach should look. Dr. Bodden covers not only the professional life but also the personal, at times taking an in-your-face approach to help people be honest with themselves. In this book, one can expect to find research-based characteristics of toxic leaders and their behaviors. Just as important are the reflective questions Dr. Bodden has provided for the readers. This book is for both victims of a toxic leader as well as for toxic leaders who need to find a way into greater personal and leadership health. If you are looking for hope out of your current situation, this is a must-read!

LISA CHRISTENSEN, PH.D.
CEO, Leadership Coach, Deeper Wells Life & Leadership, LLC
Director of Transformational Leadership
Adjunct Research Professor
Barclay College, School of Graduate Studies

Colorless, odorless carbon monoxide poisoning (CO_2) from furnaces, stoves, or cars can kill you. So can toxic leaders—if you are trapped in their room. Dr. Bodden's book is your just-in-time CO_2 alarm system.

JAY GARY, PH.D.
Associate Professor of Strategic Leadership
Oral Roberts University

Dr. Bodden's perceptive and timely message calls us to attentively and authentically consider the leadership wake we leave or experience. God's design for leadership is anything but toxic, but God's people can easily pollute their roles and responsibilities without necessary raw and realistic reflection. This book is an indispensable diagnostic tool to assist us all in taking the next step in God's purpose to be a blessing to those we lead—from the home to the public square.

JOHN MABUS, D.MIN.
Moody Bible Institute of Chicago
Assistant Professor | Applied Theology and Church Ministries
Pastoral Studies Program Head

Many leaders in today's world seem to have their leadership based on a foundation of sand, and we all know that a house built on sand simply sucks. No one wants to live in a structure with a weak foundation, just like no one wants to work in a shifting leadership environment. Often, operating on a foundation of sand leads to sliding ethical standards and serious toxicity. Not only is this hard for employees to handle, it does not produce the quality output customers demand.

Dr. Bodden brings a fresh set of eyes to this age-old challenge of values-based leadership. He unapologetically tackles the hard issues facing leaders in the modern world and offers a prescription to solidifying the shifting sands and weak foundations many face. No matter how solid any of us thinks our foundation is, a careful and reflective read of this book will make it better. We owe this introspection to our employees and our customers, but more importantly . . . we owe it to ourselves.

COLONEL ROBERT FIRMAN
United States Air Force

The church has been full of leadership failures in the recent past. There is a need for a discussion of toxic leadership that this book fills. It is full of practical suggestions and discussions of the types of leadership and followership the church needs to avoid more failures. If one follows the advice given, the church will be in a better place.

DARRELL L. BOCK, PH.D.
Executive Director for Cultural Engagement, Howard G. Hendricks
Center for Christian Leadership and Cultural Engagement
Senior Research Professor of New Testament Studies
Dallas Theological Seminary

END THE REIGN OF
PAIN

IDENTIFYING AND TREATING

TOXC
LEADERSHIP

DR. RICKARDO BODDEN

End the Reign of Pain: Identifying and Treating Toxic Leadership
©2023 Rickardo Bodden

Scripture quotations marked (ESV) are from the ESV® Bible (The Holy Bible, English
Standard Version®), copyright © 2001 by Crossway, a publishing ministry of Good
News Publishers. Used by permission. All rights reserved.

Scripture quotations are taken from the Holy Bible, New Living Translation, copyright
©1996, 2004, 2007, by Tyndale House Foundation. Used by permission of Tyndale
House Publishers, Inc., Carol Stream, Illinois 60188. All rights reserved.

Scripture taken from the NEW AMERICAN STANDARD BIBLE®,
Copyright © 1960,1962,1963,1968,1971,1972,1973,1975,1977,1995
by The Lockman Foundation. Used by permission.

Scripture taken from THE HOLY BIBLE, NEW INTERNATIONAL VERSION®, NIV®
Copyright © 1973, 1978, 1984, 2011 by Biblica, Inc.™ Used by permission.
All rights reserved worldwide.

Published by Carpenter's Son Publishing, Franklin, Tennessee

Front Cover Layout by Michael Prince

Interior Design and Cover Layout by Suzanne Lawing

Edited by Robert Irvin

Printed in the United States of America

ISBN: 978-1-956370-00-3

In honor of:
Bruce A. and Sharon A. Haynes
The Late Bishop Isaiah S. Williams Jr. D.D., D.Min.
The Late Bishop Harry R. Jackson Jr.

FOREWORD

Rickardo has done an exemplary job of presenting a thorough study on proper leadership, but he does more than that! He covers every aspect of man's relationships, both personal and in business. He does not speak just from his opinions and understanding but quotes from the experts in various areas of life. He uses more than seven hundred references.

The author's passion is to help men and women reach God's standard for leaders so that they lead people with dignity, respect, and honor. I can identify with Rickardo's passion for leadership. I am a Bishop over about four thousand ministers, a fifty-person board of governors, and many spiritual sons and daughters. I have written fifteen books; three of them deal with proper leadership where character is more important than position or title. The standard which I set for leaders is what I call the 10 M's: Manhood, Ministry, Message, Maturity, Marriage, Methods, Manners, Money, Mortality, Motive. I challenge leaders with this illustration: visualize yourself hanging over a three-thousand-foot cliff in a basket being held by a ten-link chain. One of the links is paper thin and could break anytime. Would you brag about the nine that are in great shape and ignore the one that is about to break? As the old saying goes, "A chain is no stronger than its weakest link."

Rickardo summarizes in two paragraphs what he hopes to accomplish for those who read this book.

There is much talk in the leadership industry about motivating people and motivating followers. Leaders must first know what is motivating them. As leaders, be people-centered and not self-centered. Make an earnest effort to not allow the cracks in your character and wounds of your soul to bleed on the people you lead.

Leaders must deal with their trauma, not pass that trauma on, get their eyes off the "glory" and all they think it could bring, and put their eyes on their character, on how God wants them to lead. As a leader, you are the example. Never settle to live and lead while being toxic. It is time for you to take action to justify who you really are. A leader is called to live a high standard, raise up others to at least that standard, and accomplish goals.

Bless you, Rickardo, for taking the endless time and research in writing this book to bring these truths to this generation.

DR. BILL HAMON
Bishop of Christian International Ministry Network

CONTENTS

INTRODUCTION

You are beginning a journey that will transform you. Your eyes and heart will be opened. You will see your life and leadership differently than ever before. This book, your personal education and training manual, can impact every major area of your life. Its strong advice and instruction will make you a better leader, parent, sibling, employee, and even a better person.

This book is about toxic people, toxic behaviors, and ultimately toxic leadership. Have you ever worked for a bad leader? Why are so many people unhealthy in their thinking and relationships, have no boundaries, don't care about others, and are arrogant? Have you ever wondered why people aren't aware of the problems they cause and why they are causing them? Why are people so proud to be . . . wrong? Why isn't anyone holding these people accountable and showing them a better way to live, lead, and be?

It's time to confront the poor leadership behavior people get away with far too often. My goal is to address and help solve these problems.

This book is an intense transformational trip into your soul. It will help you deal with the "whys" behind the way you think and act. You will gain a better understanding of human behavior and what drives a person. The information here is provocative, challenging, revelatory, mind-altering, and downright life changing. Practice what is in this book and it will improve and mature you.

Get ready for some of the most impactful personal and profession-al leadership training you will ever receive. Your personal makeover starts now.

One

LET'S BEGIN: WHY TOXIC LEADERSHIP, AND WHY THIS BOOK?

Warning *These paragraphs reference factual events of sexual assault, drug use, and domestic violence.*

Guilty! That was the verdict. He was convicted of drugging and raping three women. Two of them were part of the organization he led.[1] One woman he picked up at a gym. He smoked meth with her, drugged her, and raped her.[2] The second woman: for her birthday he gave her a one-hundred-and-twenty-dollar gift, then drugged and raped her.[3] She was a virgin at the time she was assaulted. The third woman said she was babysitting when he came to her location and sexually assaulted her.[4] He used his position as a community leader to lure these unsuspecting women.[5]

According to the *Dallas Observer*, this "leader" received fourteen years in prison for one assault, ten for another, and fifteen for the third—all to be served concurrently (at the same time). He was fined $30,000.[6] He was married with children. By his wife's account he was verbally, emotionally, mentally, and physically abusive.[7] One time when she walked into their bathroom, without being provoked, he backhanded her so hard she fell into the tub.[8] In another incident she went to a friend's home, essentially to "clear her head" and think about her life situation.[9] This "leader," her husband, followed her there, entered the apartment, and dragged her down the interior apartment stairs with her head hitting each step, all while her friends watched.[10]

He also faced drug charges when police found drugs and drug paraphernalia in his car during an arrest.[11]

Would it surprise you to know this man, this "leader," was a pastor?

What about this guy? Ever hear of the drug company Retrophin? In 2018, the leader of that company was sentenced to prison for seven years for securities fraud connected to two hedge funds.[12] Investors were lied to about important information and the company's poor financial market performance.[13] The executive, also known as the Pharma Bro, was ordered by a judge to give back $7.4 million and pay a $75,000 fine.[14] But let's go back further. This man was also known for his extreme price gouging. In 2015 this "leader" and businessman, who led another company he founded called Turing Pharmaceuticals, raised the price of a drug he had control of more than 5,000 percent— from $13.50 per pill to a whopping $750 per capsule![15] That is toxic greed on steroids.

What is equally as concerning is the fact that toxic leadership doesn't just take place on a large scale like this.

Let's look at leaders in the home. Did your parents expect you to be perfect, always shield you from emotional pain and disappointment, invalidate your feelings, constantly make you feel guilty or guilt-trip you into doing things, or not support you emotionally? All of these parental actions can be considered toxic behaviors.[16]

It's easy to see that not all parents are good, and not all good parents do everything well. One father helped his son smoke weed.[17] You may not think that is so bad. No, it's worse. The kid was only five years old.[18] What a horrible example to follow. Or what about the father who had ten kids with eight women?[19]

A destructive, damaging, and damning way of thinking can run its way through entire families. In 2007 the Justice Department's Bureau of Justice determined that half of about 800,000 parents behind bars had a close relative who had been in prison.[20] That's no coincidence. Toxicity was shown and taught, perhaps not entirely unlike a parent teaching their child to tie their shoes.

Many of us do not realize the power of what somebody lives or models in front of a young child. A kid's life begins with the family even before the neighborhood, friends, or classmates have an influence.[21] For example, one family from Oregon had sixty family members who had either been incarcerated, placed on probation, or been on parole at one time or another.[22] Sixty! This family had members who had committed burglaries, armed robberies, kidnapping, and even murder.[23] One "leader" passed this lack of values on to the next, which passed it on to the next, which showed it to the next . . . and on and on the cycle goes.

All of these stories are just samples of various toxic "leaders." Ever wonder how these people got to the point where they made the decisions they did? What series of thoughts, choices, and actions lead them to being toxic?

This is why I wrote this book. Because of people like these. Because of people like *us*. Because of the pain bad leadership causes. Some of the leaders you just read about are at an extreme end of the spectrum. Many of us, hopefully, will never be there.

But what about those of us who are "in between"? You may not be as toxic as these people were, but are there some toxic things in you that need to be addressed? Are you like any of these people? A word of caution: don't just automatically answer no. Stop and think about it. Awareness is the first step. Are there issues in your soul that need to be identified, dealt with, and cleaned out? We will see. Keep reading.

Again, these people are the reason I wrote this book—at least part of the reason.

Honestly, this is all very concerning to me. It's important to see what can happen with a person who has power, authority, or money at their fingertips and yet is still not dealing with their personal faults, failures, vulnerabilities, and weaknesses. The damage a person can do when they are what I call "leading while toxic" can be hazardous to others and should concern you. It's about what is already in them or what they allow into their soul. It's how they allow their heart to be turned. It's like a person dealing with unaddressed psychological needs or unhealed trauma—almost like they are bleeding on other people with their issues. They are in charge, in some form or another, but not yet intentionally identifying and dealing with their own personal problems, issues that are yet to be nursed. They are *reigning*, but in error. They are leading, but doing it wrong. They are a supervisor or boss, but doing it badly. They are panderers and conduits of needless pain.

Some people are sick, really sick. I am not talking about legitimate mental health issues or being physically ill, but many are sick in their mind. They are twisted in their soul and how they perceive and treat people.

I wrote this book to cause you to think, to analyze how you live and interact with people. And most importantly to change the way you live your life and how you lead. It's time for a self-diagnostic journey into *you*. To think about what you are doing on your job, when you're home, and in your relationships. All can be equally significant and can influence the other.

In your lifetime you will weave in and out of being either a follower or a leader. It's inescapable, inevitable. (We will talk about followership in more detail later.) In other words, sometimes you'll be leading (intentionally or unintentionally) and sometimes you will not. Somewhere, sometimes, and in some places you will follow people and lead others. You will go from observing, listening, and patterning yourself after a parent, teacher, or hero to actually being one.

With that understanding, here are some personal questions to think about. Have you considered how you live your life, lead yourself, and lead other people? Has it occurred to you that there are some things about yourself that might need to change? Does your personal or professional leadership need improvement? To jar you a little, and to put it bluntly, are you a poor follower?

Years ago, I was speaking with a friend about people and their leadership. From that conversation, a jolting question came up that I will ask you. Does your leadership suck?

Really, does it? Do not get offended, angry, or upset. What is the impact of your leadership on others? How do you influence your organization or department on your job? Specifically, in what areas, or ways, can you improve? Have you ever thought some parts of your personality, life, and leadership needed an overhaul? Are you, basically, toxic?

I know that you might be thinking at this moment: *Really? Me? I couldn't possibly be that bad.* I want to be clear. There are parts of us that are imperfect. That is part of the human experience. However, if we don't want to be or stay toxic people, we have to hold ourselves accountable.

I think you may be surprised what you find about yourself when you read this book and take a thorough inner look at yourself, your actions, and your motives. Do you conduct yourself in a way that is debilitating to those you lead, those you influence, and even yourself? Before you are quick to answer, think with me for a bit.

When I ask, "Does your leadership suck?", I mean a range of words that include but are not limited to: bad, poor, subpar, pathetic, wicked, nasty, absolutely not to be followed or emulated, crummy, dissatisfactory, substandard, unacceptable, unsatisfactory, awful, horrible, needlessly painful and stressful, crappy, dark, immoral, unethical, deplorable, pitifully weak, toxic—and many more undesirable words.

The type of language used here is not meant to be lewd, crude, rude, disrespectful, or offensive. These descriptive terms are meant to be stark examples of what can be wrong with people's leadership and the negative effects they can have on the lives of others. It is self-improvement time, and I am happy to be your guide on this tour.

Pathetic leadership has been the demise of many people, families, businesses, and even nations. Lives are negatively affected. Many seem to accept that they have poor character or are a poor leader in significant parts of their lives and that they don't care to change, no matter the cost to themselves and others. That is pathetic.

I find it important to expend the time to inform people that they need to stop doing some things, to check what's motivating them to act, and to stop saying certain things. These are vital issues to contemplate.

Before I started writing, I mentioned the idea of this book to a friend. We ended up having a lively debate. She wanted to know why I would write a book on the poor side of leadership and not just focus on the positive.

The answers are quite simple and yet profound.

There are bad leaders. Bad, but still leading. Bad in one or more significant areas of their lives. People who are legitimately leading others, but guiding them in the wrong direction. They are . . . in error.[24] So it is my firm conviction that people need to be shown what bad leadership looks like. It's not just the extreme examples, but also what it looks like in everyday life. Why? For starters, it's important that you can identify and hopefully avoid such "leadership." Often in academic or learning areas, it is recommended that a person study the bad so it is not repeated. This is done so one can tell what is good or acceptable and separate it from the bad. Only the blissfully unaware think all leaders are good leaders or that to *be* a leader you are automatically a good one.

Not true. Not even close.

Consider these questions to more fully grasp the concept. If you have a severe injury or disease, would you place your trust in a medical doctor or medical treatment professional who only treats patients *who are relatively well*? To put it another way, would you trust a medical doctor who never studied, nor had much education about disease or injury at all? Seems nonsensical, right? You may even doubt that the person is a fully qualified medical doctor.

How about taking your only vehicle, which broke down and left you stranded on the side of the road with a smoking engine and red engine light on the dashboard, to a "mechanic" who only did routine maintenance like changing engine oil, refilling windshield washer fluid, and rotating tires? A mechanic who had no advanced, refresher, or continuing education. Would you fully trust this kind of car doctor with your vehicle's significant multipart and multisystem problems?

You probably would not trust either of the people in these two situations. I definitely would not.

I would not have complete confidence in a counselor or therapist who hasn't been educated on the negative aspects of abnormal human behavior and hasn't helped bring a person back to a healthier state of mind. In many areas of life we had better learn—and not *do*—the negative so we can accentuate the positive. We need to know the negative so as to not get twisted, turned, tarnished, and tattered by it. It is easier to make wiser decisions about alcohol, drugs, pornography, selfishness, procrastination, and other similar things because one can easily see the adverse impact those things have on others.

It is worth restating that you can more easily know the wrong when you have seen the right, and vice versa. *All leaders are not good leaders.* Every leader is not worth emulating. Ignorance is not bliss. You only identify what is wrong when the right—a desired standard—is understood.[25]

To balance perspectives, the study of the bad should go with the good. It's wise to evaluate how something with a problem is supposed to work so you can identify it and fix it when it's broken. Bad leadership is a real thing. How can we stop it if we refuse to see it and study it?[26] How can you identify and correct poor leadership if you never pay attention to it? Think of the word *troubleshooter*. Here's one of its definitions: a person skilled at solving or anticipating problems or difficulties.[27] What makes you skilled at solving problems is to know the right versus the wrong, the good versus the bad, the appropriate versus the inappropriate, and the acceptable versus the unacceptable.

Printed maps, GPS, and direction apps can help you get where you want to go. They can also tell you if you are going in the wrong direction and reroute you. That is another goal of this book. Consider this book your map. It's telling you where not to go and where not to stay. Studying the good and the bad (but not doing the bad) can enrich you. It can make you wiser and more effective in life and as a leader. This is very similar to fostering a heathy diet so you keep a healthy body. This well-rounded knowledge, when put into practice, will make you better.

A MATTER OF PERSPECTIVE

A person who is seemingly successful and in a high position does not necessarily indicate that person is exhibiting behaviors and character traits that should be repeated or duplicated. As I've said, not all leaders should be followed.

This book sheds light on the fact that leadership is not always positive and bright. There is often darkness. By darkness I mean inner urges, compulsions, and dysfunctions of our personality that, at times, go unexamined or remain unknown to us until we experience an emotional outburst.[28] It is also called darkness because we are unaware of it to some degree as it is masked, or hidden, lurking in the shadows of our personality.[29] These problems stem from the flaws of mankind. Contrary to what some may think, there are bad leaders who are often still "effective" in their positions. In light of that, bad leaders and leadership need to be studied so these behaviors and actions can be identified, corrected, and avoided.

The good news is there is hope. The endgame of this book is not only to educate but to inspire and be a catalyst for change. Learning from the bad can motivate you to move on to good, and better, actions. To encourage others to be positive role models. You will see there are some paths to success and effectiveness that are not to be followed. On this exploration, you will see characteristics in yourself and others. You will be convicted to change, motivated to act and think differently, and enlightened to live and lead in different ways. So again, ask yourself: does your leadership need improvement?

Being a bad leader, or exhibiting bad leadership, takes many forms. While you read, constantly search yourself to see if any of these characteristics lie within you, and how you most need to change. Secondly, notice if you identify these characteristics in others.

You should have your heart open to be arrested by truth and your thinking open to be expanded. Begin looking for your life and leadership skills to be heightened to a greater level of maturity. This book is also a helpful tool for those of you being groomed to be leaders and developing your giftings and abilities. Your detoxification, mind-elevating, and heart-changing experience has begun. And with this experience you will also gain *toxic intelligence*.

Several different kinds of intelligences exist; for example: contextual intelligence, emotional intelligence, social intelligence, cultural intelligence, and others.[30] Several of them may be defined as the ability or capacity to give you information, understanding, or skill. I want to propose a definition of toxic intelligence as the ability to perceive or understand how leaders' and followers' negative behaviors influence each other and the harmful effects organization-wide. This book will make you aware and familiar with good and bad leadership and followership.

LEADERSHIP DEFINED

Before you continue reading, for the context of this book, let's establish an understanding of what leadership is. *Leader* and *leadership* often mean different things to different people. Many times they are used interchangeably, but they also may have separate and distinct meanings.

Leadership is a three-part process. Leadership is a system made up of people, not a single person.[31] The first part is the *leader*, the second is the *follower* (the other person or people whom the leader must engage with in order to advance or accomplish his or her goals), and the third is the *context* within which both leaders and followers are necessarily situated.[32] You will see all three facets at play.

> Leader: leaders are responsible. By responsible, I also mean accountable and liable. Leaders are ultimately responsible for the effectiveness of their organizations.[33] For example, the leader is responsible for who is hired, the organization's goals and aspirations, working conditions, who has authority over whom, allocation of resources, transparency, ethical standards, etc.[34] The very best of our leaders serve as anchors and guides to inspire us and restore hope.[35] Leaders direct (focus) people's attention.[36] The leader, depending on the situation, is not always the person with a formal title or in the highest position.

> Follower: is a subordinate who has less power, authority, and influence than their superiors.[37] Followers usually do as they are instructed.[38]

> Context: has to do with the background or framework of a situation. It is important to understanding how, when, and why leadership does, or does not, take place.[39] Being a leader or follower means different things in different contexts.

> The nuances are different. Just think how the leader and follower circumstances change in these situations: your family, job, place of worship, and the organization you volunteer with. Also, factor in these contexts: time in history, religion, politics, technology, different countries and cultures, etc.[40]

Let's continue building the ideological and philosophical foundation of this book with chapters two and three.

NOTES

NOTES

Two

———

THE PAIN AND PROBLEM OF DIFFICULT PEOPLE

"If America is so good at developing leaders, then why is America a mess?" Karl Moore said.[41] That is a question worth scrutinizing irrespective of the fact the leadership industry was first conceived in the United States.[42] Dysfunctional leadership is happening in every sector of society: from government and banking to Hollywood moguls, church leaders, and everyone in between. Reports of scandals and abuse, predatory narcissism, toxic patriarchy where women are still marginalized, and the ongoing economic disparity in relation to race and leadership in every sphere of American society are the stuff of news headlines on a regular basis.

Leadership expert Barbara Kellermann said: "Put directly, the leadership industry, in collaboration with other institutions–including corporate America and, yes, academia–has managed to make becoming a leader a mantra. It is presumed a path to money and power; a medium for achievement, both individual and institutional; and a mechanism for creating change, sometimes, though hardly always, in the interest of the common good."[43] People who mainly think of leadership as a way to wealth and influence have the wrong outlook. If that is not bad enough, for many, there is no real contingency plan for stopping or slowing the progress of a bad leader.[44] I will do my part to address that narrative. Today, leadership is much less a function of title and more about effectiveness and ethics.[45]

Let's look at some ageless information that can give us tools to change ourselves and properly lead others. One of the foundational motivations for this book can be found in the greatest book: the Bible . . . also referred to as the Scriptures. Wait! Don't close this book and put it away because you do not consider yourself "religious," a Christian, or biblically spiritual. Regardless of whether you are a follower of Christ or not, the leadership principles, overall philosophy, and rationale extracted from the Scriptures can result in eye-opening, transformative, and lifelong leadership guidance that can influence you, your family, and your organization. So keep reading, and let's search some truths from one of the most well-known and bestselling books of all time.

We begin our expedition with 2 Timothy 3:1-5 (ESV). This list is extremely telling about the types of people we will have to deal with.

> But understand this, that in the last days there will come times of difficulty. For people will be lovers of self, lovers of money, proud, arrogant, abusive, disobedient to their parents, ungrateful, unholy, heartless, unappeasable, slanderous, without self-control, brutal, not loving good, treacherous, reckless, swollen with conceit, lovers of pleasure rather than lovers of God, having the appearance of godliness, but denying its power. Avoid such people.

Because this excerpt is so important for our understanding of toxic people and leadership, let's look at this same quote again in the New Living Translation.

> You should know this . . . that in the last days there will be very difficult times. For people will love only themselves and their money. They will be boastful and proud, scoffing at God, disobedient to their parents, and ungrateful. They will consider nothing sacred. They will be unloving and unforgiving; they will

slander others and have no self-control. They will be cruel and hate what is good. They will betray their friends, be reckless, be puffed up with pride, and love pleasure rather than God. They will act religious, but they will reject the power that could make them godly. Stay away from people like that!

Another way you could read verse one is: Know this, that in today's times (or in times like these), life will be difficult, because you will have to deal with difficult people.[46] Notice "difficult times" and its direct connection to verses 2-5, wicked people. It should be an obvious conclusion that many of these people will be, well . . . *people* of all types: coworkers, family members, supervisors, friends, leaders, followers, associates, team members, etc. These kinds of people end up in all walks of life and positions.

CONTEXT

But before we continue discussing 2 Timothy 3:1-5, let's understand the context for the use of this text. This book of 2 Timothy was written by Paul to his mentee and emerging leader, Timothy. Paul was a Jew with a starred background. Before his belief in and name-changing encounter with Christ, he was formally known by the name of Saul.[47] He was a Pharisee and the son of a Pharisee—a well-known and influential Jewish sect.[48]

The unconverted Saul zealously, passionately, and consistently persecuted Christians.[49] Besides supporting their arrests, he even had a hand in murdering them.[50] He was a Greek by culture, an intelligent scholar, and a Roman citizen.[51] After Paul's conversion to be a disciple, Christ eventually appointed and sent him out to be a key leader, an apostle, to train up and establish His church at large. Paul's work is significant and manifold as a theologian, missionary, discipler, teacher, mentor, father figure, church planter, pastor, overseer, and martyr.[52]

Writing letters was one of Paul's many talents and responsibilities, and he eventually gave us many of the letters (or books) of the Bible, including 1 and 2 Timothy. In these letters, Paul instructs Timothy on the doctrine of the local church, which includes topics of responsibilities of leaders, administration, and other activities.[53]

Timothy was like a son to Paul. [54] He was influenced by Paul's ministry and accompanied him on his missionary and apostolic mission to strengthen, grow, and establish the church.[55] Timothy was Paul's right-hand man.[56]

Specifically, in the 2 Timothy letter, Paul's chief concern is for Timothy and for the success of his leadership and ecclesiastical work in a place named Ephesus.

BACK TO 2 TIMOTHY 3

In 2 Timothy chapter 3, Paul is partly warning Timothy of the vanities, consuming greed, shame, and violence that is often concealed . . . but capable of being discovered in others.[57] Paul was warning Timothy, like I am warning you in this book now. Notice Paul's comment on the "last days." Isn't it interesting that he wrote that comment to Timothy and it's still appropriate today? I will not get into all the different ways to interpret the *last days,* whether it means we are on the brink of the end of the world or metaphorically meaning the world is always passing away in light of the world that's promised to come.[58] As Professor Emeritus Thomas G. Long said, it almost doesn't matter.[59]

Paul is using this apocalyptic, or revealing and unveiling, language to get Timothy's (and now your) attention.[60] I liken it to Martin Luther's comment he made about Germany: "The world is the Devil's, and the people in it have become pure devils."[61] He also said that accursed greed and usury have utterly destroyed Germany.[62] This he said after observing Europe's changing economy.[63] He noticed old relationships were breaking down and replaced with selfishness, profit motive, and money being bought and sold by lenders at extortive rates of interest.[64] Any of this sound familiar to what's happening now or has happened in recent history? It should.

My concern is Paul's understanding of "times of difficulty," which clearly are present in every generation since the days of our human origins. This is quite a list and covers a wide spectrum of unhealthy behaviors that reveal in a very clear way how deep our alienation and estrangement is from our own call to truly be the humans we were designed to be. To say the least, Paul is describing profound toxicity here. There are nineteen things that Paul says are extremely toxic!

Scholar Luke Timothy Johnson refers to it as a *vice list*.[65] The proper way to read the list is not to obsess over each individual element, but to evaluate their overall impact.[66] The impact on themselves and others. The perpetrators or the offenders and the victims. What has been their impact on you? Besides the people, these are the traits that Timothy is to avoid in his own character and behavior.[67] Paul was forming Timothy's character, his inner life.[68] This was important instruction for Timothy, because as Paul's representative, he was responsible to role model the moral teacher and leadership in the communities where Paul sent him.[69] In a somewhat similar fashion, this book is also a character-forming tool for you.

THE SOURCE OF PERSONAL TOXICITY

In my communication with author and theo-semiotician Mark Chironna, he says dysfunction is ever-so-prevalent in the human condition . . . none of us, not even the best of leaders, arrive at adulthood without some level of wounding.[70] Entering into adulthood wounded, all of us, whether we are leaders or followers, need healing. The late Frederic Hudson, one of the premier voices in the coaching profession, and founder of The Hudson Institute of Santa Barbara, makes this profound statement regarding the wounds we incur in life:

> The slings and arrows suffered during the adult years – and earlier – may leave festering wounds from having been neglected, betrayed, abandoned, abused, wasted, rejected, or shamed. The wounds may stem from personal attitudes as well as the actions of others . . .[71]

The nature of human existence is all of us carry various degrees of wounding.[72] All leaders, who exhibit all sorts of dysfunctions, if they have not addressed their own issues prior to coming to a place of power and prestige—all of this is the very basis for toxicity in leadership and followership.[73] The good news is Jesus did not come to add to the toxicity already present in the world. He came to provide a solution to the toxicity that was present since time began, when what was once pristine and innocent was lost by man's choices that led to perverse power inequities and abuse.

Chironna reflected on the importance of comments made by psychotherapist Dr. James Hollis—we learned as children that we were quite little and that the "big people" had all the power.[74] Some of those "big people" were harsh and abusive in their power and taught us that not only did we not have power, but we had to fear power in order to survive and do whatever those in power told us.[75] Chironna believes we have all developed a relationship with power, and we have deep-rooted ways in which we are conditioned to respond to it. Believe it or not, that deep-rooted conditioning is often tied to fear-based avoidance patterns.[76] Jesus, the One who shows us what it means to be human, truly human, and what is means to actually lead in relation to love and self-sacrificial service, wants to free all of us from the fear-based mechanisms that cause us to develop strategies of avoidance and compliance, or just plain bad leadership all around. It's all toxic!

I believe the source of these ways of thinking and beliefs ultimately can be found in mankind's selfish nature and rebellion toward God. In other words: sin.[77] Sin can be defined and explained in several ways. Here are a few. According to Merriam-Webster's online dictionary, sin is defined as an offense against religious or moral law, an action that is or is felt to be highly reprehensible, a fault, a transgression of the law of God.[78]

A direct translation from the Greek language, sin can also be described as: an offense; to miss the mark, to err, to miss or wander from the path of uprightness and honor, to do or go wrong, to wander from the law of God, that which is done wrong, a violation of the divine law in thought or act.[79]

Chironna postulates that our problem is this thing called sin, which implies a deep wound in us that leads to estrangement from God, self, others, and our purpose. All of which leads to not only dysfunctional ways of living, but dysfunctional ways of thinking. The late theologian Paul Tillich wrote, sin is the great all-pervading problem of our life.[80] He suggested another way to interpret sin is: separation.[81] This stems from man's original separation from God.[82] That sin is not so much about immoral acts, but before sin is an action, it is a state of being.[83] Think about it. Have most of the corrupt behaviors and hard-hearted actions you have done occurred because you were separated from who you were really designed to be by God? If you look deeper, you may see the same is true for others.

Tillich mentioned a famous German philosopher who said: we are almost always ready to abuse everybody and everything, although often in a very refined way, for the pleasure of self-elevation, for an occasion for boasting, and for a moment of lust. To know that we are ready is to know the meaning of the separation . . . and of sin abounding.[84]

JOHN'S PERSPECTIVE

Let's look at another small section of Scripture as we link together more insights about the pain and problems of difficult people. I think Paul writing to Timothy, in 2 Timothy 3, is well connected to what John wrote in 1 John 2:15-17 (NASB):

> Do not love the world nor the things in the world. If anyone loves the world, the love of the Father is not in him. For all that is in the world, *the lust of the flesh and the lust of the eyes and the boastful pride of life*, is not from the Father, but is from the world. The world is passing away and also its lusts; but the one

who does the will of God continues to live forever. [Emphasis mine]

The New Living Translation gives us verse 16 in this way: "For the world offers only a craving for physical pleasure, a craving for everything we see, and pride in our achievements and possessions . . . "

BACKGROUND FOR 1 JOHN

John was an apostle and one of the original twelve disciples handpicked by Jesus. When originally penned by John, he wrote this letter about the concern of false teachings he knew about in the realm of Christian doctrine and ethics.[85] Specifically the problem of Gnosticism, which then was beginning to be a formalized system of teaching.[86] This false teaching taught that only spirit was good and matter was evil, and that one must free themselves from the material world and be occupied alone with spirit.[87] Gnostics wanted to obtain so-called superior knowledge by learning the mysterious secrets of the universe.[88]

BACK TO 1 JOHN 2:15-17

John wrote a warning, a strong warning against worldliness.[89] In 1 John 2:15, "Do not love the world" means we must not have the wrong affection for the anti-God culture that permeates society.[90] We must not take pleasure in the bad parts of culture nor take on perverted ways of thinking and acting.[91] Loving the corrupt and immoral world's ways is really misplaced affection. You are liking and wanting the wrong things.

The world is described in terms of the lusts and desires it stirs up: the lust of the flesh, the lust of the eyes, and the pride of life.[92] John is saying it is a matter of what a person wills, desires, wants, and trusts.[93] It's not about specific things a Christian should abstain from or condemn, but more so about the direction of their own desires and will.[94]

Notice John's strategic rejection of loyalties to characteristics of the world that would compromise devotion that belongs to God alone.[95] I hope you are realizing this simple truth—that people who have their core attention, affections, desires, and interests in the wrong areas, can add to or enable them to become more toxic.

Are you understanding the importance of John's warning? Dr. Robert Yarbrough, author of a commentary named *1—3 John*, stated that the lust of the flesh, the lust of the eyes, and the pride of life are a diabolical triad, an unholy trinity, and a toxic mix of poisons that destroys.[96] Let's briefly go over each one.

Lust of the flesh: what the body craves or yearns for.[97] The word flesh here means your self-centered human nature, not a specific reference to sexual desire.[98] If you get in touch with your own heart and understand your desires, both ordinate and inordinate, then you will know the driving force in your life that you have to contend with and learn how to regulate.[99]

Lust of the eyes: what the eyes itch to see.[100] It is the desire for what you see.[101] The eyes with the design and capacity for good can also serve evil ends.[102] The lust of the eyes can be compared with moral short-sightedness and moral bankruptcy of a spiritually blinded heart.[103] When John speaks of the desire of the eyes, certainly that seems to speak of the places where we place our attention, focus, and observation. Scripture does talk about the eyes in several ways. For example, eyes can be "haughty."[104] If our eyes are "haughty," what does that say about the state of our heart and the motives that flow from it? That could indeed be toxic.[105] If the love of God isn't perfected in me, and I am spiritually immature, my eyes are going to wander in all sorts of inappropriate places.[106]

Pride of life: what people toil to acquire.[107] This is about external expressions of a braggart's overconfidence and vain pursuit of earthly goods.[108] Again, it seems that John is offering an awareness of the toxicity of being presumptuous and overconfident. This is all too common in toxic leadership.

Leaders, the world and its ideologies are not passive, but compete for the allegiance of every person.[109] John warns people in verses 15-17 to watch out for the toxin of everyday self-centeredness that will cloud your life.[110]

When you put the flesh and selfishness in charge of your life and have no overall guiding principles (like God and His Word), you can easily focus nearly entirely on yourself and believe the world is revolving around you. You become your own god. You think you are the king, lord, judge, jury, and executioner, and other people are just stepping-stones, mere gofers, by-products to be used for your own selfish personal fulfillment.

You have no North Star, or at least not a good one. The North Star is the star of the northern hemisphere toward which the axis of the earth points.[111] The term also means a beacon of inspiration and hope.[112] It is what the trajectory of your life is based on. When you need counsel, direction, and encouragement, you look to your North Star. Self, your carnal nature, should not be your North Star. It should be Jesus Christ.

You must constantly check what's motivating you to do or not do something. Especially when you do not want to do the right thing. With the North Star comes accountability and a standard you are supposed to follow. In modern terminology, a personal North Star can be compared to your GPS or the preferred app you use to get directions.

Who or what is your North Star?

REUNION

The good news is since separation from God, sin, and the self-centeredness that closely follows are sources of personal toxicity, we have access to something greater. It is reunion . . . also known as grace. Grace is reunion, reconciliation, and acceptance all connected together.[113] Since sin separates you from God, grace is the call to reunion with God. Let's look at a couple verses of Scripture that Paul wrote to a select group in Rome.[114]

Romans 5:20-21 (NLT): God's law was given so that all people could see how sinful they were. But as people sinned more and more, God's wonderful grace became more abundant. So just as sin ruled over all people and brought them to death, now God's wonderful grace rules instead, giving us right standing with God and resulting in eternal life through Jesus Christ our Lord.

The word *law* in Romans 5:20 is referring to the Torah, which is the first five books of the of the Old Testament: Genesis, Exodus, Leviticus, Numbers, and Deuteronomy. The Torah begins with the re-telling of the ancient stories of creation, revealing that all things came into existence by the One God who revealed Himself to a particular people at a particular time to ultimately manifest Himself, and would heal all of humanity from its profound toxicity.[115] Paul contrasts law and grace so we come to realize who we are, whose we are, and how we are to become.[116] Grace trumps sin. Reunion outdoes and outmaneuvers separation.

The simple words of sin and separation, grace and reunion are not as important as your response to them.[117] What parts of your life have you kept from God and what parts do you think you have given over? Consider these words from Tillich.

In grace something is overcome; grace occurs "in spite of" something; grace occurs in spite of separation and estrangement. Grace is the reunion of life with life . . . Grace is the acceptance of that which is rejected. Grace transforms fate into a meaningful destiny; it changes guilt into confidence and courage. There is something triumphant in the word "grace": in spite of the abounding of sin grace abounds much more.[118]

It would seem that Tillich wants us to understand that Paul offers us a path to wholeness and well-being. As leaders, we need to understand our shortcomings in light of 2 Timothy 3:1-5 and 1 John 2:15-17. Often, we need to deal with our own conditions while at the same time dealing with others with their own unique circumstances.

We must understand avenues of grace, help, and assistance to move from one level of maturity to the next.

THE SUMMARY

Toxic behavior is evident in so many ways, not only in these passages we have looked at, but also in contemporary culture and contemporary leadership. It is present in men and women of every tribe, race, kindred, and tongue, because we are all fundamentally flawed and in need of healing by the presence and power of God. We cannot afford to ignore these realities as we move forward into the major changes we are facing in the twenty-first century age of rapid change and uncertainty. Even worse, many do not care how they live out their lives and how they influence and impact others. People should not think in these ways, especially leaders.

If we ignore these things we will become increasingly ignorant of how to resolve the crisis in leadership we are facing. Thinking and willing is not enough. Something radically transforming has to take place at our core. Yes, these are difficult times. Yes, there are toxic leaders. Yes, there are wolves in sheep's clothing. They aren't just in one sector of society, they are everywhere. We need to know what difficult people, bad thinking, and poor behavior looks like in and out of the home, workplace, church, or in other organizations.

We have to be responsible for who we are and who we lead. The place from which we lead internally is what matters. Our genuine sense of self has to be rooted and grounded in love, and for me that is the self-sacrificial love of God as revealed in Jesus.

After reading 1 Timothy 3:1-5 and 1 John 2:15-17, does anything stand out to you about *you*? What behaviors look most familiar to what you do? What mindset and affections do you wrestle with? Do not think about others such as your family members, supervisor, or coworkers yet. Consider yourself first.

The Scripture passages we reviewed are like an inspection checklist. When a pilot prepares to fly a jet or a surgeon performs a surgical procedure, both use a checklist as a part of their normal operating practices to identify tasks that may need to be reviewed or performed.[119] So . . . how is your personal toxic checklist looking so far? What if we made our personal checklist rooted in the ethics of Jesus, Paul, John, and the other New Testament voices that offer us a way forward in difficult times? Are you seeing too many confirmed appearances of bad behaviors based on the Scriptures provided?

To put the above Scriptures in visual perspective, see Figure 1. It shows the correlation between the toxic mindset and behaviors.

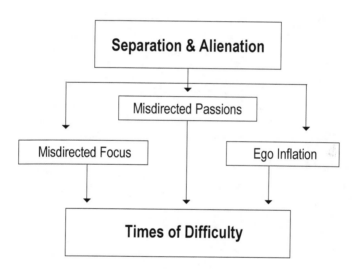

Figure 1: The connection between a person's separation and alienation, their desires, and today's times of difficulty.[121]

NOTES

Three

WHAT KIND OF PERSON ARE YOU?

I need all of us to think about some things. Who are *you*? Have you ever asked yourself this question? What do you stand for or fall for? What is your personal code? Do you *have* a personal creed or philosophy? What kind of person do you think you are, and what kind do you want to become? The answers to these questions are important because they can reveal where you are at this point in your life and what may become your life trajectory.

Ever wonder why so many companies have a code of conduct, ethical guidelines, list of core values, or credo? They have them because the codes and values are a way to tell their employees: this is the way they are to behave and these are the standards by which their actions will be judged. They are giving their employees a North Star to follow. If they are not followed, there are, often, negative consequences. So let's engage in yet another round of self and life reflection.

WHAT IS MY NATURE: NATURAL, SPIRITUAL, OR CARNAL?

Are you a person who thinks and lives by a natural, spiritual, or carnal nature? Which one of these three do you allow to be the most dominant in your life? Which one is controlling you? What are the main influences that drive your thoughts and actions? Let's consider 1 Corinthians 2:14-16, 3:1-3 (NASB).

> But a *natural person* does not accept the things of the Spirit of God, for they are foolishness to him; and he cannot understand them, because they are spiritually discerned. But the *one who is spiritual* discerns all things, yet he himself is discerned by no one. For who has known the mind of the Lord, that He will instruct Him? But we have the mind of Christ.

> And I, brothers and sisters, could not speak to you as spiritual people, but *only* as *fleshly, as to infants in Christ*. I gave you milk to drink, not solid food; for you were not yet able *to consume it*. But even now you are not yet able, for you are still fleshly. For since there is jealousy and strife among you, are you not fleshly, and are you not walking like *ordinary* people? [Emphasis mine]

In 1 Corinthians 2:14-16 you see Paul identify two of the three kinds of people. Or rather, two kinds of inner natures or states of mind. Let's start with describing the natural man. The best definition of this kind of man is *animal*: being like or living like an animal, the sensuous nature, like a brute.

The natural person does not pay attention to the spiritual things of and about God; he or she considers them foolishness. The natural person is only concerned with his or her own desires for things like eating, drinking, sex, and money. They have no spiritual understanding. This person probably doesn't pray to God, and they have no relationship with God. They choose not to believe in Him and are caught up in other simple, natural things. It's really a lower nature of thinking and allowing their appetite to rule. Have you ever tried to speak to others about God and they have no clue what you are talking about? They think things like prayer, worship, and trusting God are silly and absurd. This could be because they are only thinking with a natural mind. These kinds of people are ruled by their stomach, impulses, appetites, desires, and selfish perspectives. By definition, they are like mindless, instinctive animals. They can be violent, lack compassion, and don't make wise decisions. The spiritual person knows God is real. They know the spiritual world is real and know they can worship and be used by God to do His will for their life. He or she serves or operates as God's instrument and is filled with and governed by the Spirit of God. The spiritual person prays, thinks, considers, discerns, and asks questions of all things to make the right or best decisions.[122]

As Paul goes on in chapter 3 of this letter he mentions the third kind of nature, the carnal or fleshy person. Carnal means consisting of the flesh, *wholly given to and rooted in the flesh*. A carnal person actually intentionally or unintentionally combines the natural and spiritual natures. For example, the carnal Christian has an understanding about God and has even chosen to follow Him to a degree. However (overall, or in specific areas of their life), they are fleshy, immature, and childish. They try to enjoy their basic animal-like nature with the motivations of their stomach while they try to connect with God and be spiritual. You should never be comfortable being carnal.

This person is influenced to do or not do something if it impacts him or her in a negative way. They focus on *self*. Their hallmark is immaturity. They are childish.

Think about a carnal Christian or a carnal person like a fruit tree that doesn't bear any fruit. Or like trying to bake a cake, but it has been taken out of the oven too soon. Instead of a fully formed cake, you have hot batter. Consider a person who has a lead position in an organization, but this person controls their department as if it's for their own personal use. Carnal people are the ones who are married but still flirt with others. They are adults but throw temper tantrums like children. This is the person who does whatever nonsense they want to do and is quick to say, "Only God can judge me," when they really mean, "Leave me alone and be quiet so I can sin in peace."

Again, the carnal Christian is trying to mix both the godly and ungodly worlds. It's like a person who is supposed to be mature and pay their taxes but deliberately lies to pay less when it is time to file their taxes. It's like a Christian leader saying they stand for biblical values in their personal and professional life, but behave in ways not consistent with their faith. They profess Christ but do not look like Him in their actions.

To reiterate, which of these three natures reflects you the most? What are you motived by? What controls you? Which nature is most dominant or rules you? What is the thing or things that influence you the most? If you are heavily influenced by others, then what is influencing them?

You should not allow yourself to be ruled by the god of self, the god of your feelings, the god of your stomach, or the god of your unrestrained appetites and desires. Have there been areas that you have deliberately kept from God's control?

Now the foundation of this book has been laid. Let's keep building on it by focusing on the specific aspects of toxic leadership.

NOTES

NOTES

Four

—

WHAT DOES IT MEAN TO BE TOXIC?

The title of this chapter provides yet another self-examination question. An opportunity to look inward, much like a forensic technician researching, gathering, and analyzing evidence. Are you a toxic person? Are there parts of you that are seriously toxic? Are there parts of your personality and character that are injurious to yourself or others?

Being a toxic individual or having toxic traits affects all kinds of people in all walks of life. Some synonyms of the word toxic are harmful, deadly, noxious, poisonous, and venomous, to name a few.[123] The word toxic, according to the online Merriam-Webster dictionary, means containing or being poisonous material especially when capable of causing death or serious debilitation, exhibiting symptoms of infection, extremely harsh, malicious, or harmful.[124]

Not sure what a toxic person looks like? I'd like to present some of Jean Lipman-Blumen's perspectives on the qualities or characteristics of toxic leaders.[125] Remember, toxicity can be in anyone: from the old to the young; from the person who supervises one person to an executive director, president, and chairman of the board of directors. From a parent working a part-time home-based business all the way up to one who leads a multinational nonprofit, or a church overseer. Even your dear grandmother or doting father can be toxic.

LIPMAN-BLUMEN'S LIST OF TOXIC PERSONAL QUALITIES[126]

- Lack of integrity: marks the leader as cynical, corrupt, hypocritical, or untrustworthy

- Insatiable ambition: prompts leaders to put their own sustained power, glory, and fortunes above their followers' well-being

- Enormous egos: blinds leaders to the shortcomings of their own character

- Arrogance: prevents acknowledging mistakes, which leads to blaming others

- Amorality: makes it nearly impossible for the person to discern right from wrong

- Avarice: drives leaders to put money—and what money can buy—at the top of their priorities

- Reckless: disregard for the costs of their actions to others and themselves

- Cowardice: the leader shrinks from difficult choices

- Failure: unsuccessful to understand relevant problems and to act competently and effectively in leadership situations

These attributes could make a person even worse if combined in part, like small clusters, or grouped together.[127] Notice the similarities between 2 Timothy 3:1-5, 1 John 2:15-17, and how they are reflected in Lipman-Blumen's list of toxic characteristics. Do you see any similarities to traits in yourself?

Organizations can be toxic too. This should be obvious because of the septic nature of the people who lead them. You may have heard of the Wells Fargo Bank scandal. In 2016 the bank's toxic environment was exposed for its cross-selling tactics and intense pressure for its employees to achieve unattainable targets.[128] Since 2011, without their customers' knowledge or consent, employees created millions of unauthorized bank and credit card accounts.[129] The fake accounts added capital for the bank, which allowed employees to boost their sales figures and, as a result, earn more money under the bank's compensation structure.[130] An examination concluded Wells Fargo's sales practices were unethical, caused harm to consumers, and that management had not responded promptly to address these issues.[131]

Interesting, isn't it? It's uncanny how people can be so capable in some areas, and thus get promoted to such high levels of trust and authority, and in other areas of their life they are exploiters and even like vultures. Let's look at more characteristics often found in toxic people or leaders, as noted by Kenneth O. Gangel.[132] Do you know people who possess these traits? Do you have them?

- Deceptive leader: besides dishonesty, and deceiving and misleading people, the deceptive play people against one another and break up work teams so the power stays in the grip of the leader. Also, to keep power, the leader may create an environment of fear because they fear losing power themselves. A biblical example of a deceptive leader is found in Genesis 29:18-28. A man named Laban tricked Jacob into marrying the wrong woman.

- Overly controlling leader: leaders who desire full and total control of everything. These kinds of people are micro-managers, dictators, and overly ambitious.

- Egotistical leader: narcissists make it into this category. The arrogant, high-on-self, and high-on-their-own-ego kind of person. The person who is overly concerned with themselves to the exclusion of or harm to others.[133] Other types of egotistical people are the selfish, self-centered, and, in general, those who exaggerate their own sense of self-importance.[134]

- Cruel leader: these individuals create an environment of fear by the way they behave and treat others. The *Huffington Post* stated that cruel leaders inspire hatred because they are entirely focused on themselves and use other people to get what they want.[135] They take opportunities that could be used to inspire others to be great, then waste them by being ruthless.[136]

- Evil leader: human evil is defined as the deliberate harming of people by other people.[137] These wicked people create conditions that, in a physical or psychological way, destroy or reduce people's quality of life; i.e., their sense of self-worth, happiness, and ability to fulfill their basic material needs.[138] Evil people are basically all about intentionally harming others.[139]

- Demanding leader: the issue with demanding people is they often require too much, too soon from the people they require work from.[140] Demanding, or demandingness, can also be referred to as behavioral control.[141]

- Reckless leader: Gangel primarily refers to this kind of a leader as just plain lazy. This person knows what to do but simply refuses to do it. This is toxic because laziness creates a barrier that prevents other motivated people from accomplishing tasks or organizational goals. Lazy people slow down or stop organizational goals or the goals of others from being accomplished.

One reason I wanted to display Gangel's list of toxic leaders is so you see the similarities and interconnection of the venomous characteristics people can display. This, of course, is not an exhaustive list, but it does show some of the common ways toxic sourness is manifested through people. If any of these traits resemble you, remember that *you can change.*

WHAT LOOKS GOOD MIGHT BE BAD

Do you often think that because a person looks organized, speaks well, knows how to make money, has a charismatic personality, is physically attractive—or some combination of the above—that he or she must be a good person and have strong ethical character? If a house looks good and has great aesthetics (freshly painted, fine cabinetry, Italian marble countertops, European tile, hand-cut hardwood floors, etc.), that alone does not mean the foundation is good. It can still be cracked and grossly flawed underneath the visible surface. If that's the case, then all those fine things built atop it are in trouble. Stop thinking that just because something looks good, it *is* good. Looks do not reveal character. Great skills and abilities do not automatically mean you can trust the quality of a person's character. Your thinking that it does is equal to you eyeing a nice-looking car and assuming it has a reliable engine. In short, this is not a good way of thinking.

Think about it. How many wealthy people who seem to have it all have addictions and terrible family situations? How many times have you seen news stories or documentaries about the mass murderer next door? Again, just because something looks good does not mean it *is* good. There are plenty of foods that look and smell great that should not be eaten often, or perhaps not at all.

Consider your personal situation. You can appear as though you have it all together on the outside but have great insecurities, immaturity, and a bevy of internal issues taking place in your soul. You have to admit that many times your outward appearance and expression do not match what the inside of you is truly feeling.

Many of us wear invisible masks. We veil ourselves and try to watch our speech so others do not see the toxicity oozing from our lives like pus from an infected sore or wound. Can you see this mental image?

Many of us are like dirty bowls. Think of going to someone's home or a restaurant and eating out of a bowl. At the end of your meal there are usually leftover food particles that dry and stick to the bowl. If the bowl is not cleaned well and the remaining food residue isn't noticed, that same bowl is likely going to be used to serve other people. When used to serve someone else's meal, on top the food may look good, but on the bottom there are the leftover remnants that should have been washed away. Many of our lives can too often be like those bowls. Always taking on more and more without the inside being properly cleaned.

I need you to own this inner personal evaluation we are going through right now. It is too easy to say, "Well, no one is perfect. We are all toxic to some degree, because no one is flawless." That sounds like a cop-out and a nice way to completely avoid taking personal responsibility. You have to put in the work to be better so you can better and more positively influence others. Personal leadership should be in place first, because self-leadership is the basis for all *true* leadership.

DESTRUCTIVE LEADERS

If you are not yet identifying with the word *toxic* in all its different synonyms and various names, another term that may be easy to understand is *destructive*. There are destructive people and those who knowingly or unknowingly practice what can be called destructive leadership. Destructive leadership can be explained using five different elements.[142]

1. Don't be fooled. **Destructive leadership is often not destructive in every way.** Initially, some methods and actions from this kind of person can be appropriate or even desirable. But the overwhelming evidence left by this person's thinking and behavior ends in destruction. Consider a teacher who is a bad example to students (slanders other teachers, discredits their own leaders, is never on time and unprepared to teach the correct lesson, shows visible signs of substance abuse, and routinely embarrasses students) but can still legitimately teach the subject at hand. The

bad overwhelmingly swallows up the good. Don't be fooled by the little good that is swallowed up by the bad.

2. **Destructive leaders rely on inappropriate control and coercion rather than persuasion and commitment.** They do not believe in leadership but on complete dominance to get their way. These people are more like dictators than supervisors. Followers or staff members likely think, "I better do what they say or else I am going to get crushed and humiliated"; rather than the preferred, "I should follow this person, and they have a legitimate right to receive what they are asking from me. No problem." Destructive leaders are like tyrants rather than desirable leaders. It is not about being likable, quirky, socially awkward, or just not that great with people. Destructive leaders hurt, hinder, and hamper organizations much more than they help.

3. **These detrimental types are all about themselves.** They are selfish. It's about their goals, plans, and objectives. Not about others, those they lead, or their organizations (whether that be family, friends, or business firms). Their focus is on "me me me," "my my my," "I I I," "my way, my plans for my good, and my pleasure no matter who else is involved." This is totally antithetical to what true leadership is about: servant-leadership of and for others.

4. **The results of destructive leadership are seen in people's lives.** The simple proof of destructive leadership is those displaying it leave the people and the organizations they lead worse off. Sure, employees get a paycheck as they should. But what is a paycheck worth when you are overstressed, dealing with ulcers, cannot sleep due to worrying about the job, or possibly driven to a heart attack? When going to work is more about dodging land mines than it is about being productive and fulfilling the company's vison and mission, there may be a toxic situation happening. For example, the destructive person could be married, but it is

difficult to be happy in a marriage when that person is committing adultery, betraying trust, verbally and physically abusive, financially irresponsible, and just plain miserable to be around.

5. This last one may seem the oddest of the five: **destructive leadership is dependent on followers and environments**. Without followers there is no leadership (unless you are focusing on leading yourself, also called self-leadership). In some twisted way, people continue to work for terrible leaders. To keep following them means you are empowering them to keep doing damaging things. There are certain environments wicked leaders thrive in more than others. Without oversight that holds them accountable and responsible for their actions, these leaders can symbolically (if not literally, in the very worst of situations) get away with murder.

DESTRUCTIVE BEHAVIORS OF TOXIC LEADERS[143]

Here is yet another list of destructive behaviors that toxic leaders display. Do you notice these behaviors in yourself and others? This list encompasses some of the things not yet mentioned in this chapter.

- Leaving people worse off than they found them: deliberately undermining, demeaning, seducing, marginalizing, intimidating, threatening, demoralizing, disenfranchising, debilitating, imprisoning, manipulating, unnecessarily punishing, or even torturing, terrorizing, or killing

- Violating the basic human rights of others

- Leaders who lie to those who follow them solely to enhance their own power

- Stopping constructive criticism and teaching others to comply and not question the leader's questionable judgment or actions

- Purposefully distorting certain issues and problems (lying)

- Sabotaging processes and structures that were intended to generate truth, justice, and excellence

- Failing to nurture or mature other leaders

- Causing division or conflict by setting people against each other

- Finding other workers to take the blame for problems, and encouraging others to criticize or punish them

- Ignoring and/or promoting incompetence, corruption, and cronyism

- Convincing followers to hate or destroy other people

Any of these look familiar? Do one or more of these behaviors represent you, coworkers, mentors, or leaders you follow? Are you guilty of any of these things toward, or even with, others?

TOXIC TRIANGLE

Describing what destructive people are is just a part of the foundation of what is referred to as the toxic triangle. The toxic triangle was outlined in a leadership article (Art Padilla, Robert Hogan, and Robert Kaiser authored) titled "The toxic triangle: Destructive leaders, susceptible followers, and conducive environments." As you know, a triangle is made up of three different angles. Each line is connected to and supports the others. Each part of this triangle can be further broken out into subcategories adding even more meaning. As the title says, the triangle is made up of destructive leaders, susceptible (manipulatable) followers, and conducive circumstances or environments (Figure 2).[144] Let's look into each.

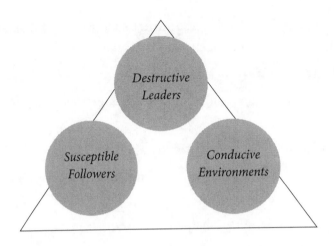

Figure 2: The three parts of the toxic triangle

When each of the three parts of the toxic triangle are in play, it makes things easier for a bad leader to take charge, assume authority, and lead people.

Besides the five elements of what describes destructive leadership, let's look specifically into the five components of destructive leaders as part of the triangle. These five factors, when used in a negative way, make a person more damaging to almost any person, cause, or company. The five puzzle pieces are: charisma, personalized power, narcissism, negative life themes, and an ideology of hate.[145]

To be fair, a person who has one or all of these factors may not necessarily be harmful to people and organizations, but it's likely they will be because the leader's mind and heart are not directed in a positive way.

Charisma: charismatic leaders can have a powerful impact because they change the way people think about their work, offer a vision of a better future, bring people together to foster cohesive and tight-knit working communities, and can enhance workers' abilities to get work done and achieve results.[146] Charismatic leaders move, motivate, and mobilize followers to action.[147] Do you see how powerful these kinds of people are? At the same time, though, do not be overbalanced in your thinking. Being charismatic does not mean you are a bad leader. However, most destructive leaders are charismatic.[148] If you think and act in wicked ways, you can use the gift of charisma to lead people in the wrong direction and set a bad example. You can do a fairly easy search throughout history and notice several leaders able to gather, motivate, and deploy people to action who were evil and harsh. Many maniacal leaders have been charismatic. These leaders are often master marketers because they talk themselves into a place of prominence, status, and importance. If an environment is hostile and threatening, the charismatic leader will promote himself or herself to build even more support for their agenda.

Personalized power: have you known someone who was power hungry? They can treat fame, accolades, fortune, and illicit sex as elixirs to their soul wounds. They can only be satisfied for a short while before they need another fix, much like a drug addict. For clarity, those who use the servant leadership style of leading are the opposite. They use their positions to do just that: serve, support, and assist others, not themselves. A destructive leader's personal job description includes using their position to fuel, feed, and fight for their selfish wants and needs.

The way they exert their influence can range from subtle manipulation to outright bold acts. Leaders with a personalized need for power have a power motivation, and this translates to a desire to increase their status and maintain their impact on others.[149] When this motivation is out of whack, it can cause the leader to make wrong decisions. Some may end up aggressively promoting themselves and their own causes to the detriment of their organization and subordinates.[150] Warning! Watch out for people who "need" power.

Narcissism: I referred to narcissism in my first book (*Leadership in the Age of Narcissism*). Narcissism consists of a person being self-absorbed, along with self-love and inflated self-views.[151] Narcissists think they are special and unique; their relationships have low levels of empathy and emotional intimacy; and they maintain overblown self-views. Narcissists seek out opportunities for attention and admiration, brag, steal credit from others, and play games in relationships.[152]

Narcissism can be further defined in two subsets: grandiose and vulnerable. Let me provide some illustrations.

The typical narcissist in the workplace is likely to be a *grandiose narcissist*, someone who is overconfident, has an extraverted personality, is high in self-esteem, dominant, seeks attention from others, and is charismatic (interpersonally skilled and charming). Yet at the same time this person is unwilling to take criticism, is aggressive, has a high sense of entitlement, lacks true empathy, exploits others, and is conceited or haughty.[153]

A *vulnerable narcissist* is likely someone who is hostile, thinks the world is unfairly stacked against him or her, and has a high sense of entitlement, but also has low self-esteem and is depressed and personally anxious.[154] Which flavor are you? Which one reminds you of someone who may be a match for that description? The narcissist does not focus on relational intimacy, fostering warmth, or other positive long-term relational results. And yet he or she is quite skilled at both initiating relationships and using relationships for their own good—to look popular, successful, and high in status.[155] Notice how close charisma and narcissism can be associated.

Beware of pride that feeds a narcissistic way of life. Pride is a life-sucking and destroying monster. Pride is a blinder. It clouds your vision and makes it much harder to see what you should, making it easier to fall and fail. Do not allow pride to tarnish your judgment, work, worship, and relationships. Gross pride often takes one down the road to failure.[156] Many maniacal leaders are pompous, proud potentates.

Negative life themes: ever meet someone who is almost always negative? Hardly anything is ever good, or good enough, for them. From parents to jobs to friendships and other relationships, it's all bad, all gloom. A car, a meal, a person, a situation, a product—none of it is ever good enough. This person may just be negative themselves. It is as if they live underneath a dark cloud. So it is with people who have negative life themes. This term is defined as when a person has a negative image of the world and their role in it.[157]

The world is bad and the negative person cannot do much to help it. For an illustration, think of this in terms of a child being raised in a broken household. The parents had little to no money and, as a child, the boy or girl has experienced abuse after abuse and hardship after hardship. After a while, when the child grows up, he or she may carry those childhood traumas, mental scars, heart hurts, and mental anguishes every day into their personal and professional way of life. Hurting people easily hurt other people. This is toxic. A person is always responsible for their behavior no matter their past. Having a hard upbringing and poor self-esteem does not help a person's situation. Some people were raised under cruelty and so become cruel to others. This is no excuse, but it's a fact—and something to remain aware of. Some people become what they have been exposed to, good and bad.

Ideology of hate: were you by any chance raised to hate someone or something? Some people are. Some people who have a favorite sports team may hate other teams and talk down about them. On a more serious note, some people are indoctrinated to hate people of other ethnicities. Prejudicial thinking, discriminatory behavior, and racism are often passed on by teaching others an ideology of hate. What a leader hears, says, and sees (their vision), and their worldview, can reveal an ideology of hate.[158]

In movies, for example, too often a theme exists that, for one reason or another, a person hates another country, people group, religious sect, or company. Then they think, "When I'm in charge, I will destroy them. I will take my revenge." Think about your own way of talking about people, places, and things, and you may realize you have a belief system of hate. Hate is in the way a person thinks. Some people hate authority because they were raised by, or worked under, a tyrannical parent or boss. A person's ideology can easily result in manifested behavior. Leaders must be careful that what they negatively experienced in the past is not intentionally or unintentionally passed on to others or heavily obscuring the way they think.

SUSCEPTIBLE FOLLOWERS

What many may not realize is the role followers play in the lives of all leaders, not just the toxic ones. Understand that, knowingly or unknowingly, people who support terrible leaders are, by default, empowering them. Destructive leaders cannot do much by themselves without the undergirding of others doing what they say. There cannot be a leader without at least one follower.[159] Followers can be defined as those who do what others want them to do.[160] Followers can be referred to as staff, subordinates, volunteers, work associates, team members, and coworkers, just to name a few.

In an article for *Harvard Business Review*, Barbara Kellerman wrote that followers may also be defined as people who are " . . . low (or lower) in the hierarchy and have less power, authority, and influence than their superiors. They generally go along to get along, particularly with those in higher positions. In the workplace, they may comply as not to put their money or stature at risk."[161] Susceptible followers can be broken out in two categories: conformers and colluders.

Conformers are people who have unmet needs, low self-esteem, and are immature. Having unmet basic needs could result in a person being more easily controlled. Those in need of basic food and safety, and who feel cut off (unable to get access to things others have), can open themselves up to oppressive leaders who take advantage of their vulnerability. I recommend to any person aspiring to lead others that they evaluate whether their own basic needs are being met so they don't seek praise, validations, security, and hero-like worship from others to fill the void in their own soul.

A person's evaluation of themselves is an important factor influencing their well-being in different life situations.[162] What you think about yourself matters. Individuals with a negative self-image or low self-esteem dislike themselves, lack confidence in their capabilities, and see themselves as powerless to affect their environments.[163] The better you feel about yourself increases the odds that you will have better satisfaction in life, higher job satisfaction and performance, and increased motivation.[164] It's easier for people with low self-esteem to follow charismatic leaders because these kinds of leaders want to control and manipulate people, and the followers believe they deserve to be controlled and manipulated.[165]

People who are not mature often do not make the best decisions. Why? Because they are immature. They do not see or perceive things properly. These people can be impulsive subordinates because they do not think things through, are rebellious, and needlessly challenge people in authority.[166] When a person does not have a strong sense of who they are, they may conform to leaders' destructive actions (they are not strong enough to stop them) and adhere to the wrong value system. They may not be able to discern who is worth following because they are still immature.

Colluders are a slightly different brand of follower. Colluders are broken down into three subsets. They are: the ambitious, those with a similar worldview, and those with bad values.

Ambition can be defined as the constant striving for success, attainment, and accomplishment.[167] Or you could define it as a desire to achieve ends, especially ends like success, power, and wealth.[168] It is about attaining outcomes.[169] I do not believe there is anything inherently wrong with simple ambition. It is fine to want things. It is okay to want more within the checks and balances of your purpose and the ability of your character to handle it. Ask yourself: why do you want more? How can you manage your ambition?

Ambition can be good, and it even provides advantages in certain healthy ways (i.e., enhancing personal status, pay, and promotions), but there is a darker side to it that many do not think about. Unfortunately, some people align themselves with destructive, narcissistic, despotic, and abusive leaders. Why? Simple: they see the advantage in it for themselves. The followers are focused on themselves and what they can get. Let me state that again. Sometimes people follow bad leaders because they see where they can personally benefit.

For instance, some ambitious people support or participate in cruel actions for status or to further their own agenda.[170] Not all bad people act alone, and not all staff is innocent. Often bad leaders have an inner circle that knows what is going on. Consider the people who are close to and support leaders who are con artists, fraudsters, abusers, drug dealers, pimps, gang leaders, tyrants, heads of criminal organizations, dictators—friends, staff, or other supporters, allowing themselves to be associated with or led by perverted leadership. Consider organizations that take advantage of children, the elderly, etc. Ambitious colluders are easy to recruit when there are opportunities to profit.[171] A wise man once said, "Do nothing from selfish ambition or conceit, but in humility count others more significant than yourselves."[172]

Be careful with colluders who have a *negative worldview*, especially when they are around destructive leaders. If they value the same, or similar, things it's quite easy for them to team up. Perverted people often team up with other perverted people. Of course, you have heard the phrase: "Birds of a feather flock together." There is definitely truth to that.

What about the phrase "Misery loves company"?[173] People who cause misery are often surrounded by a supporting cast of team members of like mind. They are comforted by people who do the same things or allow them to do these things. They are comforted by people who think the same way. Who are you supporting and comforting with your presence? The closer the leader is to the follower's beliefs or values, the stronger the bond and greater the motivation to follow and join the same cause.[174] Be careful of your affections and connections.

The third of the three kinds of colluders are *followers with bad values*. By bad values I mean things that are not socially acceptable in society. Supporters who have largely unacceptable (or bad) beliefs and values, such as greed and selfishness, are more likely to follow a depraved leader and do the same things.

ENVIRONMENTS THAT ENCOURAGE BAD LEADERS

Just as there are environments that work best for growing certain plants, flowers, raising animals, and raising children, so it is with positive leadership. On the dark side of leadership, there are certain environments that work best to allow, foster, tolerate, cultivate, and support bad leadership. The pieces that make up this fertile soil are: *instability, perceived threat, cultural values, lack of checks and balances,* and *ineffective institutions.*

Instability. In times of dysfunction or crisis, leaders find it advantageous to vie for radical change. This is when charismatic leaders come to the forefront.[175] Times of instability or unstable environments can cause or allow leaders to gain power.[176] Why? Because times of unrest and emergency call for leaders to step up and lead others. An important question to ask is: what kind of leader is taking advantage and seizing these moments? Are they moral or immoral? Are they in it for the good of the people or organization, or for their own selfish interests?

Perceived threat. When people do not feel safe in their environment they are more willing to accept people who assert themselves.[177] Threats increase followers' support for charismatic leaders.[178] Stated plainly, times of terror, coercions, and intimidations empower leaders and motivate followers to find someone to lead them.

Cultural values. Culture means beliefs and behaviors. Culture, which can also be referred to as atmosphere or environment, decides what things, ideals, and actions are allowed or important. Your home, church, business communities, people groups, countrymen, and nation all have their own specific culture. Culture shapes values and values shape culture. It's cyclical, interconnected, and one part influences the other like falling dominoes.

Beliefs and values can shape leaders for good or bad. If the social conditions are bad, those bad virtues can shape emerging leaders.[179] People are products of their environments. Corrupt cultures produce corrupt leaders. Be careful of your culture. How have the various cultures you have been exposed to (home, work, worship, others) influenced or formed you?

Lack of checks and balances, and ineffective institutions. Checks and balances, also known as accountability with boundaries, are in place to limit people's authority. This is a good thing. Due to how great, yet flawed, mankind is, limits should be considered a good thing. For example, in the world of corporate governance, the danger is that the directors or managers might act in their own interests rather than those of the shareholders.[180] Checks and balances keep leaders on course and limit their power. Again, this is a good thing.

Checks and balances can take on many designs and forms such as an independent governing board, a supervisor or manager who holds personnel accountable, restrictions on spending, boundaries on specific actions that can't be made alone without the approval and participation of other departments, and more. People held accountable to their organization's guidelines, codes, instructions, regulations, codes of conduct, core values, mission, vision, and credos—all of these are good practices. Shared responsibility and accountability act as safety nets for leaders and should catch destructive leaders before their nefarious, self-servings actions go too far. Without checks and balances destructive leaders can run wild. Limiting control means limiting the risk. Who or what are your personal and professional checks and balances?

BAD LEADERS

Just because a person is a leader or in a leadership position does not mean they are good, right, moral, and upstanding people who should be followed. More simply put: not all leaders are good ones.

Barbara Kellerman, who wrote *Bad Leadership*, has a list of several kinds of people who represent the dark side of leadership.[181] Several of them are listed below. These are the kinds of people who wield influence and power in the wrong way.

- Rigid: the leader who is inflexible and unyielding. These people either are not willing or are incapable of adjusting to new ways of doing things, to new ideas, and to new information.

- Intemperate: the person who cannot control himself or herself.

- Callous: the leader who is cold, hard-hearted, mean-spirited, or unsympathetic.

- Corrupt: the person who is unethical/crooked.

- Insular: the leader who does not care for others outside of the group or organization he or she is responsible for. This person neglects the health and welfare of others.

- Evil: the person who commits atrocities. Pain and harm (physical or psychological) are used to exert power over people.

Can you see the patterns? The cycle? See the connection from what was written in the biblical passages of 2 Timothy 3:1-5 (list of toxic behaviors represented in bad leadership), 1 John 2:15-17 (sources of toxic behaviors that manifest themselves in bad leadership), and the Gangel and Kellerman lists (bad leaders who exhibit harmful behaviors)? There is a clear link between each part in this wicked network.

Notice anything that concerns you about . . . you? About others? Has God been convicting, exposing, or showing you any of your toxic motivations, thoughts, or actions? Have comments people have made about you over the years matched some of the descriptions you have read so far? To repeat myself and to be clear: no one is perfect. No one. Perfection is not expected of anyone. But that is no excuse to exhibit behavior that can make another person's life hell on earth. There is no excuse to manipulate your way into powerful positions by taking advantage of people's vulnerabilities, bad situations, and experiences. While following God's standards and leading their institutions, leaders are to serve and support the people. Not be exploiting and constricting snakes.

Do you find yourself being a bully, threatening people, or screaming at people?[182] How about throwing things at staff associates and subordinates because you are upset? Are you the backbiting, belittling boss from hell?[183]

To make sure we are balanced in our thinking, we know it's appropriate for leaders to direct, correct, promote, demote, terminate, and hold people accountable for their actions. As a leader, I strongly encourage other leaders to hold people accountable, give guidance, and bring correction when needed. Not everything a leader does that you do not like is toxic. For example, some people think raising your voice is toxic. I do not think it is when done properly—in control and done constructively. I come from a military background, along with having worked in non- and for-profit organizations. I have learned that raising your voice can be effective at select times to bring about constructive correction, motivation, and direction. However, yelling and screaming at people to berate, belittle, harass, inappropriately punish, or embarrass is a big no.

Give some thought to your ways. Are there habits and methods you need to change so you are not a bad leader? Are you maladjusted, malcontent, malevolent, malicious, and making others' lives miserable all the while acting as though you are fine and everyone else is the problem?[184]

Here are more pointed questions.[185]

1. Have you come to realize that you don't care about the well-being of subordinates? Is everything all about you, your way, or no way (of course, excluding the basic tasks staff must do on a daily basis)?

2. When people interact with you, does it negatively impact the organizational climate? When you have a bad day, does everybody end up having a bad day just because of you?

3. Do people who follow and work with you believe you are motivated primarily by your own egomaniacal self-interests?

One of the reasons I am constantly asking questions in this book is because a significant number of leaders do not know the true impact they have with their organizations. Many never take time to reflect. Rather, they suffer from "CEO disease," which is a leader's ignorance about how his or her mood and actions appear to the organization.[186] Leaders too often take action and have no idea how they are being perceived by others.

Do you know how you are being perceived? It's not that leaders don't care how they are perceived; most do. But they incorrectly think they can interpret this information themselves.[187] What is worse is they think if they are having a negative effect on the organization someone will tell them . . . and this is wrong thinking.[188]

Are you aware of yourself and how those who work with you and for you, and other associates, see you? Do you have a realistic, sober, and practical understanding of what are the best—and not-so-pleasant—parts of your personality? Are you truly aware?

NOTES

NOTES

NOTES

Five

—

WHY FOLLOW BAD LEADERS?

Ever wonder why we follow specific kinds of people? Even more specifically, why do people follow bad leaders? Why do we seek out, sit in front of, or stay under leaders we know are bad? I'm not talking about leaders you don't like just because of personality differences. I mean leaders who are just dreadful. You should want to know why. Getting to the answers can be important in unearthing deep-seated information concerning how you think about and perceive people.

Ever think about why people are so wired to follow people? You can trace it back to many of our childhood experiences. As children, we usually follow leaders such as parents and other older family members.[189] A typical well-behaved child usually won't question the teacher even if the teacher is somehow bad.[190] When we enter adulthood, we follow the leaders on our jobs the same way. We tend to play by the rules and do as we are told even when the rules are unfair.[191]

Here are some other reasons people are geared to seek out and follow leaders whether they are good or bad.

- Our need for parental authority figures.[192] Childhood experiences with authoritarian, demanding, and controlling parents, who also loved and protected us, may condition us to accept difficult, hostile authority figures: teachers, bosses, spouses, police, clergy, judges, presidents, and more.[193] These "parental replacements" can fill a psychological void in a person yearning for an external authority figure.[194]

- Our need for security and certainty provokes us to surrender our freedom to attain them.[195] We search for replacements to our primary relationships such as parents and caregivers.[196] No longer having those relationships and no longer being in a childhood role could leave us feeling isolated, lonely, and powerless.[197] When feeling this way we tend to move toward any leader who will make us feel safe, protected, and good about ourselves.[198]

- Our preference for strong leaders.[199] Most of us want leaders to be strong and confident.[200] The problem is too many of us confuse arrogance and narcissism for strength.[201] That is wrong; research clearly shows that the very worst leaders—those who become tyrants—are extremely narcissistic and arrogant.[202]

- Our desire to feel chosen or special.[203] The concept of being in a special, chosen group has a powerful grip on humans.[204] Many toxic leaders have used this means to prompt their followers to distance themselves from others.[205] Wicked leaders who promise security and assure us that we are special attract the insecure.[206]

- Our desire to know who is responsible. A leader is a person who can be observed, is typically replaceable, and is responsible for what happens.[207] It's just easier to blame the leader for what occurs.

- Our leaders help keep things simple.[208] People obey orders in stressful situations because of their need to keep things simple.[209] It is assumed that people in charge know what they are doing.[210]

- Our need for community.[211] People have an intense need to belong.[212] To be socially ostracized, or to face social death—put out of a desired group—can be just as bad or even greater than the fear of death.[213] Even when led by a toxic leader, some people will not leave a group because they feel their community provides some kind of security and meaning.[214]

- Our belief that we are powerless to change a bad leader.[215] "I am just one person and I have no power"—this is a common thought. So we passively surrender and never challenge toxic leaders. We change ourselves to live under their rule and leave it to others to challenge these bad leaders.[216] In the end, you accept them.[217]

Followers are as driven to follow as leaders are to lead.[218] The motivation for people to follow a leader falls into two categories: *rational* and *irrational*.[219] **Rational**-inspired supporters typically hope to get money, status, power, or access through a personally meaningful situation by following a great leader, and they fear missing out on things if they don't follow.[220] With the **irrationally** motivated, these people are usually unaware they are irrational and have no control of their responses.[221] This comes from powerful images and emotions in their unconscious mind that they bring to relationships with leaders.[222] Many people may not realize they are operating in what Sigmund Freud, an Austrian neurologist and the founder of psychoanalysis, referred to as transference.[223] Simply put, transference is when you project, assign, or transfer experiences and emotions from past relationships onto the present.[224] This may be the reason people fall in love with their leader, therapist, doctor, or an executive they work for. Freud was quoted as saying, "There is no love that does not reproduce infantile stereotypes."[225] Maybe, just maybe, this notion of transference explains why so many of us choose spouses like our parents.[226]

SELF-AWARENESS

Have you heard of or read of being self-aware? When you have an understanding of your own strengths and limitations you are fostering self-awareness in your life.[227] It's an interconnected process made up of self-reflexive thinking, self-examination, and introspection.[228]

It is getting to truly see, know, and understand yourself. The basic foundation of self-awareness is focusing your attention inward and studying yourself as though you were looking in a mirror.[229]

Tasha Eurich, who authored a paper titled "What Self-Awareness Really Is (and How to Cultivate It)," stated self-awareness is explained in two parts.[230]

Internal self-awareness: this represents how clearly you see your own values, passions, aspirations, the fit with your environment, reactions (including thoughts, behaviors, strengths, and weaknesses), and the impact on others.

External self-awareness: means understanding how other people view you. People who know how others see them are more skilled at showing empathy and taking the perspectives of others. For leaders who see themselves as their employees do, their employees tend to have a better relationship with them, feel more satisfied around them, and see them as more effective in general.

Eurich goes on to explain that self-awareness can be further broken down into four distinct forms. On the lower, internal self-awareness level, there are *seekers* and *pleasers*.[231] **Seekers** are people who do not know who they are yet, don't know what they stand for, and don't understand how people see them. Seekers may feel stuck or frustrated with their own performance and relationships. **Pleasers** are focused on presenting themselves a certain way to satisfy others. As a result they could be overlooking what personally matters to themselves. On the negative side, pleasers may make decisions that are not to their benefit. They do this because they are not self-aware.

On the higher, internal self-awareness side, we have *introspectors* and *aware people*.[232] **Introspectors** know who they are but do not question their own perspective on things or search for their blind spots by getting feedback from others. This could end up harming their relationships and hindering their success. The fourth and final perspective is **aware people**, those who also know who they are, what they want to achieve, and who intentionally seek feedback from other people and value the opinions of others. This is the mindset where leaders really grasp the benefits of being self-aware.

So how do you become more knowledgeable about yourself? In short, you have to take time to critically think and ask yourself questions. Notice I stated to *critically think*. Not to be negatively critical of yourself. According to the Oxford Learning Dictionaries, critical thinking is the process of analyzing information in order to make a logical decision about it.[233] Do not be a person who lays blame and finds fault with yourself all the time. We do not want to get into a locked system of negatively thinking about ourselves. Do not make that a habit, and do not destroy the image of who God made you to be.

To help you become better at self-awareness, here are some ideas you can implement right away. I have incorporated some ideas from Anthony Tjan, who wrote on five different ways to become more self-aware.[234]

Think. As said previously, ask yourself questions. Think about how you are thinking and why. For example, do you only see things from your point of view and no one else's? Have regular moments of pause and refection. In a TEDxMileHigh talk, Eurich encouraged people to ask the "what" questions.[235] The "what" questions are those that can move you in a healthy way to your future.[236] Here are some examples: What is the goal I want to achieve? What am I doing that is working well for others and myself? What am I doing that's hindering me or slowing me down? What am I doing now that I can change? What can I do even better with a little more effort?

Write down important plans and priorities. Write down what you want to accomplish and track your progress. Journaling or having someone keep you accountable can be helpful here. Writing things down could create a historical record to help you evaluate things.

Take psychometric tests. The Collins Dictionary explains that a psychometric test is designed to test a person's personality, mental state, and thought processes.[237] Some leading tests are: Personality

Profiling; Myers-Briggs Type Indicator; Sixteen Personality Factor Questionnaire; DISC; Verbal, Numerical, and Situational Reasoning Assessments; and Situational Judgement Tests.[238]

Ask trusted people. Ask for feedback from people like friends, peers, mentors, and coaches. Tjan suggests having friends play the role of "honest mirror." They should be able to give you frank and straightforward feedback without any negative reaction from you.

Get feedback from coworkers. If your job has formal feedback sessions, use them. These kinds of sessions help you see strengths and weaknesses in your life. If your job does not have formal feedback sessions, ask for them. Realize that if you are at a high level in an organization, you may have fewer people above you to give the honest feedback you need.[239] The more power you have as a leader, people tend to not feel comfortable giving constructive feedback for fear of their careers being hindered or ruined.[240]

LISTEN

Knowing yourself better is not the only benefit to self-awareness. You can end up *thinking* differently about yourself. At times you need to, as C. Otto Scharmer wrote in "Uncovering the Blind Spot of Leadership," slow down to understand.[241] Scharmer discusses several kinds of listening. Three of the different types are *downloading listening, factual listening,* and *empathetic listening.*[242]

Downloading is about noticing. Have you slowed down to notice or listen to what you say and think you already know? It's when everything you hear confirms what you already know.[243] For example, when someone tells you something about yourself (i.e., you get so cranky when you are tired, you don't get along with others well, you get so angry at the simplest thing, you are good at a certain task), take the time to download—to closely think about—that information and match it up with what you already think or know. Some of us know we do nasty things and have awful ways of thinking. It is not a surprise to us when people notice it and say something. Downloading is about reconfirming what you already know about yourself, people, and other things.

Factual listening is when you realize what's new or different.[244] You are looking and listening for new information. You especially notice what you do not know. You can see what is different. Ever have someone ask you questions that revealed a truth you did not know? Or caused you to think to force an answer? For example: "Do you know that you often have a bad attitude when you have to see your ex for anything?" "You ever notice how anxious you get when you see your supervisor?" "Do you really trust God to help you with your problems?" "Do you realize that when your friend betrayed you, you began not trusting anyone anymore?" With questions like these, take the time to find out what information is new to you. What is factually accurate? Pay attention by download thinking and factual thinking.

Listening to a person and seeing things from their point of view is **empathetic listening**.[245] You really have to listen with an open heart to understand how another person feels. If some of us did merely this kind of listening and cared enough about what others had to say, we might change. You understand the reason a person feels the way they do. It's attempting to walk in their shoes. You are not controlled by other people's opinions, but you listen to get revelation from them, the situation, or yourself.

Let's say a person asks you one of these questions: "Why are you so mean to me all the time?" "Why are you constantly destroying things and relationships?" "Why do you enjoy screaming and yelling at people so much, and then smile about it?" At first it is easy to get defensive, but if you practice listening empathetically to understand what they see from their point of view, you can learn something about yourself, and them.

Empathetic listening might be eye-opening and even humbling since it opens you up to at least try putting yourself in the other person's place so you can better see and understand how they feel and how you are impacting them. Some of you may not be so quick to do this because no matter the situation you simply do not care what others think, and you keep doing what you want even though you know it's wrong. That is a major problem, because this attitude does not foster healthy communication and keeps negative habits and cycles in place. Change.

MOTIVATED TO AVOID

Some people give in to another kind of selfish motivation. There are people who do not want to be self-aware. They purposely do not want to confront some of the things in their own heart. Some people don't want to be confronted about the things they do. Is that you? It may be literally taking pleasure in watching and doing some things illegally, or just acting in ways that are inappropriate and just plain wrong. Some of us avoid looking in that mirror so we do not have to confront our dirt. Did you know there is something called motivated blindness?

Motivated blindness is when you choose not to see something because not dealing with it in the right way means you can keep taking advantage of it. A more formal way to explain it: your failure to notice other people's corrupt (bad, wrong, unethical) behavior because really *seeing* that behavior would harm (or not benefit) you.[246] Many of us have done this. Some of you may have known a friend was stealing from a business and chose not to say anything because you were given some of the stolen goods. Essentially, you were paid to keep quiet. Ever have a friend who worked at a restaurant and you knew they were stealing food but didn't care because they were giving you some of it? You choose not to do or say anything because, if you do, you won't get the benefits.

It's like a woman who stays in a multiyear abusive relationship and chooses not to believe her boyfriend or husband is doing anything substantially wrong. Even though she has had to go to the hospital multiple times, knows he is cheating on her, and is being verbally abusive, she—perhaps for a number of reasons—doesn't think it's too big of a problem. She may try to make excuses or justify her perspective because she still "has a man around" or "knows he is under a lot of stress." She is too busy *unseeing* to see, because seeing may mean she has to make better decisions for her life.

Sure, there are a lot of factors why people do not see what they should see and do not do what they should do. Remember, people who are not trying to see—or "unseeing" the seen—may be dealing with the psychological inclination of motivated blindness to not notice the bad. It may be another of their defense mechanisms. This may be the reason so many people keep following poor leaders. These blind followers may very well be the people who keep empowering deplorable leaders.

Remember the Enron and Arthur Andersen debacle? As an energy-trading and utilities company based in Houston, Enron committed one of the biggest accounting frauds in history.[247] Arthur Andersen once was the world's largest professional-services firm, employing 85,000 people, and, in one year, generating $9.3 billion in revenue.[248] Enron executives lied about the company's revenues with dishonest accounting practices.[249] How was the Arthur Anderson firm able to assure Enron's financial well-being during a time when Enron was hiding billions—I repeat *billions*—in debt from its investors/shareholders?[250] How? Why? Could it be because of their motivation to *not* see? It turns out Arthur Andersen earned tens of millions in lucrative contracts from Enron. How many situations can you think of in which you chose not to see what was clear, plain, and obvious? God is calling you to *see*. He is calling you to see and deal with what needs to be dealt with. Leaders are called to have proper vision. As you read, I hope the blinders are coming off. I believe God is trying to tell you what John was told in Revelations 4:1: to "come up here." God wants your perspective changed . . . so that what you see can change. As a leader, you have to be the change agent, be willing to change, and deal with what needs to be dealt with.

I am telling you these things because many of us live with a gap. The gap exists between the ethical, moral, and integrity and character values we think we have compared to how much we actually *do* have.[251] It's the gap.

The gap is the blind spot. The gap is where mediocracy lives. It is the gap between who you are and who you want to (or should) be.[252] The gap is where hypocrisy is. Moral hypocrisy happens when the opinions of your own wrongdoings are not taken as seriously as other people who do the same thing.[253] It is perverted privilege. For example, when you do something wrong you want it to be quickly forgiven and forgotten, but when someone else does the same thing, you want them held accountable and punished. As leaders, the rules must apply to you too.

Do not take the fact that you have these blind spots, or gaps, lightly. The danger of mental blindness or inattentiveness is that it can destroy, bankrupt, or shipwreck your entire organization (even your family) if not addressed and handled properly.[254]

Stated another way, your blind spot is your mental prejudice that will prevent you from seeing what is better or worse, from seeing right from wrong.

Just as with driving, what's in your blind spot can be a danger to you, or you can be a danger to what's in your blind spot. As your consultant, I recommend you take this counsel seriously and believe God to use it to revolutionize your way of thinking, parenting, leading, and how you interact with people in general. Take time to reflect and pray right now. Ask God to reveal the gaps in your thinking and to help you remove hypocrisy in the way you think and act. Write these things down. There are different kinds of blind spots a person can have. These are the ten most common according to Inc.com.[255]

1. Going it alone
   Practically, this means: Being afraid to ask for help

2. Being insensitive to the effect of your behavior on others
   Being unaware of how others perceive you

3. Having an "I know" attitude
   Valuing being right above everything else

4. Avoiding difficult conversations
   Conflict avoidance

5. Blaming others or circumstances
   Playing the victim; not taking personal responsibility

6. Treating your word/commitments casually
   Not honoring the other person's time, energy, resources

7. Conspiring against others
   Being driven by a personal agenda

8. Withholding emotional commitment
   Emotional blackmail

9. Not taking a stand
   Lack of commitment to a position

10. Tolerating "good enough"
    Low standards for performance

Any of these look familiar to your performance? *After* you carefully reflect on yourself, think about whether you see these blind spots in others. Parents, friends, coworkers? Inc.com goes on to state five ways to address your blind spots.[256]

1. Ask others for feedback.
   Ask others for the one blind spot they think you have and need to be more aware of.

2. Surround yourself with people who think differently than you with the intention that you learn from them.

You should learn from a variety of perspectives, experiences, and approaches to problem-solving.

3. Reflect; identify patterns from your past.

   Some suggested self-reflection questions are: as a leader, how have you succeeded? How have you struggled? What situations led to both desirable and undesirable results? What feedback have you received from people you trust such as mentors, coaches, or advisors regarding questionable decisions you have made that indicates a pattern?

4. Identify your triggers—defined as situations that cause you to impulsively or instinctively react without thinking.

   Every moment is filled with people, events, or circumstances that have the power to shape how we act or react. When we know and have control of our triggers, we can control our responses and make them work for us, not against us. So . . . what are your triggers?

5. Be accountable to someone.

   Ask someone to hold you accountable to change your behavior.

NOTES

NOTES

Six

—

THE EFFECTS OF TOXICITY IN EVERYDAY LIFE

So what is the big deal with all of this? Yes, wicked, twisted, warped executives and even parents are painful to work with and be around, but it's easy to just say . . . "So what?" Well, there *is no* "so what?" Especially when it is your life, friend, or loved one who is under the gun. Bad leaders, no matter the brand or style (parent, formal leader, informal leader, volunteer leader, and so on) can make another person's life a living hell. They can be life-sucking leeches who drain the creativity, life, joy, peace, and health from your being. You'll see this in more depth in this chapter.

Bad leaders tend to tolerate misconduct in themselves and others, perpetuating a culture that accepts unethical behavior as normal.[257] Their extreme bias toward results at all costs, an arrogance as to their existence and purpose, the belief in a mindset that justifies misconduct—all of this is antithetical to what leadership is supposed to be about.[258] Many leaders resort to abusive behaviors in order to obtain results. Tragic!

To keep the definition of toxic leadership before us so we can not only understand but identify and stop it in ourselves and others, allow me to provide another definition. Toxic leadership, also referred to as abusive supervision or downward bullying, is a form of workplace bullying behavior involving shaming and blaming, passive hostility, team sabotage, indifference and lack of compassion, a negative and corrosive interpersonal style and exploitation, or the appearance of using others for personal gain.[259]

Remember, abusive leadership can happen in families and among other people in and out of work. So don't think that just because you do not experience these behaviors or exhibit them on the job they can't be found in other areas of your life. So, in the workplace and out of the workplace; in church and out of church; in a volunteer group or out of the group; in friendship and out—these principles and this information applies to you.

Individuals who demonstrate a pattern of counterproductive work behaviors that seriously debilitate individuals, work teams, and organizations over the long term are toxic.[260]

Below is **Figure 3**, noted by Col. (Chaplin) Kenneth Williams. It shows some of the criteria, descriptions, and examples of toxic behavior.[261]

Element	Description	Observable Behaviors
Shaming	Humiliation, sarcasm, put-downs, jabs, blaming	• Persistently pointing out mistakes intending to reduce another's self-worth • Public embarrassment
Passive hostility	Passive-aggressive behavior; redirecting one's anger inappropriately on a target person or persons	• Resenting requests, deliberate procrastination, and intentional mistakes to serve self and avoid serving others • Complaints of injustice and lack of appreciation • Compliments that veil criticism • Always having the last word • Spreading rumors about subordinates

Team sabotage	Meddling to establish one's personal power base, resulting in decreased cohesion and performance	• Inconsistency: unclear, constantly changing expectations, and unpredictable policies, procedures, and behaviors • Dysfunctional communication: to maintain power and control, withholding key information, sharing incomplete information, or sharing partial items of information resulting in each team member having incomplete data
Indifference	An apparent lack of regard for the welfare of others, especially subordinates	• Lack of compassion and empathy • Excluding certain people • Disinterest in the successes of and unsympathetic to the suffering of others
Negativity	A corrosive interpersonal style that has a negative impact on individual or collective morale and motivation	• Malice: cruelty and degradation are more prevalent than kindness • Narcissism: uncaring abuse of others for personal gain
Exploitation	The perception of getting ahead at the expense of others	• Inequality: tolerating toxic people, who are often highly skilled but punishing others • Favoritism: special treatment for a select few • Nepotism: the hiring of unqualified friends or family

Toxic leaders lead to corrosive environments. The opposite can also be true. Corrosive environments lead to toxic people. Another way to term a toxic/poisonous environment is to call it incivility. Incivility means: the quality or state of being uncivil; rude, impolite attitude or behavior; discourteous acts.[262] Being consistently, constantly, routinely, repetitively, habitually, normally, regularly rude to people (especially the same people: spouse, children, friends, coworkers, and so on) *will* cost you.

Please be balanced in your thinking when you are taking in this information. I am not talking about having a bad day here and there or even being distraught for a relatively short while due to larger problems, pains, and life tribulations. That happens to all of us. I am not talking about impossible perfection and being forever faultless. We are human beings, so do not put yourself under the mental pressure to be perfect. That will not serve you well mentally.

When you are frequently offensive, rude, and disrespectful to people, then you have a character issue that needs to be addressed and corrected. To repeat, being harsh or sharp-tongued for a brief while due to unfortunate events is one thing, but being that way for years is an entrenched and established character problem.

Harsh, pervasively rude environments of incivility cause several negative outcomes.[263] There are tangible costs of letting this damaging environment fester:

- Nearly everyone who experiences workplace incivility responds in a negative way.

- Employees are less creative.

- Many employees quit/resign their jobs.

- A large portion decrease their work efforts or lower the quality of their work.

- Customer relationships are damaged.

- Rude workers lead to fewer customers buying the products, and customers begin to negatively brand or stereotype the organization.

In a poll of 800 managers and workers in more than fifteen industries, of employees who received incivility:[264]

- 48 percent deliberately decreased their work efforts

- 47 percent purposely decreased time spent at work

- 38 percent intentionally decreased the quality of their work
- 80 percent lost work time worrying about an incident
- 63 percent lost work time to avoid the one who offended them
- 66 percent said their performance declined
- 78 percent said their commitment to the organization declined
- 12 percent left their job because of malicious treatment
- 25 percent confessed to taking their frustration out on customers

Many leaders have tolerated these venomous environments for far too long. From the metrics you just read, I think some leaders literally cannot afford to be toxic. It's costing them too much. Too much of their purpose. Too much of their mission and vision. Too much capital, and too much of people's livelihoods. Have such bad environments affected you? How have you personally responded to toxic leaders? What has it cost you? Which of these metrics are you a part of?

Figure 4, below, describes what Col. Williams refers to as the effects and costs associated with bullying and toxic leadership.[265]

Category	Effect	Cost/Research Finding
Individual		
Psychological	Insomnia, anxiety, apathy, lack of concentration, memory loss, panic attacks, mood swings	Swedish study reported significant impact on a diverse group of public service workers
	PTSD	76 percent of targets reported symptoms of PTSD with 29 percent showing all the criteria
	Depression	75.8 percent of bullied individuals reported negative health effects; 29 percent stress; 18 percent depression
	Suicide	100 of 300 of those who committed suicide have been targets of bullying

Physiological	Psychosomatic symptoms (gastrointestinal issues, nausea, loss of appetite, hypersensitivity to sound, headache)	In a 1997 report by UNISON, a UK public service union, 75.6 percent of members stated adverse effects of bullying on health
	Respiratory, cardiac, and hypertension problems	Significant impacts on a diverse group of individuals
Performance	Absenteeism	Targets of bulling had 26 percent higher sick absences; £1.5 billion lost due to sickness
	Intent to leave	57.1 percent of military officers considered leaving their branch of service
	Job satisfaction	30 to 50 percent of US workers experience at least one negative event weekly for a six- to 12-month period
		A confirmatory factor analysis discovered strong and significant correlation between abusive supervision and perceived mobility, interactional justice, procedural justice, disruptive justice, job satisfaction, continuance commitment, work-to-family conflict, family-to-work conflict, depression, anxiety, and emotional exhaustion
Team	Isolation of individuals, impairment of cohesion, decreased perceptions and expectations of performance, degraded effectiveness, eroding team norms	Public service employees reported increased professional and personal values conflicts, cognitive conflicts, power struggles, targeting, marginalized contributions and performance; bullying resulted in perceptions of decreased cohesion and team success

Organization	Organizational performance/productivity, financial profits, organizational culture, reputation, wasted resources, replacement costs	25 percent of employees in Great Britain experience decreased productivity due to 4-7 percent bullying, accounting for a 1.5-2.0 percent total decline; estimated cost of bullying to organizations: $30,000-$100,000 per employee
		Time managing workplace conflicts: among Fortune 1000 companies: 13 percent
		£380 million lost annually due to bullying; $30,000-$100,000 for each employee who leaves due to bullying
Societal	Increased medical costs	Data unavailable
	Increased need for social services	Data unavailable
	Premature retirement	Data unavailable
	Unemployment	Data unavailable
	Impaired interpersonal relationships outside the workplace	Data unavailable
	Legal costs	Data unavailable

Have you suffered any psychological, physiological, or work performance issues because of toxic leadership? Did you spark or produce any of these issues in others? How has your team or organization been negatively affected by bullying and bad leaders?

NOTES

Seven

POISONOUS PARENTING

Let's turn the page, so to speak, to look at some leaders many people overlook: parents and guardians. To be even more clear: parents are leaders. They are family leaders.

The damage that can happen in families can be equally, or even more, unnerving. Why? Because humans are hard-wired for attachments (i.e., form a strong emotional, cognitive, and psychological bond to caregivers regardless of whether those caregivers respond in a healthy way or not).[266] Parents are the ultimate teachers because they teach their children what to think about the world, what's important and not important, self-worth, who to love, how to love, how to be loved, and how to love themselves.[267]

If not done correctly, the same things that can constitute love, care, and healthy parenting (affection, competition, teasing, humor, control, and punishment) can also become poisonous or unhealthy depending on several factors: intensity of expression, the number of times they occur, the context for expression, and the psychological and interpersonal needs and sensitivities of the child.[268] Poisonous parenting is defined as chronic toxicity at a level that will ultimately severely impair the parent/adult-child relationship.[269] But before you read through the list of problem parents, understand that these parental types can be representative of all kinds of people, not just actual fathers, mothers, or guardians. These types can also apply to people you work with, people you work for, and almost any kind of person in general. The list below represents a twisted mindset. Recognize the negative pattern behind the given name. And, do you see any of these in yourself?

Here is a hefty sampling of some styles of harmful parenting from Dunham, Dermer, and Carlson's book *Poisonous Parenting: Toxic Relationships Between Parents and Their Adult Children.*[270] Never forget that parents are leaders too, and the styles represented below can be symbolic of different kinds of leaders in other contexts outside of family.

Pageant parent: this kind of parent works to create a child who is the image of who they wish they would have become. The person lives vicariously through their child's accomplishments. Think about the father who forces his son to play football and drives him to become a top-ranked quarterback because that is what the father wants—not necessarily the son.

Showbiz parent: this type of person drives their child to become the smartest, best, most famous, and most talented, making it appear the parent (leader) only wants what is best for the child. This mentality reveals it's all about the parent and not the child's desire, purpose, or God-given plans. This can appear to be done in love, or with good intentions, but the actions are actually based on parental selfishness. It is good to want the best for anybody and everybody. But this desire has to be tempered with what is best for the person or team as a whole, or it quickly becomes all about some lust for fame and significance through another person/team.

When I lead teams, I work to bring out the best in people. I know I have their personal buy-in because they submit themselves to the mission and vision of the organization. My personal benefit comes after everyone else's. As a leader you do what's best for the organization's mission and vision while professionally taking care of the people you have. Their submission, permission, and buy-in is key. If those things are not there, it might be best for the employee to work somewhere else. People should be shown and led, not forced and manipulated.

Fictitious parent: this family leader creates a façade of who the child really is. It is based in lies and exaggerations. They may take a bit of truth and blow it out of proportion to glorify their relationship with the child or embellish the child's accomplishments, goals, or characteristics. This person may be looking to the child for their own parental self-esteem, love, and acceptance. This way of thinking is backwards and toxic; the child may be raised in a dream world that inflates their importance.

Superstar parent: ever see a parent compete with their children all the time? While constantly competing with them, the parent creates a long-term culture of "I'm better than you, and you will never be as good as me." That can wear on a child long-term and hurt their self-esteem, and that could have far-reaching and lifelong effects. The message is the child will never be as good as the parent. It's about pushing the child to be the best they can be (which can be fine, to a limit), but when mixed with needless criticism and undercutting words, they unknowingly create damaging outcomes in the child.

Dismissive parent: this kind of leader does not have a genuine connection with their child. There is no meaningful relationship. The parent could be absent in one or several ways including emotionally, physically, or financially. Have you read about, heard of, or experienced a parent who was there but *not really there*? They are around, but only "around," and not really a part of their children's lives. These parents are so absorbed in their own lives that the result is detrimental to their children's lives. These lazy or laissez-faire parents are selfish, sightless, and dismissive to the importance of their children. There is no emotional connection, no real bond. When the child is in distress, he or she may not feel comfortable going to the parent. Children in this type of situation feel they are not really important. Confident and compassionate parents engage their children emotionally. This dismissiveness can easily carry into adulthood. The parent can make themselves too busy with their own social activities (such as traveling or going out with friends), being immersed in their occupation, or in other time-consuming activities so that they do not make time for their adult children.

Stepford parent: nor is this kind of family leader emotionally invested in their children. The way this person thinks: *I do what I am supposed to do because it is expected, not because I want to.* It's more a fulfilling of parental chores or tasks, not because they are emotionally connected to their children. Those looking in from outside the home dynamic think everything is fine, but it is not. The children feel empty and disconnected.

Prerogatives parent: these individuals think parenting is a choice; they do what they want to do. They think the children ought to feel fortunate for being born and getting whatever they get due to the parent's "kindness." The parent does what works for himself or herself. Again, they are selfish in mind and intent; it is mostly about their own wants for things like support, affection, and attention. The children are, at best, thought about in second place.

Acquaintance parent: this parent lacks intimacy with their offspring. The parent does things that are more like what an acquaintance would do rather than a parent with a close relationship. Any deep love and close relationship that should seemingly develop naturally has been underdeveloped. It's a no-depth relationship. It's more of a fleeting, casual, and passing association.

Donor parent: these leaders are the real absentee parents. They are called donor parents because they donated the sperm and egg to create a baby together . . . and that is about it. They are not home much and not part of their children's lives. If they come around for a time, they do not stay around long.

Contemptuous parent: these people take responsibility and complete charge of their offspring's needs, wants, goals, and behaviors.

They are the judge of these things. They put down, complain, condemn, and emotionally intimidate their children to control them. The criticism used here may denigrate the character of the child and blanket them with negative words or labels. As a parent, at times, it is normal to get angry and correct the child. But labeling them with negative statements grouped with words of criticism and insulting them is not healthy. Assassinating the child's character is not healthy.

Zealot parent: this fanatical person is fixated on their opinion and will use their authority to control, manipulate, and exercise domination over the child. Their power base for control can be things such as money, religion, and even parent-to-child affection. These kinds of things are withheld from the child if they do not do as the parent wishes. Love is given or withheld based on whether the child does what the parent says. Threats, fear, control, and manipulation are used repeatedly so the parent gets their way.

Seesaw parent: Like a seesaw at a park or playground that goes up and down, so go these family leaders. Because of their up-and-down ways, they are not easy to understand or predict. Their level of contempt toward their offspring cycles up and down. The parents are constantly harsh, and one never really knows if they are ready for a relationship or not. Why? Because they are up and down, impossible to read. They are "sometimey." Sometimes they are good and happy toward you, and then they can be downright degrading and complaining to you and about you. They ebb and flow like waves on the seashore.

The "mommy or daddy dearest" parent: these are abusive parents, often extremely abusive. These dangerous people are vicious and cruel for even minor misbehaving. They consider anything the child does that is outside of their wishes as disrespect, and it is met with harsh reactions.

To reiterate what was previously said, the information above does not apply only to poisonous parents, nor does it apply to just children and families. In some situations, it can apply to leaders outside the home. Can you see any significant parts of the above poisons in you? Always start with yourself first. Use the tools being taught in this book to identify some important traits that need to change.

Write down what you see and the areas you need to start addressing. Then determine if you can identify any of these hazardous activities or styles of leading in others.

When you go to a medical doctor you generally are asked questions about symptoms or problems you are having coupled with your personal and family medical history of past sicknesses, ailments, surgeries, allergies, and more. You are asked questions about various things so the doctor can begin narrowing down problems you may have or could have in the future. Sometimes it is not always best or prudent to self-diagnose. Professional counselors and therapists are available. I recommend Christian counseling and therapy.

I hope you are seeing this book as a part of your education, spiritual enrichment, and edification. Toxic parenting is directly connected to toxic leadership. You may need help from others (ministers, doctors, counselors, etc.). You should at least identify some things you may be doing, thinking, and experiencing personally. You should also start to identify lapses in real leadership from others.

The process of identification is not for finger-pointing and accusing people. More so, it is there to know what to avoid and correct, and to find solutions.

NOTES

NOTES

Eight

HOW WORLDVIEW DETERMINES YOUR ACTIONS

Some people do bad things and think this is okay. Unfortunately, many people think this way. They continue to do things they know are bad, wrong—simply not right—in hopes of bringing about good. I have to tell you to stop using unrighteous, wrong, and even wicked methods to bring about a desired (good) result. To put it another way, stop doing the bad to get the good. The ends do not justify the means. Let me be clear: this way of thinking is completely wrong.

The main problem with toxic leaders is the way they think. It's like cheating on a negligent spouse to get more of their attention, so you can make up and reconcile in hopes of having a better marriage. How can you violate your vows and covenant of marriage in hopes of staying married? How ridiculous! This is childish behavior and immature reasoning. Like a kid misbehaving to get their parents' attention.

I once heard of a couple, claiming to be Christians, actively participating in spouse swapping. In other words, this married couple agreed to have sex with other people while staying married to each other. While they participated in these perverse acts and associated themselves with other swingers, they would tell these people about Christ in hopes of getting them to become Christians. They were justifying their actions to "spread the Gospel" to get people to become disciples of Christ by breaking the very marital laws that are given by God in the Bible they are supposed to believe in and follow! This may seem odd to you (and I hope it does), but some people truly have this demented way of thinking. Their desired end to get people to follow Christ is *not* righteously justified by their wicked means of breaking God's Word on sex and marriage. On the other hand, if they were to stay committed to each other and honor the biblical institution of marriage while being an example to other swingers to leave their perverse lifestyle, that would be a different story.

God does not have His children get as wicked as the people they are trying to win over.[271] God is not going to have you commit fraud to win over other white-collar criminals. He will not ask you to sell illegal drugs to win other drug dealers. People who think like this more than likely are dealing with deception, seduction, and compromise in their personal background. Stop leading by the Robin Hood Principle. Robin Hood was a character who robbed from the rich and gave to the poor.[272] Although many like the character, the bottom line is Robin Hood was still a thief.

Situations like these can be addressed by what the apostle Paul told Titus in Titus 1:16: "They profess to know God, but they deny him by their works. They are detestable, disobedient, unfit for any good work." Paul was telling Titus what kind of leaders to look for, and there were some who said they followed Christ, but by their way of living (lifestyle) they showed they were not actually following Him. They were denying His lordship in their lives. Said another way, they acted as though they didn't know God by the ways they lived, because their "wrong" actions were speaking louder than their "right" words. They disrespected the presence of God in their life by their actions. They were not standing for what God wanted them to stand for.

Notice, in the same chapter of Titus, Paul identified people who were unfit to lead, which also means they were unfit to be followed. These are people who do not need to be leaders at all. Paul labeled them as detestable (abominable), disobedient (not compliant), and unfit for any good work (worthless). See the pattern? **Bad thinking + Bad behavior = Unfit to lead**.

People with crummy, even destructive, ways of thinking tend to continually make bad decisions. Like the woman who thinks that a man's abuse—physically, emotionally, or mentally—is his way of showing true love. Wrong! An expression of love is not abuse. Love does not drive a person to create a hellish environment for the one they love. Can you see the flawed logic?

How many of you have heard of the guy who goes to strip clubs and thinks the strippers genuinely like him . . . as he gives over wads of cash. Foolishness! If you think like this, I have to break it to you that you are only getting attention from a stripper because you are paying for her attention. You are literally *paying attention*.

I hope these examples seem outrageous to you. If not, consider this a warning to the poor way you think and process information. You may be toxic in this way of thinking.

RIGIDLY RIGHTEOUS

God wants you to be rigidly righteous.[273] For every one of us, the goal is to display honesty and integrity. To be upright in character. Your character should be formed by God's Word and be the standard by which you make decisions. Your actions and decisions will change depending on the situation, but they should be based on good character, inner qualities that are unchangeable.

Yet again I remind us that so-called "good" results do not justify wicked methods to accomplish them. Romans 3:5-8 talks about how some think it's okay to sin, to do wrong, for the purpose of seeing how righteous God is. Nonsense! Paul wrote (verse 8) that the people who say such things deserve to be judged or condemned.

WHAT IS YOUR WORLDVIEW?

On important matters in your life, have you ever asked yourself: *What is my worldview?* Or, *what is my worldview based on?* You should. You may be surprised to find the foundation of what you believe or stand on is not what you think it is. How you see life and how you treat people comes from your worldview.

All people have a worldview. Here are several definitions to explain this important point. A worldview is a way of thinking about the world, your specific life philosophy, or how you see the world. Any worldview, even your personal worldview, is a combination of all you believe to be true, and what you believe becomes the driving force behind every emotion, decision, and action.[274] Another basic definition is that a worldview is a framework or structure of our most basic beliefs that shape our view of the world and becomes the basis of our decisions and actions.[275]

One author noted that your personal worldview colors every decision you make and everything you do.[276] Consider it a blueprint or map of your present reality.[277] As a blueprint, it serves two parts. One, it helps explain and interpret life.[278] Two, a worldview is the point of view from which you live your life, with your decisions and actions following (see Figure 5).

If you see people as ants who exist solely to build your plans, your kingdom, your business, and as though they are only good to follow your commands, wishes, and perspectives, do not be surprised when you start treating people like ants. People do not realize that they live and lead from the inside out. Whatever is on the inside (anger, resentment, jealousy, arrogance, fear, timidity, etc.) often leaks out in our actions and what we say to others. It's the mind-body connection. Often, what is in the heart and/or what the mind thinks manifests itself in mouth and body.[279] If you see people as garbage, don't be surprised when people feel that you treat them as garbage. Men, if you only see women as sexual objects to be conquered and used, you will probably do and say things that show you believe that. It will come out.

Without knowing it, many of us live incongruously. Incongruous means: not in harmony, incompatible, not conforming, disagreeing, inconsistent, unsuitable.[280] I remember part of a conversation I had with the late Bishop Harry R. Jackson Jr. He was speaking about some people who said they were Christians. When he heard the things they believed in, he thought: How can these people say they follow God and believe and support things totally against their Christian faith? Bishop Jackson asked, in disbelief, "Are these people really Christians?" He saw and heard the incompatibility between who they said they followed and what they actually did.

The problem is people either do not clearly know what their worldview is or don't realize what they do reflects their worldview. It can be embarrassing when you see disharmony between the two. Most men say, "I value women," but (in reality) many don't value their presence, opinion, the way they think differently, or what they bring to the table besides domestic actions. People say God is their source, not material things like money, but then do all kinds of things to show their God is actually money. Many people say their worldview is valuing people no matter their skin color, nationality, or ethnicity. They say there isn't an iota of racism in their soul. But God forbid their child wants to marry a person from another ethnic group. Then you see, and I mean *really* see, what they believe. Your actions prove your true worldview.

Consider a woman who listens to and buys music with lyrics that are perverted, violent, sexually explicit, plainly disrespect women, and treat them as sexual toys for gratification. Yet these same women will become extremely upset if they are told the same things from a father figure, minister, supervisor, coworker, or others. These women are literally paying to be disrespected. They are paying to hear lyrics that cheapen and lessen their God-given value and, at the same time, enrich the man or woman saying these things. Absurd! It's almost funny that a person will demand respect in their life and yet feed and fuel someone to talk to them as though they are worthless garbage. Stop glorifying the people who create, perpetrate, and stand by these lyrics. Stop validating these people with your time, attention, presence, and money. Fix the disharmony. Again, what is your true worldview?

Take a moment to consider the man who wants to be respected on and off the job, and especially in the company of others, but never respects anyone else. He'll go out of his way to disrespect another man's home, possessions, money, and spouse. But if that disrespect comes back to him, he'll get upset and be willing to fight to be honored and respected. This man lives in a dream world where he wants honor but does not want to give it. This sounds a lot like an immature, narcissistic child.

See the incongruity? How about this example. I know men who did not have a good father figure in their life. They say they want a father figure, and to be mentored, but will not listen to the father figures and successful men who *are* in their everyday life. How does that make any sense? Answer: it does not. If you say you want to be led and coached, but you have available leaders in front of you that you do not take advantage of—that becomes a walking contradiction. Do you have the right view?

Many times we do or say things without thinking about our motivations for doing or saying those things. It is important to ask some honest questions of ourselves. What is the foundation of my thinking and decision-making process? What is leading me? Is it God, money, fame, selfishness, or revenge? Am I driven by the opinions of others, by my ambitions, by an evil spirit, by my carnal nature? What is my worldview based on? Where does it come from?

See Figure 5, as noted by W. Gary Phillips, William E. Brown, and John Stonestreet in their book *Making Sense of Your World: A Biblical Worldview* (Salem, Wisc.: Sheffield Publishing Co., 2008).

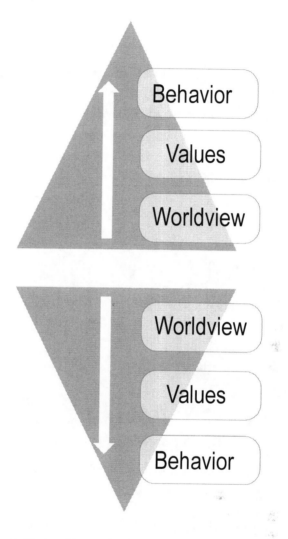

Figure 5: The Worldview Triangle: behavior, values, worldview

Here's an example of a specific kind of worldview. A biblical world-view is basically explained by its name. It is a view based on the Word of God.[281] When you believe the Bible is true and follow its teachings, you allow it to be the foundation of everything you say and do.[282] For the Christian, the worldview should be a biblically based one. There should be no separation of personal worldview from a different biblical worldview somewhere in the back of your mind. The two should be one. If you follow Christ and believe what is in the Scriptures, the Bible's view trumps, overshadows, and should change any other personal view you may be considering. You should not separate your mind from the mind of Christ.[283]

Worldview leads to culture (values, beliefs, and behaviors), and your culture leads back to worldview. It is a self-supporting cycle.

To reemphasize, you tend to live by, place value, and behave according to your worldview. For those who believe they have a biblical worldview, let's take a quick test developed by researcher George Barna. Answer these questions.

- Do absolute moral truths exist?
- Is absolute truth defined by the Bible?
- Did Jesus Christ live a sinless life?
- Is God the all-powerful and all-knowing Creator of the universe, and does He still rule it today?
- Is salvation a gift from God that cannot be earned?
- Is Satan real?
- Does a Christian have a responsibility to share his or her faith in Christ with other people?

Here is the answer key: every answer should be yes. Only 9 percent of believers answered yes to all the questions in the survey.[284] That is sad. We have Christians who say they follow Christ but do not know, or choose not to believe, what the Bible teaches. No one knows everything, but when confronted with revelation, teaching, and learning God's Word, Christians need to change to be in agreement with it. I recommend you stop the disconnect between what you know is right and what you actually do.

You may not be aware that your worldview is often the combination of several different sources of information. Some of these can provide terrible points of view. Your worldview can get polluted, diluted, or changed by secular worldviews, opinions, and perspectives that come from politics, laws, books, movies, music, the Internet, academia (schools, colleges, and universities), and people.[285] As leaders, we must believe the truth of God and live it. If not, our lifestyle will be confusing and misleading. This is important to know because many people go through life not recognizing their worldview has been deeply influenced by secular humanism, poor standards, and bad examples from other streams of thought. Again, the media and other influences affect our thinking more than we realize.[286]

A great writer once wrote, "Don't let anyone capture you with empty philosophies and high-sounding nonsense that come from human thinking and from the spiritual powers of this world, rather than from Christ."[287] Put another way, make sure no one leads you away like a prisoner (deceives you), pulling you from the truth by empty ideas and philosophies with no truth or purpose.

Caution! Be careful what you allow to influence you. For instance, if you accept more of a biblical worldview and trust it with unwavering faith, you put yourself in a better position to make the right decisions and form appropriate responses to questions on things like racial issues, abortion, same-sex marriage, what to watch and listen to, and more.[288] A worldview can be *taught*, and it can be *caught*.[289]

Read Romans 12:2 (NLT): "Don't copy the behavior and customs of this world, but let God transform you into a new person by changing the way you think. Then you will learn to know God's will for you, which is good and pleasing and perfect."

I know a mother who spends a great deal of time with her young daughter. When the two are watching TV together, if something is heard or seen that is not right, the mother will speak with her daughter about it. The mom intentionally explains what happened and teaches how to think and respond from a biblical perspective. She is actively forming her daughter's worldview. Bottom line: your behavior advertises what you think and believe.

If you as a Christian do not align yourself with God's Word and His way of thinking, your Christian faith is not worth much. God cannot trust you to truly represent Him if you "choose" to not think like He does. In Matthew 5:13 (NASB) Jesus says, "You are the salt of the earth; but if the salt has become tasteless, how can it be made salty *again*? It is no longer good for anything, except to be thrown out and trampled underfoot by people."

Jesus is speaking to His disciples in Matthew 5:14-16: "You are the light of the world. A city set on a hill cannot be hidden; nor do people light a lamp and put it under a basket, but on the lampstand, and it gives light to all who are in the house. Your light must shine before people in such a way that they may see your good works, and glorify your Father who is in heaven."

Leaders who endeavor to teach, mentor, and coach the next generations need to make sure all have the "What is your worldview?" talk. We need to emphasize a high standard in all things. Do not assume people have the same perspective about major topics of interest. Ask: what do you believe and why do you believe it?

Leaders are gatekeepers of beliefs. You stop the bad, and you should only allow what's proper and right. You are the standard-bearers.

NOT MANIPULATING OR DECEPTIVE

Matthew 7:15-20 (NIV) speaks of bad leaders. Let's look at the practical ramifications of verses 15 and 16.

"Watch out for false prophets. They come to you in sheep's clothing, but inwardly they are ferocious wolves. By their fruit you will recognize them . . ."

A prophet is, without a doubt, a type of leader. All leaders are supposed to be ambassadors for the organization they represent.[290] They are supposed to be credible representatives who embody strong values set by the organizations they support. They are to be a model for true leadership.

A signal that a leader is ready to be followed—even modeled—is proven by their behavior. Matthew 7:15 states these false prophets (or bad leaders, people who should not be followed) are like ravenous wolves (animals of prey). Remember, these people are supposed to be leaders of people, not those who would abuse and devour them. On the inside, their soul (mind, will, and emotions) is wicked. These leaders are compared to predators. They are motivated to act just as a wolf would toward a deer. This kind of leader is dangerous to your well-being. (These pathetic leadership attributes were covered in the toxic leadership chapters earlier in this book.)

You will recognize these people by their fruit (Matthew 7:16). Fruit can be explained in several ways.[291] Let's cover two. The first part is finding out what motivates the person. If a person is motivated, energized, inspired by, and interested in bad things . . . be careful. In other words, what is the original cause for their actions?

The second part of defining fruit is the end *result* of their action; i.e., the outcome, the product. Evil actions come from an evil heart. Grasp this insight: terrible leaders can be identified by what they *do*. The results of what they say and do are the telltale signs. Whether prophet or non-prophet, this leadership Scripture applies to you no matter your occupation.

My last point on Matthew 7:15 is to watch out for these deplorable leaders. These leaders come to you in a seemingly innocent way ("sheep's clothing"), just as a normal person in leadership would, but they are motivated to attack and ravage like a beast. You will recognize them by seeing what they do—their fruit. Again, what a person says and does is a product of *what they think.*

NOTES

NOTES

Nine

TYPES AND SOURCES OF LEADERSHIP POWER

Temporarily putting aside the toxicity issue, let's cover what the proper leader, follower, and familial relationship or association should be based on. Gary Yukl, who wrote *Leadership in Organizations*, noted there are different facets of power a leader may gain access to.[292] These types of power are subdivided into two categories, *position power* and *personal power*.

After we go through these categories, take time to reflect and/or journal how you interact with people on the basis of these two divisions of power.

Position power comes from having a rank, or formal position, in an organization. The higher up you are placed or promoted to in an organization, the more power you tend to have.[293] **Personal power** is realized when a leader is likeable and knowledgeable.[294] Here are Yukl's suggestions or guidelines for some of the bases of power.[295]

- Position Power
    - Legitimate power
    - Reward power
    - Coercive power
    - Information power

- Personal Power
  - Referent power
  - Expert power

According to Yukl, a leader has *legitimate power* when he or she has formal authority over another's work activities. To put it simply, your supervisor can legitimately, legally, and with valid grounds tell you what to do because of their legitimate position of control. The nuances may vary a tad in other kinds of organizations, but legitimacy tends to hold true all the same.

Legitimate power works similarly in the family unit. For example, the parent normally has oversight, control, and authority over the children. Generally, we expect children to listen to their parents. It's normal, typical, and customary that parents are in charge and children follow. (In many homes, even, it is not uncommon for older siblings to have some kind of perceived legitimate authority over younger siblings.)

In volunteer organizations legitimate power still has a place. You follow the guidance of the team leader or department head because they really are the team leader or department head. Formalized or structured positions tend to give those in charge legitimate power with, and over, others. What organizations are you part of that gives others legitimate power over you, and who do you have legitimate power over?

Suggested guidelines for leaders using legitimate power:

- Make clear requests.

- Don't exceed your level of authority.

- If necessary, confirm or reconfirm your legitimate authority and require compliance.

- Follow proper organizational processes.

- Follow up to confirm your instructions are being followed.

Reward power comes from the ability of a person to offer a positive incentive. For example, consistently doing a good job at work could earn you a pay raise, promotion, bonus, or special work privilege.[296] The leader finds out what motivates the targeted person and uses it to the advantage of both parties. Advised guidelines for using reward power:

- Offer rewards that are fair, ethical, and what people want.
- Only promise what you can deliver.
- Explain the criteria for giving rewards.
- If requirements are met, provide rewards as promised.
- Do not use rewards in a manipulative way (use them to reinforce good behavior).

Coercive power is similar to, but separate and distinct from, reward power. Both have the ability to control monetary and non-monetary compensation and punishment.[297] Coercion, however, is the ability to give a person things he or she does not desire or to remove or decrease things that are desired.[298] Understand that leaders who use coercive power are not necessarily bullies, but most (if not all) workplace bullies use or lead with coercive power. Recommended guidance for using coercive power (in a proper way, to maintain discipline) are:

- Explain rules and requirements, and ensure people understand the consequences of violations.
- Respond to noncompliance promptly and consistently without showing favoritism to anyone.
- Investigate: get the facts, avoid jumping to conclusions or making assumptions, and avoid placing blame too fast.
- Except for the most serious violations, provide adequate oral and written warnings before starting punishment.

- Generally, give warnings and reprimands in private; there should be no rash threats.

- Stay calm and avoid the appearance of hostility or personal attacks.

- Show a sincere desire to help the person comply with expectations.

- Ask the person to suggest ways to correct the problem, then agree on a corrective plan.

- After warnings have been made, administer punishment if non-compliance continues.

- Use punishments that are legitimate, fair, and match the seriousness of the infraction.

Information power is the control of information. It is about controlling, and about giving access to information that people need or want.[299] People who wield this type of power have access to information others do not. For example, people who are senior managers have access to information that customer service and first-level supervisors do not. Associates in the workplace's management division may have access to information that those in the maintenance or information technology departments do not. Senior sales representatives often know more than the junior ones. At times, this type of power will be in demand more than others because of what people want to know.

Referent power is the desire to please another person for whom you have strong feelings of affection, admiration, and loyalty.[300] No formal legitimate authority or association is needed. Simply put, people listen to, follow, and accomplish tasks for people they respect and appreciate. Celebrities, and political and spiritual leaders, often have this as a strong power base. Yukl's general guidelines to obtain and use referent power are:

- Show acceptance and concern.

- Be helpful and caring.

- Keep your promises and commitments.

- Make self-sacrifices to help others, not yourself.

- Practice self-leadership; lead by example; be the role model.

Expert power is when a person possesses unique knowledge about the best way to perform a task or solve a problem.[301] This is often the main base of power that mentors, coaches, and consultants use. Experts administer information, knowledge, or expertise.[302] We value their opinion and insight because of their vast experience or exposure to things we want to know. Recommended guiding principles for the use of expert power:

- Explain the reasons for a request or suggestion and why it is important.

- Provide evidence that a proposed action will be successful.

- Be sober-minded, clear-headed, and consistent, and do not make rash, careless statements.

- Integrity always: don't lie or misrepresent facts.

- Listen to the person's concerns and suggestions.

- Be confident and decisive in a crisis.

In any given personal, professional, and volunteer association, you may find several of these power bases overlapping and intersecting. For example, if you have a supervisor, most likely *legitimate, reward, coercive,* and *informational* power are already working simultaneously. If you admire your supervisor, you can add *referent* power to the mix. If you are the smartest person in the group, the best at what you do in the department, and the majority of people do what you say, you are most likely operating under *expert* power.

Knowing these general social bases of power and influence that go back and forth between personal and business relationships can make you more socially aware. Notice I used the words *social* and *socially*. The business of leadership is a social one. It involves people and lives—human beings. Some leaders seem to ignore or forget that.

People who are in charge can fall prey to the "It's all about me" mindset. To some degree it *is* about them, but leadership is *mainly* about others. Leadership is about the interaction between leader and follower. To lead people is to influence, inspire, and guide them.[303]

Leadership is defined in many ways. James Kouzes and Barry Posner wrote in *The Leadership Challenge* that leadership really is a relationship.[304] They explain the best leadership experiences are not stories of solo performances, but leaders who activate others to action to accomplish a shared goal. Restating: leadership is a relationship between those who lead and those who follow.[305] The bases of power described previously can help you develop or fine-tune your relationship with those you lead or those who lead you. The bases of power also act as boundaries for those with whom you work.

Here are some more definitions of leadership.

- "The process of getting people to do their best to achieve a desired result . . . the ability to persuade others willingly to behave differently. Leadership involves developing and communicating a vision for the future, motivating people, and securing their engagement to the task they are expected to do."[306]

- The process of producing direction, alignment, and commitment in others.[307]

- A process where an individual influences a group of individuals to achieve a common goal.[308]

I hope you are seeing the simple fact that leadership is a process that involves others. Those who believe leadership is a one-way street, one that is about themselves only, are bound to have the wrong mindset and ultimately do the wrong things.

For there to be leadership, there have to be followers. To be a credible leader, you need people following you. Again, by *followers* I mean:

people who do what others want them to do and who usually have less influence than their superiors.[309] And, people who typically follow voluntarily due to one of the power bases stated previously.

What if you have no one following you? Can you still be a leader? Yes. I believe there is an exception, and it's the practice of self-leadership.

In my first book (*Leadership in the Age of Narcissism*), I describe self-leadership as the practice of intentionally and proactively influencing your own thinking, behavior, and feelings to achieve your goals.[310] It is you first leading yourself. You follow your own instructions and make proper decisions on your way to your goal. You lead yourself before you try to lead anyone else. If a person claims to be a leader but is derelict in their duties to lead themselves first, they discredit the foundation of their own headship.

Think about it. If you were out of shape, would you hire an overweight personal trainer? Would you hire a financial advisor if you found out they do not follow their own advice? Would you trust the advice of someone who wants to coach you on taking care of your children, but they do not have a good record of taking care of their own? Would you rely on a dentist who wants you as a patient, but has no regard for his/her own oral health? Isn't it interesting to see a supervisor who is always telling work associates to be on time and follow the company's code of conduct but who never seems to follow the same guidance?

Be extremely careful of people who say one thing in a wholesale manner and yet live another. I am not talking about a mistake, an occasional oversight, or a temporary loss of focus. I am referring to a complete disregard for the principles they teach. See the point?

You must be properly self-led before you try to lead others. You should first be an advocate and an ambassador of the principles you believe are important before you request or require anyone else to live up to them. If you don't, you leave yourself open to being needlessly questioned, and you create a foundation of a lack of credibility and trustworthiness. In 1 Corinthians 9:27, even the apostle Paul said he needed to discipline himself to follow what he told others to do. Otherwise, he would be considered worthless (unfit to lead).

Let's finish at the main point. One of the reasons I explained all the sources of power (legitimate, reward, coercive, information, referent, and expert) is to show you what most working relationships in profit and nonprofit, volunteer and professional working relationships, associations, interactions, connections, and affiliations are (or should be) based on. These are the appropriate bases of power or influence that occur in many relationships. All the bullying, overreaching, abusing, berating, harassing, poisonous, oppressing, and corrupt behaviors are totally unnecessary. They are truly toxic. I hope you understand the differences.

Let's end this chapter with three important questions.

- What bases of power are you functioning under at work, school, and home?

- Do any of these bases of power come into operation in your more intimate and familial relationships?

- If you are in charge of people, which power bases most define your relationships? How can you improve them?

Take some time now to reflect.

NOTES

NOTES

Ten

—

LINGERING, LASTING, LASCIVIOUS LUSTS

Lust. We covered portions of it in a previous chapter. But there is so much more to cover about lust and the poison that can infect a person's life. It's a binding, wicked spiritual force that will drive you, take you where you shouldn't go, and keep you where you shouldn't stay.[311] Lust has many synonyms, and a number of these can give us a fuller meaning of what it is and provide a more well-rounded definition.

The Collins Dictionary states that a lust for something (person, place, thing, ideology, etc.) is a strong and eager desire to have that thing; excessive sexual desire; seeking unrestrained gratification.[312] Merriam-Webster says lust is an unusually intense or unbridled sexual desire; lasciviousness; an intense longing or craving; to have an intense desire or need.[313] The Cambridge Dictionary describes it as a very strong sexual desire, and a powerful feeling of wanting something.[314]

Lust has a lot to do with sex or sexual desire, but it's important to understand that lust deals with many different areas besides sexual desire. Review the definitions again and you will see that lust is far more than only relating to sex. Another definition is that lust is a psychological drive that produces intense desire, one that makes a person desperately need to obtain an object or secure a circumstance (i.e., getting something he or she wants or wants to see happen).[315] When the object has been obtained or the circumstance secured, there is only temporary relief.[316] Lust can get so extreme that it becomes extraordinary. To put it another way: it implies an intensity to acquire, achieve, and/or consume, a desire that is just not ordinary.[317]

When left unchecked, or if a person has unaddressed or unhealed soul wounds, lust cannot be satisfied; it is unappeasable and insatiable. It can be constant or chronic, like the desire or need for food and water. No matter how much you fill your stomach or gorge yourself, you are bound to be hungry and thirsty again soon. It is never satisfied, never at complete rest, and always has an appetite for more.[318]

Your lust will not stop unless you or something stops it.

Notice what the Scriptures say in James 1:14-15 (NLT): "Temptation comes from our own desires, which entice us and drag us away. These desires give birth to sinful actions. And when sin is allowed to grow, it gives birth to death." Did you realize that verse 14 says a person is *lured* (tempted, trapped, and attracted) by "his own desire"? Desire, lust, and the like is specific to the person. A lust or struggle for you may not be the same for another.

Lust goes way beyond sex. Just as mankind is a dynamic being who can have a multitude of needs, wants, and desires, so too can mankind's lusts be numerous or multifaceted. You can have multiple lusts running at the same time in your life.

Take some time to reflect before reading further. In what areas of your life do you believe you are harboring lusts? After that, let's cover a few areas that may bring some revelation and understanding.

POWER LUST

Author Joseph Haroutunian, who wrote *Lust for Power: A Study of the Misuse of Power*, said this.

It is strangely gratifying to make people come and go at our bidding, to overrule their minds and their wills, to take away their power and thus virtually to annihilate them. There is an "irrational" but nonetheless soul-filling self-fulfillment in mastery over human beings. There is no pleasure quite like it; and for its sake, men have risked every good and done every conceivable evil. It is well to remember these facts and to take them seriously. Now, this "lust for power" is irrational and wicked . . . some people are possessed of a lust for power. It is not prudent to say it publicly, but in truth a great many people, perhaps most people, love power for its own sake.[319]

Haroutunian goes on to say several things about the lust for power.[320]

- The lust for power is not natural and is a corruption of nature.

- The end goal of lust is its own gratification; the lust for power is the pursuit (the going after, the chase, the tracking down) of its own desires (it wants what it wants and does not care about others). Lust of power is not used to serve the greater good of anyone else.

- Pride, ambition, and greed lead to lust.

- Influences that may push people to lust for power are when they experience exploitation, segregation, defamation, and/or unfair treatment.

See anything familiar? Think of this power lust as an unending craving to control. This brand of lust can be broken down in two different ways: autonomy and influence.[321] Autonomy power means to ignore or resist other people's demands (i.e., requests, orders, assignments given, terms, or stipulations).[322] The second part, power of influence, is to have control over yourself and others.[323] The lust for power as influence can be problematic because your appetite for it can grow. It's like eating your favorite food, one you become addicted to. The more you eat it, the more you want it. That is a fundamental problem with lusts. *They cannot be ultimately satisfied when you feed them.*

A point of balance is to remind ourselves that the concentration of this book is to teach about the negative sides of power. There are, of course, healthy (unharmful) sides. People can do, and have done, great things with the gifts of leadership and power entrusted to them. When handled properly with the right heart and perspective, people in charge can do much good. However, you must be educated and aware of the bad to identify it and avoid it.

Power in the hands of the untrained, unskilled, evil, proud, and selfish-minded person is like putting a small, untrained child behind the wheel of a speeding car. Pain and destruction are often imminent. Think about the concept of the paradox of power. The paradox of power says that *the very traits that helped leaders accumulate control (power) in the first place disappear once they rise to power.*[324]

Think about a person who was once kind, disciplined, and hard-working, who later became disrespectful, lazy, and disorderly. What about the man who's married? Just a few years ago when he was dating or courting his fiancée, he took her out on dates, bought her thoughtful gifts, attended to her needs, spoke to her often, and did all the things she loved. Only to finally get married, and now he no longer does any of the things that attracted her to him in the first place. Quite the paradox.

What is your largest paradox? What are your paradoxes? What good did you formerly do that you have now stopped? What support, assistance, aide, and help did you provide others that you have since stopped? When and why did you stop? Think about it and write down your leadership and life paradoxes. Identification is crucial before you can properly address the paradoxes. It's needed before you can change. A sad point: it is consistently found that when a number of people gain power, they start acting like fools.[325]

As leaders, we need to take a while and think about what ground we've given up. What moral ground, what integrity ground, and what work ground have we lost? What were the inspired things you knew you should do that you are no longer doing because now, "I am in charge"? I am not talking about duties you need to pass on to a subordinate due to your position requirements. I'm talking about a change that would cause a leader to do something today that they thought unthinkable in years prior: speaking inappropriately to others, sexually harassing another, breaking furniture in fits of rage, going on temper and pride tantrums. How many of you have simply stopped being nice and hardworking? What switched your mentality from supporting others to now being a type of god, one imposing your egotistical rule on others?

Psychologists believe one of the problems with authority is it makes people less sympathetic to the concerns and emotions of others.[326] Studies found that people in positions of authority often rely on stereotypes and generalizations when judging other people; it is harder to imagine the world from someone else's perspective.[327]

What does perverted power or the grab for power look like? Consider Xi Jinping, the Chinese Communist Party's vice president from 2008-2013 who became President of the People's Republic of China in 2013. One of Xi's first initiatives was a nationwide anti-corruption campaign that removed thousands of high and low officials.[328] This may seem like a good thing, but along with the fact that more than one million corrupt officials were punished by late 2017, the campaign also removed many of Xi's political rivals, strengthening his efforts to eliminate opposition and maintain his grip on power.[329] Under his administration, The National People's Congress, China's constitution was amended to change the term limits for the country's president and vice president, and this allows Xi to remain in office beyond 2023 when, originally, he would have had to step down.[330] Xi believes in what he thinks is a superior form of government: a totalitarian, closed society where the individual is subordinated to the one-party state.[331] Not only does Xi intend to break the established system of presidential succession and remain president for life, he wants at least another decade to concentrate the power of the state and military in his hands.[332] He knows there is opposition to his plans, and he wants to make sure those opponents won't have the ability to resist him.[333]

Think about Russian President Vladimir Putin, who is called by several names: a modern-day Joseph Stalin, czar, killer, even a schoolkid with an attitude.[334] All these nicknames have one thing in common: power. They describe a man with a hard-fisted, iron-rule mentality.[335]

Dictators dominate others and employ what is called an authoritarian or autocratic leadership style, but not all authoritarian or autocratic leaders are dictators. Dictators and the regimes they cultivate will have malicious and insidious actions, harshness, and cruelty mixed in. Tyrants look out for their own advantage rather than the well-being of their followers, and in the process are more than willing, and able, to employ extreme and cruel tactics.[336] Tyrants are narcissistic in thinking they are the exception to the rules that apply to others. They think themselves above others and imbued with special traits or gifts. Dictators from the past century (Stalin, Adolf Hitler, Saddam Hussein) said they would create a new social order, erected statues or monuments to themselves, and changed their titles and roles to suit their own desires.[337]

Are you a dictator? You do not have to be an extreme one to be one. Who has been a dictator, totalitarian leader, harsh ruler, tyrant, or destructive leader in your life? Again, is it you? To be clear, I am not against strong leaders. I am not against sweeping reforms or actions when needed. Strength, decisiveness, and making bold moves doesn't have to be mixed with brutal behavior and viciousness. But the insidious and harsh edge is what truly tips things into full-blown dictatorship.

Tyrants will do whatever it takes to gain and maintain power. Rivals or threats are removed.[338] You can read about many dictators and see how they used various tactics to eliminate people to secure power.

I ask again: are you a tyrant? You could be. On a lesser scale, you could be a tyrant at home, in the workplace, or in relationships. Just because you are not a well-known leader doesn't mean you are not a dictator. There are plenty of harsh leaders in corporate America, churches, nonprofits, and in homes. This ranges from CEOs to front-line and first-level supervisors. This person could be a family member, politician, gang member, or tyrannical law enforcement official. These lust-for-power leaders are bullies in lead roles.

BULLIES

A bully is a person who hurts, frightens, threatens, or tyrannizes those who are smaller or weaker.[339] Of course, not all leaders are bullies, and not every bully is in a leadership position. A bully leader will strategically select ways to make a particular point (or convey an image) to put people in a submissive and powerless position where they are more easily influenced or controlled so the bully can achieve personal or organizational objectives.[340] Notice the word *strategic.*

The three typical types of bullying are verbal, physical, and relational.[341] Verbal bullying is the most common form of bullying and is used by both men and women.[342] Physical bullying is the most recognized type and is usually (though not always) done by males. Relational bullying is often used by women. This relational intimidation is about denying another person access to relationships or, rather, blocking others from associations, friendships, and being accepted.[343]

Bullies consider how and what to do to get their desired result. A bully's actions are typically implemented to fit a specific situation, environment, and person. It is strategic and thought-out, not random. For example, to get their way this person may fire or demote, yell, hit, shame, harass, be overbearing, be intentionally difficult, and use other planned tactics to get the recipient to bend to the bully's will. Clearly, bullies intimidate others to get their way. Do you see the selfishness theme showing up again?

Don't be fooled by looks. Bullies are not always people who appear inflexible and strict with cold personalities. A bully's intent is to demean you and use toxic ways to bend you to their will.

Let's spend some time reflecting once more. Are you a bully to the people you lead? Are you bullied by other leaders or coworkers? Do you bully your family members? I am not talking about having proper boundaries, holding people accountable, and disciplining or correcting your children. But are you bullying them? Identifying things like this are important so they can be dealt with and people can achieve healing.

Another problem with bullies is the success some of them have is used to justify their poor behavior and treatment of others. They use hurtful ways to attempt to bring about good results. It is sad, really sad, for a person, institution, or society to ignore a person who is allowed to strong-arm, heckle, oppress, threaten, and push around others just because they get the job done. It is sad that companies let people like this be successful. Simply "winning" does not fix everything. The way you do it matters.

As an example of strategic bullying, remember basketball coach Bobby Knight? Under his tutelage, Indiana University won 11 Big Ten Conference titles and three National Collegiate Athletic Association national championships.[344] Knight was fired in 2000 when he violated a zero-tolerance policy after years (I repeat, years) of high-tempered outbursts and accusations of physical abuse and racial comments.[345] Knight was a strategic bully who combined his ability to read his players and adjust his behavior and style to affect team performance.[346]

Some may say this is the positive side of bullying. *No!* Wrong. Do not use harmful tactics to justify good results. For those of you who do that, as your leadership coach I am advising you to stop. People who think this way help bullying continue. Evil means do not justify positive ends. There is no justification for evil ways even if they result in "good things" happening after them. For example, imagine that you are an event coordinator. To lie about what's going to happen at an upcoming event to get more people to come so you can pump up attendance numbers is wrong. Imagine you are a restaurant cook. Undercooking food to fill orders so people can pick up their food quicker and cut down on wait times is wrong. Lying to someone to not hurt their feelings is still lying. It's wrong. Wrong is wrong.

Being abusive to people in your department just to get work done on time is not a justifiable tactic. Guide followers by living the company standards others are required to meet, hold people accountable to their tasks, implement a code of conduct, and hold to the organization's values. If you need to fire people, do so. If you have to demote, move an employee to another position suitable to their skill set, or if you need to reprimand them, do so. Do not step into the realms of lying, abusive supervision, shaming, violence, and unprofessional aggression.

Unethical behavior is wrong. Stop verbally insulting people about their height, weight, sex, socioeconomic status, religion, or intellect. Even if you are winning awards and keeping the company in the black, this is not right. Preying on the weak, or bullying people to make budget, is still, at the end of the day, bullying. You can be successful and not be a tyrant. The two are not inextricably tied together.

As leaders and leaders in training, let's do our best to live a respectable and higher standard. Be transformative, not toxic. As servant-leaders we are called to have a positive impact, not an insufferable one. We are called to be a blessing to people, not bullies. Have you been guilty of any bullying tactics?

MONEY LUST

This type of lust is an endless desire to accumulate more and more wealth.[347] Greed is an insatiable longing for more than just money, but also for other goods and resources.[348]

The problem with greediness is what people will do to get what they want. For instance, drug cartels, gangs, criminals, and other unrestrained people will do all kinds of things to get money. They'll murder, rob, cheat, steal, extort, con people, keep back what belongs to others, and lie to get and keep money and possessions. Greed and the insatiable lust for more have been responsible for entire wars.[349] When nations are rich, instead of being content with what they have, their lust for money and possessions makes them covetous to gain more and more.[350] The never-satisfied appetite increases ambitions that have no limit, no restraint, incite jealousy, and stir up predatory instincts.[351] Any of this look familiar?

I think at times money acts like a highlighting marker, an amplifier or exposer. It amplifies what is already inside a person. Could this be why the apostle John wrote, in 3 John 1:2, "Beloved, I pray that all may go well with you and that you may be in good health, as it goes well with your soul"? By digging into the Greek wording of this Scripture, you can reread it like this: Dear well-beloved, I pray to God that in and above all things you prosper and be successful, be well and in good health, even as (or, just as) your soul (mind, heart, desires, feelings, affections, emotions) prospers and is successful.

See any connections? To be successful in all things and to be healthy even as our soul prospers and is successful—this is the goal. One of the things to highlight in this Scripture is the connection between being successful and prospering with your mind. The two should go together.

A prospering ministry, business, wallet, or bank account should be in lockstep with a prospering mind. A rich man with a broke and poor mind is at risk or even in danger. There have been athletes who have earned millions of dollars in a relatively short time and have gone broke thanks to a meager, untrained, undisciplined, and uneducated mentality. Don't be a rich man with a poor mentality or a wealthy man with a worthless mentality.

The wrong mindset could end up in you losing money or being unable to hold onto it for very long—something like a water bucket with holes in it. Having access to riches with the wrong mindset is like being married but having a single person's mentality. There will be problems and hindrances. Reflect on this quote from L. P. Jacks.[352]

> At the same time it is indisputable that morality, by which I mean justice and wisdom, has not advanced, anywhere, in the degree that is needed to deal justly and wisely with the enormous accession of riches which has suddenly fallen to the lot of the human race. Material prosperity has taken the world unawares; morally the nations were unprepared for it; some of them made ready for war, but none of them made ready for the greater dangers of peace. The nations have acquired all this wealth, but in the deepest sense they don't know what to do with it; they don't know how it ought to be handled; they don't know how to make it a blessing, or even how to prevent it from being a curse. This disparity between the moral and the economic development is the prime cause of our present trouble.

For long-term success, your character is your ceiling. For many of you, your character can dictate and determine how high you will go or how successful you can be. It will determine how long you stay successful. The word *character* can be defined several ways. It can be made of: integrity, trustworthiness, emotional intelligence, openness (to people, ideas, and experiences), and motivation.[353] Your character may very well be the cap on your personal development. The news, various media, and social media are filled with what appear to be successful people whose actions caused their failures. They self-destructed.

How many times have you earned genuine successes and accomplishments in your life, all to be destroyed, overlooked, and forgotten due to lapses in character? Why? Because your character is your ceiling. You cannot progress pass your ceiling.

How many relationships (professional and personal) have been broken due to your cruelness, selfishness, immaturity, cheating, lying, and foolish neglect? How many times have you passed on the same toxicity you experienced from one person to someone else? Your character may well be your ceiling, roof, boundary line, limiting factor ... your leash, your handcuffs, your foot restraints, your self-allowed and self-imposed traps. Your character is your ceiling, and your ceiling is your character. Prosper and be in good health equal to how your soul is prospering and successful.[354]

Prospering your soul is achieved in part by the quality of what you read, watch, listen to, your friends, and the environment you choose to put or keep yourself in. You become more valuable to yourself and others by educating yourself, changing for the better, and making yourself a real asset.

Proverbs 4:23 (NLT) says, "Guard your heart above all else, for it determines the course of your life." Said another way: watch over (preserve, or guard from danger) your mind, will, and emotions like a guard on a post, because from them are the limits of your life.

Money can be a curse if you don't know how to handle yourself or handle it. Do not, ever, confuse a person's financial wealth with wealth of character. You could win the lottery, be the recipient of a trust fund, inherit money, or secure intellectual property that could net you so much money it could change your family's lives for generations. And you could still be poor in character and poor in the way you treat people. Money does not make you good, godly, or great. It just makes you a person with money. Never be impressed by a person because of their assets.

I once read from an unknown author that lust, greed, and envy work together to twist a leader's sense of right and wrong. Here's a quick story to reflect on. Let's look at a man in the Scriptures named Gehazi, in the book of Second Kings, chapter 5. Simply put, and in today's more modern understanding, Gehazi was an administrative assistant to a leader named Elisha.

In the Second Kings account, Naaman was commander of the Syrian army. He had a disease called leprosy which affects the skin and nerves. Naaman went to see Elisha so he could get healed. After some initial reluctance, Naaman finally does what Elisha told him to do, and God healed him. After he is cured, Naaman returned to see Elisha to give him a thank you gift.

Elisha would not take anything from Naaman. After seeing all this, Gehazi (the assistant) revealed what was in his heart: greed and deception. Those two things go hand in hand more than we realize. People who have greed in their soul may be more willing to be deceptive to get what they want.

To complete the story, Naaman eventually left Elisha to travel to his next destination. Gehazi, without telling Elisha what he was doing, went to Naaman privately and lied about Elisha now wanting some money and clothes. Naaman was glad to give the items to Gehazi in honor of Elisha and for what God had done for him.

When Gehazi returned, Elisha asked him where he had gone. Gehazi lied once more, saying he hadn't gone anywhere. Elisha knew he was lying, and Gehazi was punished by God for his greed and deception.

Briefly consider another Bible story—this one is in the book of Acts, chapter 5, verses 1-11. I encourage you to read this short, but powerful, story for yourself. It's about a couple named Ananias and Sapphira. The story reveals both of them were greedy and deceptive before they both ended up literally dropping dead. Again, we see lust for money and deception working together. The focus of the story is clearly when the couple lied about a financial transaction. Their punishment was swift and final. I will not get into all the possible meanings of why both suddenly passed away, but any reader can clearly see the results of their greed and dishonesty.

Greed and deception work together like left and right feet. Like left and right hands. You can see them paired, working together, all the time. For instance, this is why some people lie or cheat on their taxes, or file false insurance and disability claims. This is why some deceive the elderly and even steal from family members. It is based on greed and deception. Let us pause for a few minutes. Check your soul. Think about your life right now for areas of greed and deception.

Think of the times people may have gotten or taken things from you because of their lust for money. Although it is the focus of this section, remember greed goes far beyond simply money.

To be balanced and clear, there is nothing wrong with being wealthy. There is nothing wrong with riches, nor launching, leading, and appropriately having the benefits of a successful organization, ministry, nonprofit, or for-profit company. There are obvious benefits to having money. But does money control, lead, bind, and tell you what to do? You may have heard of the passage in 1 Timothy 6:10. It says, "For the love of money is a root of all kinds of evils. It is through this craving that some have wandered away from the faith and pierced themselves with many pangs." Put another way: when people have excessive, insatiable, bottomless desires to gain, or for wealth, it is the cause, origin, or source of all kinds of evil things. This is the reason you have to constantly practice self-awareness. You have to guard your heart.[355] Just as a store manager takes inventory of what is on the store shelves, likewise you must constantly consider the way you have been thinking and what is in your heart. Don't just categorize the things in your life that are good and bad. Begin to detail the steps you will take to deal with the problem areas.

When people love money too much it can create more and more havoc even on a national and global scale. For example, the 2008 financial crisis was caused by lust for money.[356] This great recession led to some of the highest recorded unemployment rates and home foreclosures in the U.S. since the Great Depression in the first half of the twentieth century.[357] It's said one reason for the housing industry collapse was that lenders of subprime mortgages passed off risky mortgage-backed securities to investors.[358] The banks did not care if they loaned to borrowers who were likely to default.[359] Another reason for the industry collapse was that financial institutions sought risky mortgage loans to get more profits from high-paying securities.[360]

The results of the recession lasted eighteen months. Net worth of U.S. households declined, erasing $19.2 trillion in wealth. Gross domestic product had the largest decline in sixty years, falling 4.3 percent in October 2009. The unemployment rate reached 10 percent (rates were higher among Black and Hispanic households). From July 2008 to March 2009 the U.S. lost $7.4 trillion in stock wealth, and home foreclosures soared—nearly three million a year in 2009 and 2010.[361]

SEX LUST

People with this kind of lust go on continual hunts for sexual satisfaction.[362] Always searching for or having experiences, but never fulfilled. God created the human body and all its many parts and systems. God created sex. Sexual intercourse between a natural-born man and woman, joined together in marriage, is God's mandated structure for sex to be experienced and enjoyed.

I know some might think this is old-fashioned and out of touch. It is not. God's commandments and principles are the standards to be followed regardless of how old-fashioned some may think they are. This is God's normal. If things are done outside of God's plan and purpose, they are abnormal.

By the way, normal does not mean boring, mundane, unexciting, or uninteresting. It's simply the preferred situation for your optimum use and benefit. When you buy a car, electronic device, or appliances, the manufacturer typically sends instructions on how to use the product so you don't damage it and it won't damage you. God, as your manufacturer and designer, has given you your purpose, gifts, and destiny and is calling you to follow His instructions in all things.

The degradation of biblical marriage and sexual intercourse we see in these times of outlandish lusts—swapping sexual partners, orgies, pedophilia, living a promiscuous lifestyle, bestiality, prostitution, molestation, incest, and other abominable and deviant immorality—none of these are God's plan.[363] The Bible is God's original intent. It is the standard. Just because a group of people say it's okay to do something, change the political climate, and pass a new law does not mean those things are okay in God's eyes. They are not. They are not okay even if your favorite leader, spiritual leader, politician, or your friend says they're okay. God's Word is His law. God's Word trumps all. There are some important chapters in the Scriptures to give you a greater understanding of God's perspective on these things. Genesis 19; Exodus 20; Leviticus 18 and 20; Judges 19; 1 Kings 14 and 15; 2 Kings 23; Proverbs 5 and 6; Romans 1; 1 Corinthians 6; 1 Timothy 1; and Jude 7 (which is a single verse) will provide you a strong start.

Because lusts are already over the top, outsized, disproportionate, and excessive, it's easy to understand these desires are too powerful and can lead you into addictions. These licentious (i.e., lacking legal or moral restraints; ignoring sexual restraints) patterns of thinking, including the spiritual effects, are like being in a car going downhill with no breaks. You are not in full control and you cannot stop. At least not in any safe, non-harmful way.

I am not saying every person who lusts for sex is fated to be addicted to something. I am saying that you do not need to play around with sexual lust as though it is not a big deal or is insignificant. Sexual lust has derailed marriages, ministries, careers, relationships, and more. Addiction and destruction could be at your door, so do not feed and let this hunger continue to grow unchecked. It's like trying to walk around with a wild, full-grown tiger on a short leash. When it gets going, no circus whip or small stick can stop it. You will get mauled.

The lie is you think you can control it, but it is really controlling you. Put this lust where it belongs. Gone. Kill it! In spiritual terms, lusts may be the result of an evil/negative spiritual force motivating, energizing, and driving you to do things to temporarily satisfy urges that ultimately will never be tamed. Let's briefly look at the case of Harvey Weinstein, who, I believe, among many other issues, has a sex lust problem. Weinstein was said to be one of the most influential movie producers in Hollywood.[364] In February 2020 he was found guilty of two felony sex crimes, criminal sexual assault in the first degree and rape in the third degree.[365] From that trial, held in New York City, he was given a twenty-three-year prison sentence.[366]

After the New York trial was completed, he was extradited to Los Angeles to face another round of charges. The Los Angeles County district attorney said that anyone who abuses their influence and power to prey on others will be brought to justice. After the trail in LA, in 2023 Weinstein was sentenced to an additional sixteen years in prison for rape and assault charges on a lady identified as Jane Doe 1.[367] This assault occurred ten years prior.[368] Do you see the toxicity of a person like Weinstein?[369]

Some may think: I am no Harvey Weinstein. I am not a powerful Hollywood mogul, and I do not assault people. That is likely true, but there is still something you should notice and can learn from his example. Look at where a man with his lusts can be led. Look what happens to a person who has a lifestyle (fame and money) that many want, but cannot keep his private parts in his pants. As we have read, unchecked power can be dangerous, and so can unchecked lust for sex. These two kinds of lusts can be separate but also connected. Appetites can grow with repeated occurrences, especially if you think you are getting away with them. Obviously, lust for sex is not only a male problem. But for men, power poisoning all too often manifests in penis poisoning.[370] In other words, their male organ stands up and they do ridiculous things that damage themselves, families, and organizations.[371] Allow me to list a few of these symptoms.[372]

SYMPTOMS OF POWER POISONING

- Focusing more and more on your own wants and needs and less on the wants and needs of others.

- Having less empathy (the ability to relate, understand, and have compassion) for other people.

- Behaving as if the rules do not apply to you (entitlement, thinking you automatically have rights to and deserve something when you do not).
- Showing an increasing lack of self-control.

STAY OUT OF MY BEDROOM

Some may say, "Stay out of my personal life." You should think carefully before taking that position. I believe the wisdom found in this book can speak to important areas in your life.

No area is off limits if it is holding, hindering, and limiting your life from growing and going forward. Like a caring father speaking to his children, the information may not always be what you want to hear, but it may be necessary and even vital for you to hear it and make the changes needed to better your life and leadership.

If your lust is overtaking you, driving you, controlling you, and leading your life down a detrimental path, you should be open to seeing that areas of your personal and private life are examined. Nothing should be off limits.

Do not let shame, pride, or resistance be your defense mechanism. That's the easy way out. If you are going to be the leader you are designed to be, that you should be, that you can be, you must be open to change. It is change you may not want, but change you *need*.

If you are doing things in the confines of your home or even thinking things in the confines of your mind that negatively influence and affect other people, these are areas in which you need information, ministry, counsel, advice, healing, and liberation. Don't let pride keep you in prison. Let's take the humble path and be open to hear, listen, consider, reflect, think, and chart a path to sustained change. Chart a path to being less corrosive, less toxic, and ultimately a better person and leader.

Of course, there are many different kinds of addictions. Having a sex obsession is a component of lust. An addiction is a chronic disorder with biological, psychological, social, and environmental factors.[373] An addiction is much more than just an intense interest in something or someone.[374] It is a medical condition that changes the brain, the body, and causes the person to feel bound to continue doing an activity or using a substance even when doing so is harmful.[375] Millions are addicted to pornography.[376] Pornography is defined as material showing erotic behavior (as in images, pictures, writings, books, and media) intended to cause sexual excitement.[377] If you are not sure what a pornography addiction looks like, consider this information. Watching pornography can cause a person's sex life to become less satisfying, cause relationship issues, make a person feel less satisfied with their partner, and lead a person to engage in risky behavior to view pornography, such as watching it at work.[378]

Other signs that pornography is a problem:[379]

- You ignore other responsibilities (work, appointments, and other obligations) to view it.

- You get yourself in deeper and deeper—you increasingly view more extreme pornography to get the same release that less extreme porn used to give you.

- No matter how it makes you feel, you keep going back to it. You feel frustrated or ashamed after viewing it, but continue to do so.

- You can't stop yourself. People at this stage often want to stop using pornography, but cannot.

- You spend large sums of money on pornography.

Any of this lust for sex feel convicting? Think about yourself first before you begin to think about another person who might need this information.

Another example of a person with a lust for sex problem is Silvio Berlusconi. Let's briefly review some information about this charismatic Italian's life. Berlusconi, a media tycoon, three times was prime minister of Italy.[380] He built a media group named Fininvest into a large company.[381] Berlusconi was convicted of tax fraud in 2014 and convicted in 2015 of bribing a former senator.[382] He was initially banned from running for political office until 2019. Later, an Italian court lifted the ban early, in May 2018, and he subsequently won a seat in the European Parliament in 2019.[383]

Berlusconi was often entangled in sex scandals including allegations of involvement with a teenage model.[384] In February 2011 he was ordered to stand trial for allegedly soliciting sex from a seventeen-year-old prostitute and abusing his power in a cover-up.[385] An Italian constitutional court trial opened in April 2011, but it was stopped shortly after it began.[386] One author wrote that Berlusconi is a powerful man with a promiscuous lifestyle.[387] There were many reports that he used his position to entice women into sexual relations, often under the guise of aiding their professional advancement.[388] Berlusconi's second ex-wife accused him of consorting with minors.[389] One reporter said the prime minister was known to have sex parties at his villa.[390] Photographs of Berlusconi's private mansion in Sardinia showed skimpily dressed young girls entertaining him and other famous guests, including an entirely naked Mirek Topolanek, former Czech prime minister.[391] One editor-in-chief of an Italian publication, *La Republica*, stated that the prime minister had a potent mixture of the personal and political that became his undoing.[392] Did you notice the word mixture? Do you see how Berlusconi's personal life affected his public image and leadership? The revelations about his extramarital affairs, abuses of power, and allegations about his consorting with minors affected the stability of his brand.[393]

Do you see the obvious issues with the prime minister's public and private life? See any toxicity, corruption, undercutting, and lack of integrity? Do you see any similar toxicities in . . . *you*? Could you imagine the type of person you would be if you were in charge of an entire country? Would it surprise you to know you might be a lot like how you are now, just on a larger platform?

Just as an electronic amplifier increases the sound it's connected to . . . how would your life be viewed if it were amplified and displayed on a public stage? Does just thinking about that make you nervous? Under such amplification, what areas of your personality would be fine, and what areas would need work?

SUCCESS LUST

Do you lust to accomplish certain things or *be* someone? Not just want or like those things, but have an actual lust for them? Are you obsessed with being successful? You accomplish and accomplish and accomplish. It's not just a goal we are talking about. For example, your lust is more than just wanting to get a degree so you can get a certain job and a certain level of pay, or to have your own business and, with it, make a certain amount each year. You lust to accomplish for accomplishment's sake. You are never satisfied. It is a never-ending lust for more, and then more, more, and more. Get the idea?

Let's use basketball star Lebron James as an example. James is one of the wealthiest athletes in the world. According to Forbes, at the time of this writing his net worth is said to be 1 billion dollars.[394] In 2021, before paying taxes and agent fees, he earned 121 million dollars.[395] According to the National Basketball Association, here are some of James's major awards and accomplishments.[396]

18 All NBA awards
6 All-League Defensive Team awards
1 All-Rookie Team
3 NBA All-Star Most Valuable Player awards
4 NBA Finals Most Valuable Player awards
39 NBA Player of the Month awards
64 NBA Player of the Week awards
6 NBA Rookie of the Month awards
1 NBA Rookie of the Year award
1 NBA *Sporting News* Most Valuable Player of the Year

1 NBA *Sporting News* Rookie of the Year

1 Olympic bronze medal

2 Olympic gold medals

On February 7, 2023, James became the NBA all-time leading scorer.[397] He was once quoted as saying, "Whatever success I have had is never enough. I always want more."[398] Seeing that quote initially, it can be viewed as motivating, as reflecting on the drive this man has. Let's reflect on this on a deeper level. Whatever success you have is never enough? *Never?* This statement is both a notification and warning that lust is present. Imagine James's life. One of the greatest athletes around, he has earned many accolades, is world famous, earns more than most people will ever make in several lifetimes, won medals for representing the United States in the Olympics, and it's *still* not enough? Really? This is the very definition of a lust for success.

Do you lust to achieve? What impact has it had on you and your family, for good and for bad?

It's necessary to repeat that lust does not always lead to bad or terrible things. But it can and often does. Knowing the kind of lust you, your child, coworker, or supervisor has is important. It can reveal the whys of what people do, and how people think.

When is enough, enough? Do you find yourself always moving the finish line? Do you even *have* a finish line? I am not presuming that you should just settle in life. It's always good to have goals to work toward. But are you ever truly satisfied? Do you get drunk from seeing a continual list of your successes? Are you addicted to accomplishments with no end in sight? Is there a purpose for the things you accomplish? Is the pride of seeing a list of self-fulfilled accolades what gets you up in the morning?

OTHER LUSTS

As mentioned, there can be many types of lusts, especially since there are so many people thinking and desiring so many different things. Maybe you have a lust to leave some kind of legacy. *Legacy lust* is defined as a person who desires to leave an imprint of some kind that is lifelong or permanent.[399] Anyone can have this lust, but you may find it easier to see in presidents and business and spiritual leaders.

Maybe you have a *lust for legitimacy*. Leaders with this extreme passion have an overarching drive to diligently claim an identity and demand equity with others.[400] This lust may have you doing things in an attempt to prove your worth. This manifests itself in trying to prove to people that you are not worthless, that you are not the negative things that some people have said about you, or that you have gotten better since your past mistakes and have a desire to prove to others you are worthy of respect. That you are, in fact, legitimate. The list can go on and on.

Is it a *lust to be liked* that pushes you? Is it wanting to be accepted that has you bending over backward and allowing yourself to be taken advantage of so you can be liked? What gaping holes in your soul have caused you to be walked on by others and treated like a doormat so they accept you?

Are there other kinds of lusts you deal with? Do some analysis of yourself and others. Write down your findings.

NOTES

NOTES

NOTES

Eleven

MORE SHORT TALES OF TOXIC LEADERS

Warning *These paragraphs reference factual events of child sexual abuse.*

Serial molester. Pedophile. That's what he was. This man was absolutely wicked! This deviant had a history of destruction. It was known he had a problem with boys.[401] It was also said that the damage he did to hundreds of children is almost impossible to calculate.[402] Reported complaints about James Porter began in 1963 in River Falls, Massachusetts. Throughout his career he demonstrated devilish behavior. What makes matters worse is this horrific leader's actions were known by his *leaders* as he was transferred from one work location to another over the course of years.[403]

At one grammar school location, when James would walk around, the girls would warn each other he was coming.[404] Then the girls would find a place to stand against a wall so their backs were not toward him when he walked by. Why? He would sneak up behind them and fondle them.[405] If they did not turn their backs from him, he could get his violating hands under their skirts.[406]

This shadow of a man and disgraceful leader molested more than two hundred boys and girls while performing his profession. He committed crimes from masturbation (him on the children and them on him) to vaginal and anal rape.[407] For some, these horrific encounters did not happen just once; some children were repeatedly abused, often from his work locations and even in the children's homes. At his prison sentencing this man said he needed treatment and was not aware what led him to do the things he did . . . and that he was not cured.[408] James was supposed to be a Catholic priest. He was much more like a pedophile wearing priest's clothing.

TERRIBLE BOSSES

How would you like to work for a supervisor who required you to ask for bathroom breaks and then denied your requests 90 percent of the time?[409] Sounds ridiculous.

A man named George Pullman would fire his employees if their house wasn't clean enough.[410]

Some bosses merely embarrass you in meetings or in front of your coworkers. But a man named Alex Campbell would demand the women who worked for him get his birthdate tattooed on their back.[411] He was literally branding his employees.

Scott Rudlin, a theater and film producer, was named "Worst Boss of 2007."[412] He had a habit of screaming and throwing things at staff and firing people randomly . . . only for them to be rehired.[413] Everyone had to be reachable every day and at any hour.[414]

A woman once named the meanest member of Congress, Sheila Jackson Lee, burned through eleven chiefs of staff. She has been called the boss from hell.[415]

An employee of a large corporation was once called into the office by the CEO and CFO to discuss the workman's pay. The problem was he was being asked to keep quiet and be a part of a direct deposit scheme to take small amounts of money from other workers' paychecks. They were routinely robbing thousands of their employees by taking just a few cents up to one dollar (per each paycheck), hoping their victims would not notice.

What about the unapologetic supervisor who regularly intimidates, embarrasses, and backstabs their employees because he or she is jealous of them and does not really want them to succeed, or at least become better than them?[416]

Using what you have learned to this point, what toxic leaders have you worked with? What terrible bosses have you encountered? Have you led people in the wrong way? What true stories would you write about?

NOTES

Twelve

FOLLOWERSHIP

No one governs alone. No one. No one is able to rule alone. You cannot sustain leadership without followers or followership (unless you are practicing self-leadership). The study of followership is largely unknown because the focus has mostly been on leaders.[417] A focus on followership better helps our understanding of the leadership process.[418] How and why? It's because without followers there are no leaders. Organizations stand or fall on the basis of how well their leaders lead and how well their followers follow.[419]

Since the concept of followership may be a new one, let's begin with a few definitions of followership and followers. Followership is the other side of leadership.[420] Followership is the ability to take or follow direction well, to get in line behind a program or decision, and to be part of a team to deliver what is expected of you.[421] Another definition of followership is the ability to effectively follow directives and support the efforts of a leader to maximize a structured organization.[422] A third but closely related definition: followers are subordinates who have less power, authority, and influence than their superiors and do as they are instructed.[423]

There is nothing wrong with being a follower. Many of us go in and out of leadership and followership roles and responsibilities in what seems a mere blink of an eye. It all depends on how our lives are arranged: i.e., our positions in work, family, church, and volunteer situations. At different points in their careers, even at different times of the working day, many people play both roles.[424] As life takes you from moment to moment and situation to situation, you will find out you have no choice but to lead in one situation and follow in another. Even when we have subordinates, we still have supervisors and other leaders over us.[425]

Bosses are not necessarily good leaders, and subordinates are not necessarily effective followers.[426] **Understand this important point: how well followers follow is probably just as important as how well leaders lead.**[427] Characteristics that distinguish an effective from an ineffective follower are enthusiastic, intelligent, and self-reliant participation while accomplishing an organizational goal.[428] Being an excellent follower could leave you accomplishing more for an organization than being the big boss or someone in a key lead position. Using a basketball analogy, making the assist (a strong pass to someone who then scores the basket) is often just as important as the score. The importance of followers is huge, and you should not overlook it.

Consider this quote taken from a paper titled "A Fresh Look at Followership: A Model for Matching Followership and Leadership Styles."[429]

Dishwashing in a college cafeteria—it just doesn't get more important than that . . . think of the impact those students were going to have on the world. Business leaders, doctors, social scientists, world leaders, researchers. One load of unclean, bacteria-infected dishes could have wiped out a whole class. Look at it in terms of human impact . . . Students arrived tired, hungry, and . . . lonely. You were an important part of the chain that provided joy and nourishment . . . What a wonderful gift to give another human being.

If a dishwasher at a cafeteria can see how important his role is, so can you. Nothing gets done in organizations without followers; they are the people closest to the customers and issues, the ones creating the products, taking orders, collecting payments.[430]

Do you see how significant followers are? I hope so. The people who work under the leader to make an organization run are actually running the organization. No matter how great a pilot is, he or she cannot fly a plane for long without aircraft mechanics and a myriad of other technicians. I once heard a motto from some airmen in the Air Force that specialized in the aerial refueling of aircraft: "No one kicks butt without tanker gas." They know no matter how advanced the jet or cargo onboard, no one is getting anywhere or doing anything without the jet fuel they provide. People often focus on the airmen, soldiers, sailors, and marines who do the actual combat operations of dropping bombs, shooting bullets, attacking people, or defending territory. What many do not pay attention to is the amount of support it takes to make those things happen.

Think of the medical professionals who take care of, treat, and implement preventive medicine to keep people healthy. The cooks who prepare meal after meal. The sergeants who dedicate hour upon hour of training and supervision, and the huge logistics apparatus that gets everyone their equipment and transports personnel to and from destinations. Also, consider the list of civilian and other military personnel and departments—the people who work long hours before a single trigger gets pulled.

People are not ants to be abused and stepped on so leaders (and those who want to be leaders) can progress higher. Just because you are not the general, commander, departmental supervisor, president, vice president, CEO, CFO, COO, or CIO does not mean you are not important. All must work together to bring about the desired mission and vision. Again, people are not insects; they are the engine that makes organizations work.

What church could function well without supporting ministries, assistants, and volunteers? What good could they do without people gifted in administration, finance, and other management skills to keep a ministry going? The same applies to nonprofits and corporations. Leaders, I need you to see *beyond*. See beyond viewing only other leaders as the important ones.

Effective followers have different motivations for following and how they see their role.[431] Some choose to follow as their main role at work and take satisfaction in helping further a cause, idea, product, service, ministry, or even a person.[432] Others, as mentioned, are leaders in some situations but choose the follower role in another context.[433] Both of these groups view the role of follower as legitimate, honorable, and inherently valuable.[434]

Important point: there are no bad leaders who stay in position long without bad followers. For instance, if there is an executive who is known to be toxic, flies into fits of rage, throws objects in anger at employees, gropes or otherwise sexually harasses members of the staff, and frequently says inappropriate things, there must be followers who keep following and doing what is asked of them despite the corrosive environment. Anytime you hear about any leader, realize that they were able to accomplish what they did for as long as they did because there were people following them or turning a blind eye to their leadership. Toxic leaders stay in power only because of the people who support them. It is really difficult to be at the top of a criminal enterprise without a supporting network of people carrying out your instructions.

Think back to the Watergate scandal. On June 17, 1972, five burglars were arrested at the Democratic National Committee headquarters in the Watergate office-apartment-hotel complex in Washington, D.C.[435] Four of the men had been involved in Central Intelligence Agency (CIA) activities against Fidel Castro in Cuba. The fifth burglar was the security chief of the Committee to Re-elect the President.[436] The break-in was connected to President Richard Nixon's reelection campaign, and the burglars were caught wiretapping phones and stealing documents.[437]

In August of that year, President Nixon gave a speech swearing his White House staff was not involved in the break-in.[438] He was lying. A few days after the break-in, he provided hundreds of thousands of dollars to the burglars to keep them from talking to authorities.[439] Nixon and his aides devised a plan to instruct the CIA to impede the Federal Bureau of Investigation's research of the crime.[440] This was an obvious abuse of presidential power and a deliberate obstruction of justice. Eventually the House Judiciary Committee voted to impeach Nixon for obstruction of justice, abuse of power, criminal cover-up, and several other constitutional violations.[441] On August 8, 1974, Nixon became the first U.S. president to resign.[442] A president of the United States was involved in illegal activities, and yet he needed, and had to enlist the help of, others to accomplish the task. They were following his lead.

This bad leader could not have done what he did without people following his directions. The burglars and White House staff supported the president's illegal activities. They knew what they were doing was wrong. When there are wicked people in power, there are often wicked people supporting them. Some maybe unknowingly, but many know exactly what they are doing and for whom they are doing it.

As an aside, of course I am referring to the leaders who show their toxicity and live their lusts out loud, like Italian Prime Minister Berlusconi. No follower can be blamed for supporting a leader they did not know is being corrupt. But most destructive leaders are able to stay destructive because they have destructive followers who help them carry out their damaging ways. Don't be that kind of follower.

Followers can be separated into several types. Knowing where you stand as a follower in your family, business, church, nonprofit, or other organization is not just about knowledge. It is about gaining insight. You could realize you are in the wrong place and need to change the way you follow. As you read these different categories of followers, as always, think about where you see yourself first. You may realize you need to move to another group. Then start thinking about where those who work for you are—and where they should be. You may find out you are not the right follower for a particular situation. You can continue this analysis to include peers, coworkers, supervisors, family members, and others.

You will know what kind of follower you are in your family. You can decipher what kind of follower you are on your job or in a business you support. You can see what type of follower you may be in your church, area of worship, or volunteer organization.

Once you know where you are (how you are following) in key areas of your life, then you need to answer these questions: am I in the right place? Am I following as I should? Do I need to step up to another tier or take it down a level? See Figure 6. This illustrates five kinds of followers with different levels of commitment or engagement to their organizations.[443]

Progressively Lower	(Level of Engagement)		Progressively Higher	
Isolates	Bystanders	Participants	Activists	Diehards
Completely detached	Observers only	Engaged	Feel strongly and act accordingly, both with and against leaders	Deeply devoted

Figure 6: *Different followers' styles ranked by their level of engagement*

Kellerman, in *Followership: How Followers are Creating Change and Changing Leaders*, wrote of five kinds of followers compared to their level of engagement with their leader and organization.

FOLLOWERS: LEVEL OF ENGAGEMENT[444]

Isolates. This kind of follower is entirely detached. They do not care about their leaders, really don't know anything about them, and neither do they respond to them. This is the perfect follower for a toxic leader because isolates know nothing and do nothing. Their nonparticipation strengthens leaders who have the upper hand. Isolates are silent because they are disconnected/detached and separate from what's going on.

Isolates are a problem. Isolates know very little and care even less. They think they are powerless and are not motivated to pay attention to what is taking place. Isolates are unmotivated, uninformed, and uninterested. They are alienated from the system, group, or organization.

An example of an isolate is the American voter. Or should I say the American nonvoter? These are the Americans who are eligible to vote but never do. In the 2020 Presidential Election, 80 million eligible people did not vote.[445] Among the top reasons: not being registered to vote, not interested in politics, not liking the candidates, a feeling their vote wouldn't have made a difference, and being undecided on whom to vote for.[446] The nonvoters were disengaged and disaffected; they don't believe politics can make a difference in their lives.[447]

Bystanders. They observe but do not get involved or participate. Bystanders choose to stay neutral, which basically is implied support for whomever or whatever the present circumstances are. They intentionally and deliberately decide to stand aside, stand by, and disengage from their leader or group. These kinds of people decide to do nothing even when doing something is not particularly costly or risky.

They go along with the group. They go with the flow, the flow of their leaders and other followers. The handiwork of bystanders could be seen in Nazi Germany. Many did not get involved in spreading discrimination, prejudice, or hostility toward Jews (anti-Semitism).[448]

However, they also stood by and did nothing. They said nothing. They gave their tacit support as the Nazis did their heinous work.

A well-known quote, often attributed to eighteenth-century Irish philosopher and statesman Edmund Burke, says, "The only thing necessary for the triumph of evil is for good men to do nothing."[449] See any truth to that statement? The story of Nazi Germany and, in particular, the Holocaust is about seemingly good men and women who did nothing in the face of evil.[450]

Participants. They are engaged in some way. They either favor their leaders, groups, and organizations or are clearly opposed to them.[451] They care enough to invest some of their resources (time, energy, etc.). They try to make an impact. As their name says, they actively participate—to some degree.

Generally speaking, leaders want participants. Participants can be (a) in support of you, (b) against you, or (c) go their own way. When participants support you, they are like gas to an automobile; they fuel the engine. They provide the energy that creates a good group or organization to empower leaders to do what they want to do.

An example of participants can be found by examining the approval, marketing, and distribution of the drug Vioxx by the Merck pharmaceutical company. Vioxx was developed to be a painkiller, but a study showed patients taking the drug long term faced twice the risk of a heart attack compared with patients who received a placebo.[452] The drug was available and promoted in eighty countries. The CEO at the time, Raymond V. Gilmartin, was not a scientist, nor did he have experience in the pharmaceutical industry. Author Kellerman notes that Gilmartin's lack of expertise left him relying on his subordinates (followers) to run the company and provide guidance on drugs such as Vioxx. The participant-followers wanted the drug to be successful. They did what they could to convince people inside and outside the company that Vioxx was safe. They knew it was not. Participants helped the leader go down a wrong path. See how important followers are?

Activists. This type of follower feels strongly about their leaders and they show it. They tend to be go-getters, eager, energetic, involved. Because of their genuine personal and professional investment in people and processes, they tend to work harder on behalf of their leader—or, conversely, to weaken and remove them. You should know that activists are determined to create change. They care a great deal about the issue, person, or organization they are an activist for.

A great example of activists can be seen by studying the Voice of the Faithful (VOTF). VOTF is a lay organization of Catholics, organized in 2002, in response to the sexual abuse crisis in the Catholic Church.[453] Its mission is to accomplish three goals: support survivors of clergy sexual abuse, support priests of integrity, and shape structural change within the Catholic Church.[454] This group, which started in a church basement in Wellesley, Massachusetts, has grown to more than 30,000 members.[455] People were tired of and angry at the Catholic Church's silence and lack of action when it came to the horrible actions of its priests who abused and molested children year after year. VOTF fights for transparency and accountability.

Diehards. This sort of follower is prepared to die for their cause if necessary, whether an individual, idea, or both. They are deeply devoted to their leaders. Their followership and devotion explains who they are and determines what they do.[456] On the other side, by any means necessary, they are ready to remove leaders from positions of authority, influence, and power. The dedication of diehards is what sets them apart: their willingness to risk their lives. It is who they are and what they do.

A great example of a diehard is Martin Luther King Jr., whose original name was Michael King Jr. King, of course, was the Baptist minister and social activist who led the civil rights movement in the U.S. from the mid-1950s until his death by assassination in April 1968.[457] His leadership was vital to the movement's success in ending the legal segregation of African-Americans in the South and other parts of the United States.[458] King promoted nonviolent tactics to achieve civil rights.[459] He was awarded the Nobel Peace Prize in 1964. The night before his assassination, King told a group of striking sanitation workers in Memphis, Tennessee: "We've got to give ourselves to this struggle until the end. Nothing would be more tragic than to stop at this point in Memphis. We've got to see it through."[460]

In the military you find diehards. You can find many who have put their lives on the line for their country and brothers and sisters in arms. A perfect example of a group of them is to look up those who have been awarded the Medal of Honor. The award is for military service members (Air Force, Army, Navy, Marines, and Coast Guard) who distinguished themselves by gallantry at the risk of their life above and beyond the call of duty.[461]

Consider the true story of John A. Chapman, an Air Force Special Operations member who died on March 4, 2002. Part of his Medal of Honor citation reads:[462]

> Technical Sergeant John A. Chapman distinguished himself by extraordinary heroism as an Air Force Special Tactics Combat Controller, attached to a Navy Sea, Air, and Land (SEAL) Team conducting reconnaissance operations in Takur Ghar, Afghanistan, on March 4, 2002. During insertion, the team's helicopter was ambushed causing a teammate to fall into an entrenched group of enemy combatants below. Sergeant Chapman and the team voluntarily reinserted onto the snow-capped mountain, into the heart of a known enemy stronghold to rescue one of their own. Without regard for his own safety, Sergeant Chapman . . . [moved] in the direction of the closest enemy position despite coming under heavy fire from multiple directions. He fearlessly charged an enemy bunker, up a steep incline in thigh-deep snow, and into hostile fire, directly engaging the enemy. Upon reaching the bunker, Sergeant Chapman assaulted and cleared the position, killing all enemy occupants. With complete disregard for his own life, Sergeant Chapman deliberately moved from cover . . . and exposed himself once again to attack a second bunker . . . During this assault from an exposed position directly in the line of intense fire, Sergeant

Chapman was struck and injured by enemy fire. Despite severe, mortal wounds, he continued to fight relentlessly, sustaining a violent engagement with multiple enemy personnel before making the ultimate sacrifice.

Diehards will give their life, if needed, for a person or cause they passionately believe in and consider worthy.

Leadership and followership are connected to or often a by-product of context. Context will include factors that influence the situation. Some people respond well to context and some do not. Understand that not all levels of engagement are needed in every context or situation. For example, you do not need to be a diehard in every area of your life, just as you should not be a bystander in significant parts of your life.

Here are some questions to take some time to think about and seriously answer. In what areas are you an isolate, bystander, participant, activist, or diehard? Which of the five apply to different parts of your life: family, work/business, worship, volunteer organizations, and other areas? Now, after you have identified the different areas and how these five ways of following apply, ask yourself if you are the right kind of follower in those areas. Do some self-diagnostics. In your family, are you a bystander, but you should at least be a participant? At church, are you an isolate but you should at least be a participant or activist? Where are you at each place, and what *should* you be? Are you a participant where you should be an activist or nonviolent diehard?

Another way to analyze is to explain these steps to important people in your life and ask them to give you feedback. For example, ask your supervisor what type of follower he or she sees you as. Do you have a pastor, or are you committed to an accountability group for spiritual and social fellowship and accountability? If so, ask your leader, or ask other people in the group.

And by all means, ask people who follow you for their opinion.

EXEMPLARY, CONFORMIST, PASSIVE, ALIENATED, AND PRAGMATIST FOLLOWERSHIP

Robert Kelley devised another followership model I believe you should personally and professionally know. He noted five kinds of followers: exemplary, conformist, passive, alienated, and pragmatist.[463] What's unique about Kelley's research is he focused on people who specifically *want to follow*, not lead. The goal in his research was to encourage followers to be the kind of people no leader or group can do without.[464]

Effective followers have the vision to see the short term (tactical) and the broader view (strategic), the social skills to work well with others, the strength of character to succeed without constant praise, the moral and mental balance to pursue personal and corporate goals at no cost to either one, and, most of all, the desire to work with a team to accomplish a greater purpose.[465] Before we get into specifics, it's important to know that Kelley wrote his model based on a two-dimensional way of thinking.

Kelley based his followership model in two ways to describe the ways that people follow.[466] The first dimension is independent, critical thinking versus dependent, uncritical thinking.[467] Independent, critical-thinking followers can think for themselves and do not always need people to tell them what to do. They can evaluate a situation such as considering the impact of their actions on the organization and are willing to be creative and offer constructive criticism.[468] Dependent, uncritical thinkers go by the leader's thinking and do what the leader tells them to do.[469] Are you more of an independent, critical thinker or a dependent, uncritical thinker?

The second dimension is followers with active versus passive behaviors.[470] Active followers normally take the initiative in decision making, accomplish tasks without constant direction or feedback from the leader, and actively participate in performing their duties.[471] They go above and beyond. This means they do more than their job requires to achieve goals, and this leads to increased job satisfaction and commitment.[472] Passive followers wait to be told what to do.[473] They are truly passive and do not take the initiative.

Which describes you? Are you an initiator? Are you proactive? Or do you find yourself always waiting to be told what to do, then only do the specific task?

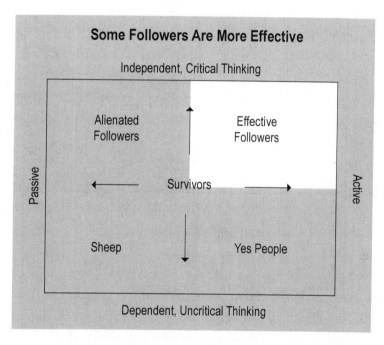

Figure 7: Robert Kelly's followership styles[474]

Here are Kelley's five styles of followership.[475]

Alienated followers think independently and critically. They do not participate in the groups or organizations they belong to. Although they rate high on independent thinking, these kinds of followers rate low in active engagement. They don't willingly commit to a leader.[476] They are competent but cynical and passive in their roles.[477] Alienated followers are prone to have job dissatisfaction, which may lead to high absenteeism, theft, low organizational commitment, low motivation, and low performance.[478] Do you know anyone like this?

Exemplary followers are just that, exemplary (i.e., effective). They perform well in every aspect. These kinds of followers are independent and critical thinkers and are actively engaged. Exemplary followers are innovative and willing to question the leadership.[479] This type of follower is vital to organizational success because they are ideal in many ways.[480] They think things through by considering the consequences of tasks before they carry them out.[481] They have social adaptability skills by treating everyone in the organization the same way, they get along well with their colleagues, and they provide support and intelligent criticism to the leader.[482] They serve the best interest of the organization, are likely to function very well in self-managed teams, complement the leaders' efforts, and can be depended upon to relieve the leader of many tasks.[483]

Conformist followers are satisfied with just taking orders and defer to their leaders (to do the real thinking). They are high on actively engaging with their leader and organization, but low on independent thinking. No critical thinking with these people.[484] Conformists are the "yes people."[485] When they are around you, that is essentially what you will hear. Again, they will just take orders. They are prepared to do everything to keep a good relationship with their leader and, as a result, will carry out orders without questioning or thinking.[486] Conformists require constant feedback from leaders.[487] They lack enthusiasm, self-confidence, creativity, initiative, courage, and ambition.[488] They may also be loyalists, meaning they are loyal to the organization and therefore prepared to give up or compromise their own needs to satisfy the organization.[489]

Passive followers let their leaders do the thinking for them, which means they need constant supervision. They are like sheep. They are low in independent thinking and also low in engagement. They are not creative or ambitious.[490] Passive followers are not good workers.[491] Don't expect them to put in extra time to complete given tasks; they leave whether or not they have completed tasks when the day is over.[492]

Pragmatist followers, symbolically speaking, stay in the middle of the road. They survive. They rate in the middle. They are average. They are in the middle when it comes to independent thinking and engagement.[493] Not high or low, just in the middle. They may have the qualities of the other four types and will use any style to benefit their position and reduce their risk.[494]

Can you see yourself in one or two of Kelley's followership styles? Are you in the right place? Are you using the best style to fit your current situation for where you want to go in life? If you see yourself as alienated or passive, why? What about you, your job, or situation needs to change? Can you see any of the dominant styles in those you work with? In your family?

THE CURPHY-ROELLIG FOLLOWERSHIP MODEL

Consider this third followership model, from Gordy Curphy and Mark Roellig. The authors of this model believe followership should be viewed as more of a role, not a position.[495] As I have stated, the same person can fill both leadership and followership roles.[496] In addition, the values, personality traits, mental abilities, and behaviors that describe effective leaders can also be used to describe effective followers.[497]

Practicing good followership principles helps make you a good leader, and the other way around is just as true. Again, the most effective people in any organization are those who are equally proficient playing both leadership and followership roles. Workers perceived to be the most effective are those likely to be asked to take a leadership role when opportunities arise.[498] The bottom line is being effective can help improve a person's career.[499] This is how you get promoted. Be a good follower so you can be primed to be a good leader.

Here is information from the Curphy-Roellig Followership explanations.[500]

The Curphy-Roellig Followership Model builds on some of the earlier followership research of the likes of Barbara Kellerman, Robert Kelley, and more. It consists of four followership types and two independent dimensions. The two dimensions of the model are Critical Thinking and Engagement. Critical Thinking is about the follower's ability to challenge the status quo, identify and balance what is important and what is not, ask good questions, identify problems, and develop practical solutions. High scorers on Critical Thinking are constantly identifying ways to improve productivity or efficiency, increase sales, reduce costs, and more. Those with lower scores believe it is the role of management to identify and solve problems, so they essentially turn their brains off at the door and won't turn them back on until they leave work. Engagement is concerned with the level of effort workers put forth at work. High scorers are energetic, excited about being part of the team, driven to achieve results, persist at difficult tasks for long periods of time, help others, and willingly adapt to changing situations; low scorers are lazy, unenthusiastic, give up too easy, are unwilling to help others or adapt to new demands, and basically would rather be doing anything but the task at hand. Engaged employees come to work to "win" compared to coming to work "to play the game." It is important to understand that engagement does not necessarily mean working 70-80 hours a week, as people can be highly engaged and only work part-time. What a person does at work is often more important than the number of hours worked, but in general, highly engaged employees tend to spend more time focusing on the challenges at hand than disengaged employees.

Figure 8 illustrates the Curphy-Roellig Followership Model. Use this model to plot what category you and others are grouped in by comparing critical thinking and the level of engagement.

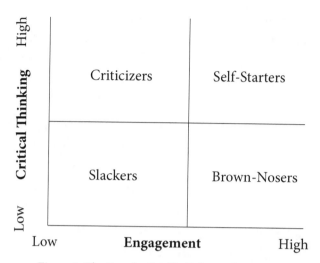

Figure 8: The Curphy-Roellig Followership Model

Here are Curphy-Roellig's explanations of the four followership styles.[501] Which style describes you best? Which style fits the people who follow you? Which style explains the leaders who supervise you?

Self-Starters: are those who are passionate about the team and will exert significant effort to make it successful. They are also constantly thinking of ways to improve team performance, raise issues, develop solutions, and enthusiastically carry out change initiatives. When encountering problems, self-starters are ready and able to resolve issues and then tell their leaders what they did rather than waiting to be told what to do. This type also helps to improve their leaders' performance by giving their opinions prior to decisions being made and giving constructive feedback after bad decisions are made. They are the most effective follower type.

Brown-Nosers: share a strong work ethic but lack the critical thinking skills of self-starters. This insincere type of follower is manipulative because he or she gives excessive praise and compliments to specifically gain the leader's favor.[502] Brown-nosers are obedient, conscientious, and loyal employees who will do whatever their leaders ask them to do. They never point out problems, raise objections, or cause any difficulties, and they do whatever they can to please their bosses. Brown-nosers constantly check in with their leaders by seeking permission to do things. Many leaders surround themselves with brown-nosers because these individuals are constantly flattering and telling everyone how lucky they are to be working for such great bosses. (Careful: this could highlight a toxic problem in the leader.) Warning: they can also create compelling reasons to take inappropriate or unethical actions. Brown-nosers often go far in organizations, particularly in those not having good performance metrics. They work hard to have no enemies and can play work politics very well.

Slackers: by their very name you know they are not hard workers, nor do they exert much effort toward work. They believe they are entitled to a paycheck for just showing up, and that it is management's job to solve problems. Slackers avoid work and often disappear for hours on end, make it a practice to look busy but get little done, have many excuses for not getting projects accomplished, and spend more time concocting ways to avoid getting tasks completed than just getting them done. Just like the military has stealth aircraft that are hard to see under certain circumstances, likewise slackers are "stealth employees" who are very content to spend the entire day surfing the Internet, shopping online, gossiping with coworkers, or taking breaks rather than being productive at work. In the end, slackers want to stay off their boss's radar screens, so they do just enough to stay out of trouble but never more than their peers.

Criticizers: are disengaged from work yet possess strong critical thinking skills. Rather than directing their problem identification and resolution skills toward work-related issues, criticizers are motivated to find fault in anything their leaders or organizations do. They make it a point of telling coworkers what their leaders are doing wrong, how efforts to make changes in the business are doomed to failure, how bad their organizations are compared to competitors, and how management shoots down any suggestions for improvement. These pessimistic individuals are constantly complaining, whining, and moaning about what is happening. Warning: criticizers are often the most dangerous of the four types because they frequently are the first to greet new employees and "tell them how things really work around here." They can contaminate and infect people. If not effectively managed, criticizers can take over teams and entire departments and be among the most difficult challenges leaders face.

ADDITIONAL ASPECTS OF THE CURPHY-ROELLIG FOLLOWERSHIP MODEL[503]

- This model can help leaders assess follower types to determine where they are and where they have been.

- Followership types or styles can change depending on the situation. You can track how one's followership type changes as he or she switches jobs, inherits different bosses, is given different responsibilities, etc.

- Self-starters are the strongest contributors to organizational success, and leaders have a direct influence on the followership types of their direct reports. In order to create teams of self-starters: set clear expectations around engagement and critical thinking, role model the behaviors of self-starters (live it), treat people fairly, create an environment where people feel safe to offer solutions, clear obstacles and provide needed resources, articulate a vision of the future, and hold staff members accountable for self-starter behavior.

- Organizations can train people how to be self-starters. Training should include the four followership types, what it takes to be a self-starter, and provide feedback on what type is currently being displayed. Trainees should learn what they need to do to become self-starters, such as how to identify problems, generate and present solutions, and how to get engaged and get things done at work. Training people on followership and having leaders develop effective followership is a relatively easy way to improve organizational effectiveness.

- Be mindful of what you are or becoming. Why? Because organizations are more likely to hire brown-nosers and self-starters than criticizers and slackers. Research has shown the longer people stay in an organization, the more likely they will be criticizers. It's only a matter of time before those critical thinking skills get directed at leaders, teams, and organizations. Do not let yourself become a bitter, critical worker.

- Department heads and people in positions of authority also play followership roles; they need to realize how their own followership type affects how they lead others. In other words, how you work will impact others. For example, leaders who are self-starters are likely to set high standards and expectations, reward others for taking initiative, and give top performers plenty of latitude and needed resources. Leaders who are brown-nosers will suppress objections and demand direct reports to constantly check in. They want employees to do what they are told, not to create any issues, and to be loyal lapdogs whose sole purpose is to please their superiors. Leaders who are slackers are just lazy or laissez-faire leaders who are not involved at work, unresponsive to followers' requests, unavailable, and lead teams that get little accomplished. Leaders who are criticizers will complain about their organizations and also direct their critical thinking skills toward employees. Be aware, these leaders tend to manage by finding fault in everything their followers do.

In this chapter you've been given a foundational understanding of followership. You've been given definitions combined with three types of followership models. These models can help you understand what kind of follower you, your coworkers, volunteers, and even those in your family can be. Which model do you think works best for you and why? **Remember this important point: followers who knowingly, intentionally, deliberately commit themselves to follow bad leaders are themselves bad.**[504]

AM I A GOOD OR BAD FOLLOWER?

From Kellerman's book on followership, here are some strong general rules.[505] These basic points help you distinguish if you and/or others are acting as good or bad followers.[506]

- To do nothing (to not be involved) . . . is to be a bad follower.

- To support a leader who is good (effective and ethical) . . . is to be a good follower.

- To support a leader who is bad (ineffective and/or unethical) . . . is to be a bad follower.

- To oppose a leader who is good (effective and ethical) . . . is to be a bad follower.

- To oppose a leader who is bad (ineffective and/or unethical) . . . is to be a good follower.

HOW TO BE A GREAT FOLLOWER

I would be remiss if I did not give you some essential clues and guidance on how to be an effective follower. These are guidelines that just about every leader would want. Followers who are trusted, consistent, reliable, excellent in their work, and believe in the mission and vision of their group or business are wanted. To close this chapter, use these points, written by Ira Chaleff, author of *The Courageous Follower*, to gain wisdom so you can be a better, more effective, and even exemplary worker.[507]

- *The courage to assume responsibility.* Workers assume responsibility for themselves (self-leadership) and the organization. Courageous followers discover opportunities to fulfill their potential and maximize their value to the organization. These workers accept the personal responsibility to act to achieve the organization's goals and even look for new ways to do things without relying on permission to do every task.[508]

- *The courage to serve.* These people are not afraid of hard work. They willingly assume new or additional responsibilities to assist the leader and serve the organization. Workers are passionate and will use their strengths to help.

- *The courage to challenge.* Courageous followers speak up if they feel the leader's behaviors or policies conflict with what they believe is right. When appropriate, they are willing to stand up, stand out, and even risk being rejected. It is implied that these workers would be discreet and handled in a way to maintain working harmony with the organization and their leader as much as possible.[509]

- *The courage to participate in transformation.* Working with their leader, courageous followers help recognize the need for transformation and assist with helping the organization change. They examine themselves and are willing to personally change . . . not just focus on others who need to change. These workers are actively a part of the transformation process.

- *The courage to take moral action.* If the leader or firm is doing illegal, unethical, and immoral things or just doing something not deemed right, the courageous follower will take a stand. Taking a stand may look like refusing to obey a direct order, appealing the order to the next level of authority, or tendering one's resignation. Their moral courage leads them to take a stand by answering to a higher set of values. Actions like these are done to stop a morally objectionable situation.

To add to your education and training, here is another source of information to evaluate yourself and others as a follower. Few places talk, teach, and train followers and followership with such intentionality as the U.S. military. Consider *The Ten Rules of Good Followership* by Col. Phillip S. Meilinger.[510] In the statements below, do you see any similarities to what you have read so far? Which ones stand out and are important to you? Which ones illustrate how you serve others and how others work for you? How would you prioritize them?

1. Do not blame your boss for an unpopular decision or policy; your job is to support, not undermine.

2. Debate with your boss, if necessary; but do it in private. Avoid embarrassing situations, and never reveal to others what was discussed.

3. Make the decision, then run it past the boss; use your initiative.

4. Accept responsibility whenever it is offered.

5. Tell the truth and don't whine or make excuses; your boss will be giving advice up the chain of command (to his or her superiors) based on what you said.

6. Do your homework; give your boss all the information needed to make a decision. Also, anticipate possible questions.

7. When making a recommendation, remember who will have to implement it. Your recommendation may impact other people or departments. You must know your limitations, weaknesses, and strengths.

8. Keep your boss informed of what's going on in the department or organization; people may be reluctant to tell him or her their problems and successes. You should do it for them.

9. If you see a problem, fix it. Be proactive. Don't worry about who would have gotten the blame or who gets the praise.

10. Put in more than an honest day's work, but don't forget the needs of your family. If they are unhappy, you will be too, and your job performance will suffer.

Leaders and emerging leaders: followers were questioned about what they need from their leaders. These three stand out.[511]

One: give clear goals and direction.[512] Followers need to know where the team, project, or organization is going and why.[513]

Two: give frequent, specific, and immediate feedback.[514] When a leader provides feedback, it shows the leader cares about the follower's growth and career development and wants to help the person achieve their potential.[515] Feedback is a route to improvement and development, nothing to be afraid of.[516]

Three: coach to develop potential.[517] Coaching is a method of directing or supporting a follower with the aim of improving specific skills or achieving a development goal.[518] Coaching involves empowering followers to understand, learn, explore, provide support, and remove obstacles that stand in the way of their ability to grow and excel.[519]

Lead the best you can. Follow the best you can. Be as excellent as you can be no matter which role you are in.

NOTES

NOTES

Thirteen

MEN: MASCULINITY IS NOT TOXIC, SO DON'T HAVE TOXIC MASCULINITY

We have been examining all types of toxicity, in several forms and practices. I thought it prudent to give some words about toxic masculinity. We will not go very deep into this topic, but as leaders, emerging leaders, family leaders, and followers it's a good idea to have a solid understanding of a subject many talk about but might not quite understand. Your understanding of this matter can impact your leadership, followership, how you perceive the way people are behaving and the way others perceive you. The goal is to give you enough information so you have a foundational understanding of what toxic masculinity is . . . and what it is not.

For a starting point, toxic masculinity is not just about behaving like a man.[520] Among the many definitions you can find through research, and in pop culture channels, there is a consensus that toxic masculinity has three parts. The three core components are toughness (the belief men should be physically strong, emotionally callous, and behaviorally aggressive); anti-femininity (men should reject anything that is considered to be feminine or womanlike, such as showing emotion or accepting help); and power (the belief men need to work toward obtaining social and financial power and status to gain the respect of others).[521] Be honest. Do you think this way? If you do, a lot of what you may be thinking or assuming is wrong. That alone is toxic.

One issue is that men are learning masculinity from horrible role models. From the untaught or fatherless man, to constantly seeing drunk, strung-out, lazy, and jobless men who did not have a clue on how to live right or treat people. Consider your role models. Consider the TV and online programs you've watched of men you idolized who did not teach the correct life principles to follow. Some of us were taught to like the villain or bad men and not the hero. Some of us were taught to love evil and hate the good.

What things about manhood and masculinity were you taught that you now know are wrong? Did you, or do you, have to *unlearn* anything? For example, did you have to learn a proper view of women? That no real man is going to agree with or condone violence against women? Or, unless your lifestyle or environment is extreme, no one should be emotionally callous and behaviorally aggressive all the time? What about knowing it's okay to show emotions? I mean emotions other than anger. Men tend to be very good at showing that one.

Alert to men: you are an emotional being. You were not made to be capable of only showing one emotion. Showing emotions, which includes crying, is okay. It's not a sign of weakness or a mark of femininity. It shows you are human. If you are sad or disappointed over some significant situation, it's okay; you are a human being. More on this point later.

Men, often, have a wrong view of their worth. For instance, you do not base how valuable you are on a temporary job. If you are solely basing your relevance as a man on a job—the title you have and how much money you make—you have a wrong view of manhood. You are more than your money or occupation. You are a great deal more. Men who think like that may also believe the only thing they can provide a woman is sex and money. That is it? That is all men are good for? Although those are often important in a marriage, they are not,

I repeat not, everything. There are plenty of couples who had good sex and/or were more financially stable than most who still ended up getting divorced.

I need you to think past the flawed logic of the warped culture we live in and see the truth that God created men to be just that: men. The standard to base your manliness on is Scripture, not politically incorrect pop culture with its ever-changing social trends.

A second definition of masculinity that becomes toxic is when men feel they must follow erroneous, rigid gender rules.[522] These cultural norms include acting like a bully to maintain a competitive advantage, avoiding losing no matter the cost, restraining your emotions except for anger and pride (the only acceptable masculine emotions a man can show), and dominating women and other men.[523]

To be fair, not everything a man learns from culture is automatically bad. It just depends on what culture you learned from. In many cultures, a male becomes a "man" by behaving in ways that fit with traditional beliefs about what men are like. For example, being dominant, tough, risk-taking, aggressive, and rule-breaking.[524] In psychological research, masculine norms—the way people view being masculine and "manlike"—include specific ways men are told they should behave, such as staying in control, being a provider, and many more.[525] Essentially, you are taught to think men are strong and women are weak.[526] These norms influence the way men seek help (or not) and what men say when stressed or in distress from a stressful event.[527] Upholding this rigid, stern, cold, hard, emotionless existence where you have to be relentlessly self-reliant can lead to poor mental health . . . because men will often not reach out for help or accept support when it is offered.[528] Men, do not cut yourself off from support.

Are you seeing that the real toxicity is upholding a wrong image and living out that image? Many men should be nominated for Emmy Awards: best performance by an actor. Why? If this is you, it is because you are acting. You are pretending to be a man that you are not.

You are not perfect, but you act like you are to uphold a perfect image, one that, honestly, is not realistic.

You are pretending to be strong when you feel week, confident when you feel deep insecurity, and you act tough when you are genuinely hurting.[529] You have been putting on a pretty good show, but aren't you tired?[530] Isn't it exhausting to be "the man" and "man enough" for everyone, every day, all the time? Are you tired of performing? Many of us men are great actors.

To be balanced, some of the attributes of honest masculinity are positive if they are used at the right place at the right time. For instance, at times you have to hold off on being emotional so your strong logic and decisiveness can come to the forefront of your mind so necessary decisions can be made. There are times when being aggressive to protect your family from danger or being assertive, by working hard, to create a stable financial future is the right thing to do.

There was a time I was in a leadership role at a nonprofit company. When the CEO suddenly passed away, I had to make decisions rather rapidly and did my best to be logical and not emotional in that moment. Why? Because the staff and organizational stakeholders needed me to be. I could be emotional later, but not at the specific moment I was needed to step up and lead. Thankfully, I was prepared to operate that way as a by-product of my previous military training. I responded to the situation with thoughtful action rather than just reaction.

You can talk about what is hurting or bothering you, release emotion, talk about your feelings, and still be a real man. Yes, men . . . you have feelings. Thinking these things are more for women is likely adding to your toxic thinking about yourself, and this can spill over onto others. Doing those things does not mean you are effeminate or soft. It may mean that you are more emotionally and communicatively mature. Here, balance is key. Balance, men, is needed. Yes, be stoic when you have to be so you can lead or follow in the moment as needed. Know when to balance it out by letting out the mounting steam from the pressure cooker called life, and trusting people such as wise friends, ministers, counselors, or therapists.

If you need to talk, talk. Letting your tears flow because a long-time friend, parent, or sibling passed away does not make you soft. It makes you human. You are a human who has human experiences. Again, men: balance. You may have heard the old joke about when men are driving, if they are lost, they won't ask for directions. Imagine the thread of truth in that joke: you in a car lost on the journey of life and ending up in places you shouldn't be and taking longer to get to your desired destination, because you are lost and need help. Ask for help! Men: bury, kill, destroy, ignore, and get rid of your foolish pride and the spoken and unspoken idea that you cannot ask for help. Don't follow the impulse that says you cannot admit when you are in personal and physical pain and need others. Let me remind you that people are social creatures and not meant to be separated from others. We are not meant to be alone.[531]

Can you admit that you need help? For example, can you acknowledge that you don't have a good idea of how to raise your kids or maintain a marriage? Can you admit that you need help with your finances? That you struggle with success or depression? Can you be honest and face the fact that even though you look like everything is going great and you seem to have symbols of success, there is a war going on in your soul and you need help? Can you be honest about being addicted to pornography or bound by sexual addiction? Can you talk about having cold sweats because you crave drugs or alcohol? That even though you are a leader, a grown man, and head of the household . . . you are still dealing with trauma and hurts from your childhood like rejection and abandonment? Help is not a bad four-letter word. Ask for it. Use it.

Stop struggling in silence. Stop suffering in silence. I remember when I was a kid, my mother yelled at me for something because she thought I was too quiet about it. She said, "Open your mouth and say something!" What inner secret are you struggling with? Is the reason you have not asked for help because you are afraid, downright terrified, that people will see you differently? That they will see you as weak, a disappointment or coward? Are you afraid to face certain things about yourself? Come to terms with the reality that you are not a superhero with no faults and vulnerabilities. You cannot run from *you*. Stop trying to drink it out, sex it out, sports it out, go to your job to work it out, or any other avoidance tactic.

Look at this list, from *Inc. Magazine*, of things people do not want to admit about themselves.[532] Any of these reflect your reality?

1. You chase success because without money or degrees your deep-seated fear of being a failure is confirmed—who or what would you be without your accomplishments?

2. You care more about what other people think than about what you think, and it's destroying your confidence—when your focus is external, you lose your internal strength.

3. You desperately want approval from others and are willing to sacrifice aspects of your true self to receive it. Life is a series of decisions; make sure you are making the right ones.

4. You're terrified of the sense of emptiness inside yourself, so you fill your life with distractions to keep yourself occupied: watching TV, online shopping, and spending time on social media can all be used as escapes to keep you from engaging in deep self-reflection.

5. You blame other people for your problems so you can feel better about your own shortcomings—not dealing with your issues and putting them on other people helps you avoid self-accountability.

6. You get angry at aspects and traits of others you identify with. The next time you get really angry at someone, think about what makes you angry, and then think about how you may have done something similar in the past. Don't deflect, reflect.

7. You avoid dealing with your emotional issues despite knowing they cause problems for everyone. Take your emotional well-being seriously.

8. You are petrified of being seen for who you really are so you wear a mask or put up a façade that helps you feel more accepted. Showing others what they want to see isn't you being authentic, it's fear, it's masquerading.

9. You enhance your image on social media to mask your feelings of inadequacy. Is the truth that every like, comment, and share is a short-lived ego boost for you?

10. You pressure yourself to be perfect or care for others because that was the only way you could receive love and attention as a child. Get to the root and address your issues. Practice healthier ways of thinking and behaving.

11. You chase happiness by buying things—all your excessive material wealth serves your ego and protects your wounded inner child.

12. You allow your inner critic to ridicule you over and over again because it's the only way you can motivate yourself. Hurtful motivation harms your well-being.

13. You create problems to solve because it's the only way you know how to be. You think keeping your mind busy keeps you safe from expectations and disappointments.

14. You stick with what's known and suffer with it instead of trying something new because you are terrified of uncertainty. You choose to live by sight and what you can see and control.

15. You won't practice the advice you give others. You would rather fit in instead of practicing what you preach and stand out. Stop allowing the wrong people and wrong culture to weaken you and destroy your integrity.

16. You won't engage in therapy because you would be forced to admit you're not okay and everything isn't in your control; the illusion of control is false security.

17. You give fake smiles to people because you think your feelings are not important to others. When looking the part is more important than acknowledging your feelings, you are being a social robot.

18. You hate the way your body looks, and you have a fear of death. You are insecure.

19. You don't engage in deep conversations because you're afraid to confess that you have no idea what you're doing in life. You use things like the weather, sports, stocks, and other hobbies to distract yourself from what is important.

20. You pretend that you know the "right way" of doing things but you fear that you have it all wrong; stop pretending and start questioning. Be courageous and acknowledge your shortcomings, then take action to create change in yourself.

Many men have no problem talking about surface things like their work, sports, politics, or women, but they never seek to get deeper about what's really bothering them such as their insecurities, self-doubts, worries, and more.[533] Some men would rather die than ask for help.[534] To let another person know you need to talk is painful. And I mean really talking about real issues. Breaking news! You do not have to die. Ask for help. If the person you ask says no or does not know how to listen well to help you, ask someone else.

Men, are you brave enough to be vulnerable, strong enough to be sensitive when it's needed, confident enough to listen to others in your life (yes, even women) who have more wisdom than you? Will you be man enough to stop the trash talk that you and your friends say about people and things that are untrue, perverted, vile, nasty, and lustful?[535] It goes without saying: you should discuss your personal issues with trustworthy people whether they are professional or nonprofessional. When wisdom and helpful information are being taught, are you man enough, humble enough, to be quiet and listen?[536] Be man enough to treat people with the same dignity and respect that you desire.

I hope reading this book, to this point, has been enlightening, eye-opening, convicting, challenging, and motivating. This motivation should move you to process and progress. By process, I mean it should be causing you to think like a child who's connecting the dots in a picture workbook, or working a problem like a computer tabulating information. By progress, I mean you are changing and seeing things with greater vision and insight. Progress is about movement. Sometimes it's fast and sometimes it's slow. Sometimes painfully slow. But progress is progress.

For a case in point, consider the great civil rights movement of the 1950s/1960s to this day. Fortunately, many laws have changed to end some legal racial segregation and discrimination (on paper), but unfortunately often still have not changed the way a lot of people think about African-Americans/Blacks or other ethnic minorities in general.[537] Things changed on paper but not always in people's heads and hearts. We as a people still need change. We still need progress. Again, progress is often slow. How have you been progressing lately?

Back to toxic masculinity. Who is responsible for the slow progress and toxic foolishness with the gender pay gap? By some level of default, some men have privilege. The privilege to get paid more than a woman. It is an established fact that men and women are not paid equally.[538] In the U.S., U.K., and around the world, studies on average pay reveal stark earning differences between male and female.[539]

According to Pew Research Center, the gender gap in pay has remained fairly stable in the U.S. for more than fifteen years.[540] In 2020, women earned 84 percent of what men earned, according to an analysis of hourly earnings of both full- and part-time workers.[541] You don't think that is a big deal? It is. Based on this assessment, it would take a woman an extra forty-two days of work, in 2020, to earn what a man did.[542]

As of 2021, The World Economic Forum said the gender gap is expected to take another 267.6 years to close.[543] This slow progress is due to conflicting trends . . . even though the proportion of women among skilled professionals continues to increase, income inequalities continue, and few women are represented in managerial positions.[544] In 2021, the uncontrolled gender pay gap revealed women made only 82 cents for every dollar a man made, which is one cent more than they made in 2020.[545] Then there is the controlled gender pay gap, which specifically researches for job title, years of experience, education, industry, location, and other factors. It showed women made 98 cents for every dollar a man made, meaning that women are still making less than men even when doing the same job.[546] You might say it doesn't matter because it's a mere two-cent difference. I disagree because that two-cent difference could end up being a lot of lost pay when spread across an annual income, a career, or time of employment. It shows a woman will still get paid less than a man despite factors and qualifications being equal.

You might think education is the problem-solver. Wrong. A woman's higher education does not lead to pay equity. For example, women with a Master of Business Administration degree take home 76 cents for every dollar men with MBAs make.[547] This gap might be there because of the "motherhood penalty," general bias against highly educated women, or women in particular occupations.[548]

Never heard of the motherhood penalty? Hiring managers are less likely to hire mothers compared to other women who don't have children, and when employers do make an offer to a mother, they offer a lower salary than they do other women.[549] The gap gets worse for minority women compared with white men.

I once met a woman from another country who worked for a multibillion-dollar U.S. firm. She found out that in several cases the minorities who worked for the company were not paid as much as their Caucasian/white counterparts (male and female). Also, in several cases, the minorities were more highly educated (with confirmed and earned degrees) than their white counterparts. Do you see how ludicrous this is? Do you see the toxic, discriminatory mindset? It is a problem that even factoring in the same job skills, experience, and more, men will be paid more than a woman just because she has breasts and a womb. It is unjust that minorities can be paid less just because their color, accent, or country of birth is different. This is heartless and senseless. Pay a person what they should be paid due to their qualifications, skills, experience, and other legitimate criteria. Being a male or female, a person's color or nation of origin should *not* bias what they are entitled to be paid.

Men, do not let your masculinity be toxic. Men, when you are leading, do not let your leadership be toxic. Close the gap.

DO NOT BE EMASCULATED

Men, everything about you is not wrong. God made you with attributes and equipment that women do not have. There is nothing wrong with that. There is nothing wrong with you having the testosterone God gave you. But . . . as with anything else of value, these things must be stewarded properly. Be careful what you do with them. People should celebrate traditional aspects of masculinity like being responsible, assertive, and competitive (in limited ways) as well as other things such as compassion, humility, and kindness.[550]

A problem is men are seemingly penalized, punished, and looked down on for doing just those things: showing aspects of their humanity that are not traditionally seen as masculine. For example, a set of studies found that when male leaders asked for help (which we all need at times), they were viewed as less capable and less competent! This is ridiculous. Why? Not asking for help when you need it will inevitably lead to mistakes.[551] How are you going to get better at something if you don't ask for assistance? Sure, you can learn it yourself and get development in other ways, but you cut off a readily available resource of help. In short, there you go again, doing everything yourself.

You do not need to do everything yourself. Even God does not believe in you doing everything yourself! Look at Scripture, which says it is not good for a man to be alone, and that he, in effect, needs help.[552] Look at Jesus Christ, who asked twelve men to follow Him. Men He personally taught, trained, commissioned, and sent out to be His representatives to the earth.

You can get toxic quickly if you need help, want help, see help available, and yet don't ask for it. Because, if you do, it will hurt your standing in the organization.

There is more. How about being nice? Do you like working with nice people? Of course. I think most do, at least being nice with each other as coworkers, supervisors, subordinates, and associated staff members and contractors. It just makes the work life, which is a major part of our lives, easier. However, research finds that men who are more agreeable (notice I said *agreeable*, not a "yes man") make less money than the stereotypical macho masculine male![553] By being nice, I mean to have a warm personality, to be caring and supportive—these are the things that make it easier for people to work with you, make you a good follower, a good servant-leader, and even help you be a better husband and father outside of work.[554] But no! The issue is when men attempt these positive behaviors and attributes, they get upstaged by the macho-macho man. So men—and women—what kind of example are we setting for other men to follow?

How about being empathetic? That's good, right? I know the value of it from leading others and being led. Empathy (which can be a remedy to many leaders who are self-absorbed, narcissistic, and clueless of how they act) is about understanding or being aware of another person's point of view and their feelings, thoughts, and experiences.[555] This quality is part of the emotional intelligence grouping of skills leaders need. Empathy is not only a beneficial characteristic to have professionally, it aids any person personally. You are able to see things from another person's point of view, and this can influence the way you deal with a situation or interact with a person. Unfortunately, women are the only ones who get "kudos" for being empathetic.[556]

What about modesty? How does that factor into this toxic masculinity scheme of things?

Who likes a leader who is peacocking all the time? Generally, no one. No one likes a showoff, at least not all the time. So, men who exhibit modesty are in safe territory, right? Not really. Men who were humble when talking about their qualifications were noted as less likeable, and even weaker, than modest women.[557] Humble men are seen as less competent and less desirable to hire than women with the same characteristics.[558]

Men, we need to set a new standard. One in which it's okay to do these things and still be real men. We can express more than just rage. We need to be real men who are not allowing culture to dictate to us that we cannot show some of the same characteristics that even Jesus Himself exhibited in His life on earth. Men, set and live a better standard.

FROM A SOLDIER'S PAIN TO CRYING LIKE A MAN

Once, when I was overseas, I spoke with a soldier who was on his way to the U.S. from Iraq. Let's refer to him as Smith. We spoke about several things and even played a video game they had in the aircraft hangar while he was waiting for his plane to arrive so he and his fellow soldiers could get back home. I asked about some of the things he experienced in Iraq, and he began to talk about a time he was guarding a checkpoint (entrance gate).

One day while guarding the checkpoint, Smith and other soldiers were attacked. In the ensuing gun battle he killed at least one attacker. During the attack, Smith's friend was mortally wounded by the enemy. After the fighting ended, he had to grab his injured friend and put him in the back of a pickup truck to get him to a medical tent. After getting to the tent, his friend was taken from the vehicle, and Smith was told to wash away the blood from the back of the truck. His friend and fellow soldier died that day.

When I spoke to him about the details of this moment, he tried his best to hold back tears and keep his composure. As the tears welled up, however, he started to apologize to me and said, more than once, "I thought I was strong." He thought he was being weak because he was getting emotional about having to kill someone and watching his friend die. Adding to all this, as Smith was dealing with the aftermath of this disturbing moment, he was realizing he also could have been killed.

I looked at him and told him it was okay for him to feel what he was feeling and to not hold back. I encouraged him to release what he needed to release before he *exploded*. I verbally validated that he was a man and it's okay to cry. As I started to talk with him more, and even began to pray for him, I can tell you I had never seen a man cry like he did. He cried like a man. I had not heard a man yell out in soul anguish like that before. Never, ever—not for a moment—did I think he was less than a man, soft, weak, or effeminate for being emotional. He is human.

On another note, I did not think my friend was a wimp when he cried before he got married, because he really wanted his marriage to be a strong one and last. I do not think when men cry because their child is born that it's womanlike. We must deal with this toxic thinking.

Some men go through hard, heavy, and heart-wrenching experiences and are not able to talk or release emotions in a healthy way. Imagine all this happening at the same time: a man is physically sick, going through a bitter divorce, kids won't talk and want nothing to do with him, he just lost his job, his dog gets run over, he is evicted from his recently foreclosed house, finds out all his money is stolen, his much-loved mother just passed away, his cell phone gets cut off, his barely working car is being repossessed and towed away, the police are investigating him for something he did not do, and the IRS is auditing him. With all that going on, his only friend (who knows all this is happening to him) gives him a handshake and says, "Stay strong." And the man replies, "I'm okay." No, no. You are not okay. Do not let society bully you into thinking you have to be silent in pain, do it all, be all, and get it all right to uphold some false image. Do not be battered into thinking showing any emotion is effeminate. That is not true. And "stay strong"? This is the type of pitiful advice you get from people who are drowning in their own toxic thinking.

From the information I've presented, you can see men do not always get a fair shake when it comes to what are and are not acceptable behavioral traits. Do not be bullied, men. Just because someone does not like you and does not have your best interest at heart does not mean everything you do is necessarily toxic. Have you noticed there is a war going on for the male image? That is why you are reading a book like this, to check yourself. Masculinity and testosterone are being attacked more and more in this society.[559] I like what Paul said in 1 Corinthians 16:13: "Be on the alert, stand firm in the faith, act like men, be strong" (NASB).

EMOTIONALLY CAGED

Many men are caged. Maybe not physically or literally, but nonetheless, many are in prison. Are you one of them? Are you suffering with emotional incarceration? Emotional incarceration is defined by Jason Wilson, author of *Battle Cry*, as self-imposed mental imprisonment.[560] It's when a man locks up his so-called non-masculine emotions and isolates his heart from the world. It is a by-product of not being in environments where it's acceptable to actually communicate and express emotions.[561] Notice: this prison is self-imposed. You put yourself there. Most importantly, you keep yourself there. I understand why. It's probably because of the poor role models you've seen, or other things happening like you experiencing shame, being made fun of for saying your feelings were hurt, or being heartbroken by a relationship ending. There are so many scenarios that can take place. The end result of all of them is personal pain.

Your psychological injury or pain, defined as trauma, needs to be dealt with. Stop allowing personal, perpetual, perennial, persistent, penetrating pain to fester like an oozing, infected, itching sore of the soul.[562] Wilson says that if we do not have an outlet for our emotional responses they begin to pile up until we feel buried, overcome, and bitter.[563]

This is where ministers/pastors, Christian counselors, social workers, psychologists, psychiatrists, life coaches, leadership coaches and consultants, and mentors can be helpful sources of support. Other outlets (even just to vent some steam) are too numerous to name, but include going to the gym, cooking, cleaning, praying, worshiping, listening to music, getting outdoors, receiving a healthy (legitimate) massage, having clean fun, and anything else healthy that you find therapeutic.

I met a man who likes coffee. I mean *really* likes coffee. He buys expensive coffee beans from around the world. He then grinds his own beans and slowly pours and manually filters each cup. He thoroughly enjoys this process of making his one to two cups of premium coffee a day. He told me: "It's therapeutic." What do you do that's therapeutic, allows you to vent, and is a good stress reliever?

Outlets are different for all kinds of people but all should be healthy. Not the unhealthy outlets such as binge drinking, over-eating, over-spending, smoking substances, and abusing others. Pay attention to your emotions, men, because the quality of your life is governed by the quality of your emotions.[564]

Wilson, the author, said, "Unfortunately, suppression leads to depression. . . . The more unresolved anger, anxiety, and distress we harbor in our hearts, the less capable we are of abundantly living in the present. When emotional issues go unaddressed, they become mental and behavioral issues."

YOU CAN'T SEX YOUR WAY INTO MANHOOD

Listen up, men. You cannot sex your way into manhood. Having sex with a lot of women does not make you manlier. Stop living by toxic knowledge learned on the streets and by people without honor and integrity. Many men have experienced trauma that has led them from one negative place in their life to another. For example, consider the child who, for one reason or another, felt powerless in his youth, only to grow older to crave power to prove his "I'm-the-man" masculine mentality and lord it over others. The emotionally incarcerated male will voluntarily keep himself in prison even though he needs help.

Consider the man who is on a never-ending journey to prove that "I am a man" by trying to have as much "meaningful"—and yet really meaningless—sex with as many women as possible. Maybe as a child you were molested, or as a man you were violated/assaulted, by a man . . . and to combat that you are having sex with multiple women to prove your manliness. Men, are you seeking to dominate as many sexual partners as you can to cover up for the times you were abused? You cannot sex your way into significance. You cannot erase your past by trying to make yourself a macho, hyper-masculine, manly man by *sexing* your way to filling a wounded and violated soul. Sex cannot fill a hurting heart. You need ministry; you need help.

If you are in any of these traps, you may need prayer, counseling, therapy, or all of the above. In its original and intended context, I believe sex is meant to be used in marriage for not only procreation but also great enjoyment.[565] It is not to be used as a bandage to give you a confidence booster, like temporarily inflating a leaking balloon with air. Some men have had sex with so many women the numbers are embarrassing. Saying you've had sex with multiple women and that you have multiple kids outside of marriage is nothing to be proud of. You get no badge of courage or honor by going through women like a man with the flu goes through tissue. If you continue that kind of behavior, you will lose your soul. I'll say it once more: having sex does not make you a man, nor does it increase your manhood.

EMOTIONS ARE EQUAL OPPORTUNISTS

Have you seen a job application where the company states they are an equal opportunity employer? It is rather common to see. Being an equal opportunity employer means an employer will not discriminate against any employee or job applicant because of their race, color, religion, national origin, sex, physical disability, mental disability, or age.[566] Men, feelings and emotions are equal opportunity employers. It does not matter who you are. Feelings, passions, and moods can be felt by anyone. It does not matter if you are young or old, rich or poor, upper-class, middle-class, lower-class, African-American/Black, White, Indian, Asian, Hispanic/Latino, self-employed, employed, retired, civilian, or military. Emotions are equal opportunity employers. They can be had by all. Everyone experiences moods and emotions. Many of us just do not admit it. It may be comical to say, but there is no formal Board of Directors on Emotions, Board of Approvals for Feelings, Board of Governors on Moods, Council of Emotions, or any Executive Committee on Feelings that approve the emotions men are allowed to have versus emotions only women can have. Let's take a commonsense approach.

Men and women can mutually experience: admiration, adoration, appreciation of beauty, amusement, anger, rage, anxiety, awe, awkwardness, boredom, loneliness, calmness, confusion, craving, disgust, pain, excitement, fear, horror, interest, joy, nostalgia, relief, sadness, grief, depression, satisfaction, betrayal, surprise, and more.[567] Men and women can and do experience both. Wilson notes that the truth is God did not create specific emotions for men and others for women. He created humans, and all emotions are available to both male and female.[568]

Men need to be comprehensive. Not just masculine. Many masculine men are bound, or restricted, to live by certain emotions that are only "culturally acceptable" for men to live by.[569] A comprehensive man can express a range of emotions and is not restricted by the typical cultural norms or the usual stereotypes of what a man can express.[570] For example, a man can be strong but sensitive and kindhearted; a leader but also one who follows and supports as needed; a lion but also a lamb; bold and outspoken yet also discreet and tactful. Again, read about the life of Jesus in the four Gospels to see how wide-ranging He was. Are you a comprehensive man, or are you bound to express and communicate only in a couple of ways?

NEEDED: REAL MASCULINE MEN

Dr. Steve Farrar, author of *King Me: What Every Son Wants and Needs from His Father*, wrote that boys need a man in their life to show them what masculinity is supposed to look like.[571] Men need to be the masculine models they were designed to be. Farrar writes this about masculinity.

> So what is masculinity? It's a willingness to lead, assume responsibility, and be a self-starter. Masculine men take initiative. It's an inclination to despise passivity and do the right thing. It's a willingness to stand alone and be unpopular. It is a desire to protect and provide for one's family and those who are weak and disadvantaged. It requires courage, honor, and the willingness to sacrifice, even if necessary, one's own life for the good of others. That's masculinity. . . . A truly masculine man honors God and blesses all who are led by Him.

Men, masculine males *can* have a range of qualities and characteristics. I will bring up a point I made earlier. Notice in the first book to the Corinthian church, 16:13, the apostle said, "Be watchful, stand firm in the faith, act like men, be strong." There is a difference in the way men behave. In our culture there are things men "do not do." Men should "act like men." When needed, be brave, courageous, a leader, a teacher, the example. Be, and act like, men. Here is a short list of some things men should do: protect, provide, lead your family in worship, and, when needed, be courageous, develop others, and lead.[572]

NOTES

NOTES

Fourteen

WOMEN: FEMININITY IS NOT TOXIC, SO DON'T HAVE TOXIC FEMININITY

It is my hope this chapter adds context and balance to the topic of toxic femininity. Let's begin with some baseline information. Toxic femininity can be explained as women expressing stereotypically feminine traits such as passivity, empathy, sensuality, patience, tenderness, and receptivity that results in individuals ignoring their mental or physical needs to sustain those around them.[573] It's when a woman works to the benefit of others (usually men) but to the detriment of herself.[574] One contributing writer for *Forbes* stated that, in the workplace, toxic femininity is passive aggression.[575] It's when women allow relationships and productivity to suffer because they are not being honest about their own objectives, or when they are assuming they know best.[576] It's being entitled or demanding while manipulating other people.[577] What do you think of these definitions? Do you agree with them?

For clarity's sake, when demonstrated rightly, there is nothing wrong with a woman being soft-natured, soft-spoken, empathetic, patient, tender, and friendly to others. All have their place and can be utilized in the right contexts. If those characteristics describe you, be confident you are on solid ground. There is nothing wrong with the way you are behaving. The issue, made clear by the second definition, is when you do those things to your own personal harm. One example is being silent when living with abuse because that is what a woman "is supposed to do." Or staying in a codependent situation with another person's lethal addictions.

From birth many of us have discovered, or others have discovered for us, noticeable or dominant gifts or bents in our personality—like the ones listed previously. The problems arise when (as the initial definition described) good characteristics and giftings are used too much, for too long, or abused. (I'd like to think most parents, especially mothers, know the responsibility of sacrificing things like sleep, time, and energy when raising their children. However, we really are not thinking about those kinds of things here.)

One view of toxic femininity is when women manipulate men with charm and sexuality.[578] Of course, men want an attractive and appealing woman based on their own particular tastes. However, the point here is the selfish manipulation. It is a woman getting what she wants to another person's detriment. This is especially heightened in business settings. See the difference? That is toxic. Using sex appeal to control men and climb the corporate ladder is wrong. It's just as wrong for men to do this. Does it seem fair to be an advocate for women's rights and then use toxic, noxious, underhanded, and manipulative means to get your way? Playing the "sex card" for promotions and to get your way is just as bad as a man manipulating, intimidating, stepping on, and blackmailing people to move up the ranks. Wrong is wrong no matter the gender. Bad behavior is bad behavior no matter the sex.

Dr. Carrie Gress noticed a closeness of toxic femininity to the extremes of the feminist movement.[579]

Women have always desired equality and respect, but our current culture . . . seeks this equality and respect through the vices of Machiavelli: rage, intimidation, tantrums, bullying, raw emotion, and absence of logic. It is this aggressive impulse—

this toxic femininity—that finds pride in calling oneself "nasty," feels empowered by dressing as a vagina, (and) belittles men . . .

Gress goes on to write that rage, indignation, vulgarity, and pride all short-circuit a woman's greatest gifts, which include wisdom, prudence, patience, unflappable peace, intuition, her ability to weave together the fabric of society, and her capacity for a genuine relationship with God.[580]

The more extreme side of feminism is being blamed for the destruction of the family, rising divorce rate, and the apathy and moral delinquency of young people.[581] If you are not careful you may believe the narrative that equality feminists are pushing: a belief that motherhood is parasitic and being a housewife is a leech.[582] Many pockets of the feminist movement think it is bad for a woman to be a mother and a housewife if she wants to. Nonsense. Both are fine decisions if that is her choice. What are your thoughts about feminism?

If you believe there is still a great deal of work to do for women's rights and equality, I agree. With all the positive changes, although too slow, going on, just make sure that you personally are changing, learning, and maturing into the right kind of person.

If you desire to be single, that is okay. If you desire to be married, that is fine. If you want to be a stay-at-home wife and mother, and both you and your husband agree to this, then that is good. If both of you desire to work and have a two-income household, that's fine too. The point: do not let hard-core, staunch feminists look down on you and make you feel bad about how you and your husband agree to live your lives. It is not toxic to be single, get married and have children, work or not work, go to college or not go to college, homeschool your children or send them to school.

Furthermore, ladies, if you are called to run for president, lead a company, be a venture capitalist, get on the governing boards of Fortune 500 companies, start and lead a ministry, or the million other things you can be and do with your God-given abilities, gifts, and purpose, then do them! Do what God has put you on earth to do. Just avoid toxicity while doing it, and stay true to your North Star. Do not let a low-moral-standard society poke, push, and prod you into doing things that are not good for you and your family. There is nothing wrong with sacrificing, or, for a limited time, ignoring your needs for others, for your family, and working toward their benefit. My mother did this for years to support her children. Even my father made significant choices when he was younger so he could be around to raise his children. Not all sacrifices in life are toxic. Just know that sacrificing time, effort, money, and other resources can become toxic if done for the wrong reason, for too long, and to your harm.

Ladies, as I wrote in the previous chapter when discussing toxic masculinity, it's important to know about toxic femininity because having it influence you could very well impact your ability to lead, follow, and cloud your interactions with others.

ANOTHER LOOK AT FEMININITY

So consider another perspective on femininity. Femininity is not a bad thing. Femininity is not a weakness. To be very clear, God made both men and women. The book of beginnings states this.[583] If there is confusion on some of the original designs for men and women, consult the book of Genesis. God made male and female. Which means He made the masculine and feminine. There is a difference between the two.

Men and women can do many things alike, but understand male and female will never be exactly the same. Think about it. By the design of God, we are not supposed to be the same! For example, look at the physical bodies of men and women. Naturally, the genitalia of men and women are not the same, and never will be. Women have breasts and a womb, and this means they are biologically built for the capability of having children. This is something naturally born men will never be able to do.

216

Femininity at its basic level is not about a personality.[584] Just like a man can show more emotions than just one—anger—and still be masculine, likewise a woman can love sports, martial arts, hunting, fishing, camping, and cars, and be just as feminine, just as ladylike, as the woman who loves interior design, shopping, makeup, and shoes.[585] Think about it. Femininity is deeply rooted in who God has created the woman to be through her biological composition and inward spirit, not one based on interests, hobbies, or personality.[586] A woman's composition is meant to reproduce, sustain, and nurture life.[587] The ability to bear children is not the only point of femininity but cannot be overlooked either.

The deepest purposes of a woman, like those of a man, are too numerous to mention and go beyond the scope of this book. One more characteristic worth mentioning is a women's relational capacity.[588] Women, like men, are meant for relationship. Look at the context between men and women found in Genesis chapter 2. A woman is meant to be different—from the biological to the visual. From the way women think differently to the way they act differently. The differences in a woman are strengths, not weaknesses. So stop trying to be like a man, and just be the best woman you were designed to be. We will never all be exactly the same; even our unique fingerprints prove that.

Women, strive to be what God made you to be. Maximize your gifts, talents, and abilities. Keep God's Word as your North Star and be careful not to take familial advice from anyone who does not love God, honor life, honor marriage, and uphold family.

NOTES

Fifteen

TREATMENT: PREVENTIVE
AND DETOX MEDICINE

Help is here. We have identified major areas of toxicity that many of us have encountered. You have already read a lot of information that can help you understand and identify what toxic leadership and followership is. You have read several helpful points on how to deal with it and remove it from your life. In this chapter we will concentrate more on soul medicine to help you treat the virus of pride, selfishness, and lust that's affected the mind, will, and emotions. I do not only want to help treat the toxic soul. I also want to recommend some detoxification advice to counteract the poison.

I believe the guidance provided here can help you walk through and even out of some things to correct and overhaul the way you think and behave. Remember, leaders set the standard. Leaders are the models others imitate. Leaders pave the way for others. Live like you are being watched, because you are.

Let's take the next steps to get and be better. Maximize yourself. Stop settling. Make progress. The time for change is now. Stop running and ignoring your issues. You may not think people notice, but you would be surprised who sees the dark or more hidden sides of your life.

LET'S GET THE FILTH OUT

Admit it. Many of us have been operating in a "mixed spirit" or "mixed mindset." To be good leaders we need to work to get the mixture out of our lives. The next obvious question is: what is a mixed spirit? I'll explain it in several ways. In the bartending profession, in its simplest form, a mixed drink is when you mix alcoholic and non-alcoholic beverages and/or ingredients together. Thus, it's a mixture.

Just like a drink can have mixed spirits (mixed alcohols and other elements), you also can have a mixed spirit. In this context, spirit means your inner life or soul. It is the things you cannot always see (what/who energies you, the way you think, your desires, your will and passions). What Paul said to the disciples at Ephesus applies to all of us. Ephesians 4:22-24 says to stop your old behavior or way of living which is corrupted by lust and deception. Instead, let the Spirit reform or change your thoughts and attitudes. Put on your new nature.

The carnal Christian operates by his or her fleshly desires. They take their fleshly mindset and immaturity and mix it with their more mature and godly sides. Confusing? Essentially, what you end up with is a big baby on your hands. It's like mixing the sacred with the secular . . . you end up with one big compromise. A mixed spirit is like mixing oil with water, and those two never mix well.

You may be the person who has Bible verses on the bumper of your car and email signature block, but on social media you are doing, liking, posting, following all kinds of lewd, crude, and inappropriate photos, videos, and behaviors. There is a mixture happening. Many parents and business leaders misuse their place of leadership in the home and in their place of business. They take the privilege and responsibility of leadership and waste it, misuse it, and abuse it by focusing on themselves and their own selfish agendas. Stop doing that.

When you mix equal parts of a hot and a cold drink, it's liable to come out lukewarm. A mixed spirit is like mixing the profane with the sacred or the good with the bad. Now it's neither truly good nor truly bad. It's a big compromise.

By now I hope you've identified some toxicity in your life that you know you need to uproot, clean up, and clear out. There is progress that God is requiring you to make in one or more areas in your life. If you have not realized this by now, the older you get, the more mature you should be. The two do not necessarily mean the same thing.

For Christians, the longer you serve God, read His Word, and pray, the more He will refine you.[589] You are like an onion being lovingly, but intentionally, peeled layer by layer. You will forever be on the potter's wheel. In other words, the Potter (God) is shaping and molding you constantly to make you into an honorable vessel fit for His use.[590] The fit you were ten years ago may not necessarily be the fit He needs you to be now. You are in God's school of lifelong learning.

A mixed spirit can be further explained with the example given previously about being married and swapping spouses for sex with other people. Another example would be not standing up for biblical truths just because it's not popular and giving way to the spirit of worldliness and perversion. It is like being a married man and still deliberately flirting with other women. It's like saying you love people, but do nothing to care for others. It's like saying you want to be a leader, but instead of leading you dishonor, disrespect, abuse, and inappropriately use people. That is not what being a leader is about. See the disconnect? If not, here are still more examples.

It's like saying you love God and hate wicked things but actively watch and support pornography and, by default, support the sex slave industry. Think about it. Are you mixed? A mixed spirit is like having the Spirit of Christ and the spirit of the world joined together. It's a corrupt cocktail with the world and a lack of honor for God (misdirected passions, misdirected focus, and ego inflation)—all while adding in a sprinkling of Jesus.

Go to war with your flesh. Go the opposite direction of where your compromising carnality wants you to go. You need to bend your will to obey God. Then the Holy Spirit will help you. When you go by the will of the flesh, you get demonically inspired assistance to feed and even grow your toxic appetites. You have the will to choose, and it's your choices that will lead you to personal victory or into trouble. Make a continuous choice to go in the right direction. Choose life.[591]

Many of us do what is written in 2 Samuel 12:9. We despise what the Lord says should be a standard to live by and simply do what is wrong or evil. God is calling you to accountability, humility, and to honor His way. If God is bringing some things to your remembrance right now, stop and begin to pray, repent (change your mind and go in a better direction; more on this in the next chapter), and ask God to minister to your hardened heart. After doing some terrible things (2 Samuel 11), David was confronted by the prophet Nathan, and this brought him to the realization that he needed to repent to God, change his way of thinking, and go in another direction.

Are you the person who needs to do that right now? Is this your "Nathan moment"? What is God confronting in your heart and life . . . right now? Do not ignore Him. In many parts of this book, whether you've realized it or not, God has been challenging you to change your ways.

I am not pushing you to unattainable perfection, but I am encouraging you to be processed. Processed by God. Processed to understand and get in alignment with His ways of doing things.

Don't continue to compromise by thinking, *I'm a little toxic, but it's no big deal.* It's the little things that can have a big effect. It's the little things that can trip you up as much as the big things. What is wrong is simply wrong. Sometimes it's just easier to justify trying to overlook the small things. I believe a little bit of sin, a little bit of soul poison, should be viewed as much of a threat as the big stuff. The Bible says a little leaven can leaven the whole lump (1 Corinthians 5:6; Galatians 5:9). Leaven can be viewed as yeast or sin. A little yeast causes the whole loaf of bread to rise or spreads through the whole batch of dough. A little unrepentant and unchecked sin can alter the course of your life. Why? Because it could grow in you. A little problem can turn into a big problem if not dealt with. A little bit of child pornography can turn your life in a bad direction just as a rudder on a ship turns it in a wrong direction.

A little bit of abuse is still abuse, and wrong. Do not overlook it. A little bit of illegal drugs might be just enough to derail your entire life and cause you to chase a euphoric high over and over again. A small gambling problem could grow into a big gambling problem. A little bit of inappropriate flirting could end up getting you caught in a situation you should never be in. A little bit of pride or willful and prolonged disobedience could cause you to ruin your faith.

Stop thinking "a little" is permissible when it can lead to a lot. A little cheating in a relationship could destroy a longtime marriage. A little cheating on a standardized test, if discovered, can cause you to fail an entire class or worse. A little snake venom can kill you. A little, a little, a little. Stop with the "a little" thoughts and comments and deal with the leaven of your soul. Let's move from a polluted, contaminated, dirty, mixed spirit to a more pure spirit and excellent spirit (Matthew 5:8; Psalm 24:3-4; Daniel 5:12, 6:3).

Try your best to see the proper reflection of yourself in light of this book. How are you looking? Try your best to operate with good character and not just your gifts and talents. Put another way, stop relying on your ability to do and get things done without taking into account how you are treating and handling the best asset you have: other people. Gifts and abilities without fruit, or character and control, are not good for any leader.

By fruit (Galatians 5:22-23) I am referring to the evidence that God is in your life as a life-influencing force. The fruit (or attributes) of godliness are: love, joy, peace, patience, kindness, goodness, faithfulness, gentleness, and self-control. Are you seeing the truth yet? What we are missing from many of our parents/family leaders, teachers, mentors, coaches, captains of industries, business leaders, department heads, political figures, congressional leaders, police officers, public officials, and ministers is *fruit*. The ability to respond to life's situations in a nontoxic, proper way.

Having power, abilities, gifts, and talents without fruit could be compared with being a Harvard University graduate and yet still being responsible for high-level fraudulent business crimes.[592] It is the equivalent of being high on ability and intellect, but low on character. High on smarts, but low on integrity and trustworthiness. Top-notch abilities, but low morality.

Harvard graduates have gone on to be responsible for terrorism, embezzlement, and other white color crimes.[593] One CEO wrote that we need to stop putting so much weight on where leaders and aspiring leaders went to school and focus more on their character, ability, and prior record of success.[594] Notice that *character* is, and should be, at the top of the list.

At least work to make your level of skill equal with fruit—i.e., your character, decency, and honor. You need your gifts wrapped with fruit. Just like chocolate covers a candy bar, so you need your talents and skills wrapped with a fruitlike covering. I hope you are getting the illustration that character—good fruit—should cover you to keep your life from being toxic.

THE VITAMIN M COMPLEX

According to the National Institute on Aging, vitamins are one of the main types of nutrients the body needs to stay healthy.[595] Vitamins perform different jobs to help keep the body working as it should.[596] If you do not get enough nutrients in your food, you may run into problems. Research shows that vitamin deficiencies can cause things like eye problems.[597] Not getting the right nutrients can cause you to see incorrectly.

In close comparison, neglect, or not putting the right things into your life to build character, can cause you problems. This is especially true in the area of leadership. If you are not taking in the right supplements, this will not only affect you but others as well. I recommend some "vitamins" for the soul and spirit. M vitamins. No, not magnesium, manganese, or molybdenum, but some vitamins recommended by Dr. Bill Hamon.[598] Dr. Hamon has served as a bishop to more than nine hundred ministers and churches in the United States as well as more than three thousand ministries overseas.[599]

Every key word in the M vitamin complex developed by Dr. Hamon starts with the letter M. These Ms represent your development, or what you need to mature in, for your personal life, which will benefit your leadership and professional life. Remember, leadership is not just telling people what to do and how you command teams and organizations. It's also about leading yourself as well. As mentioned previously, and repeatedly, leadership starts with you first. The components of the M vitamin complex follow.[600] I encourage you to take these supplements seriously; they can have a lifelong beneficial impact. Consider which of these M vitamins you need most.

Manhood/Womanhood: Being a mature person in how you handle your affairs is more important than any leadership position, title, or job. As already covered in this book, your greatest leadership role can easily be overpowered by your personal issues that can destroy it. Examples of this are the poor treatment of people and prolonged breaches of integrity. It's best to stop holding people to a standard you are not upholding yourself. Otherwise, you make yourself out to be a hypocrite. Practice the "evaluate yourself first" principle found in Matthew 7:3-5.

You are a man or woman first. Not a title or a position first. You are responsible for your own example *before* you don the position or title of boss, supervisor, manager, CEO, vice president, regional manager, bishop, elder, minister, department head, team leader, or any other similar title. You develop your relationship with God first. You uphold high standards first before requiring others to do so. You uphold the standards of the organization you are leading before requiring others to do so. Read Genesis 1:26-27. You were made in the image of God. Let your life be the best reflection of Him it can be.[601] The goal is to be like Jesus, not a maniacal, self-serving, self-indulging person. Your highest calling or goal is to be Christlike in character, thinking, and behavior. He is the ultimate leader.

Maturity: In what areas of your life are you mature, and in what areas immature? Immaturity can cause lots of problems, especially when dealing with people. You've seen the terrible circumstances resulting from people who are immature in marriage or finances or both, or immature with other people's personal business or feelings. Immaturity can be costly and painful. For those of you who desire to be married, promoted at your job, receive large pay raises; to be endowed with greater gifts, anointings, and graces; and to receive more and more notoriety, and all the great things you want for your life . . . all those desires should serve as signals to be mature in those areas so you can handle those gifts and responsibilities. Be sober minded. Understand the purpose behind you receiving these things. Can you handle them if you do receive them?

Get educated. Obtain the wisest counsel you can from people who have what you want or have done what you want to achieve. If you cannot be around them personally, learn from them online or through social media. Read their books. Most importantly, ask God for wisdom.[602] Imagine giving a million dollars to an immature person whose life is consumed with partying, video games, and dead-end jobs. What is the likelihood he or she will make wise decisions with that money with no mature outside assistance?

Maturity in any area you are involved in (or want) does not automatically guarantee success, but it can increase the probability of your success. It does put things in your favor. Why? Because you will not be making the immature mistakes that often lead to people's failures. The apostle Paul told Timothy (1 Timothy 3:6) not to put an immature person in leadership because pride comes knocking at their door to damage their life. Maturing is not—I emphasize *not*—so much about age as it is about spiritual and mental soberness. It is about developing good character.

Part of maturity is taking care of your delegated and designated responsibilities. It's having a sense of levelheadedness and ownership to take care of what is under your span of control. Be leery of the person who does not want to take care of his or her children, manage their finances, take care of their home, fulfill their work responsibilities, take care of their personal affairs, who treats people poorly, and then wants to lead you. Do not put that person in positions of power. They are not mature.

As we've said, maturity includes the character-forming goals: the fruit of the Spirit. Galatians 5:22-24 lists them. Does the fruit of your life look like love, joy, peace, patience, kindness, goodness, faithfulness, gentleness, and self-control? Do you respond with these attributes in everyday situations? If not, then you have work to do. In this context, one way in which to define the word *fruit*: the result of, or the end result of. To clarify, you know you are maturing when you respond to people and situations with love, joy, peace, patience, kindness, goodness, faithfulness, gentleness, and self-control. It's not about being flawless. It's about being intentional to be so filled and influenced by God that it comes out in how you represent yourself as a man, woman, and leader. The attributes of the Spirit are not the only markings of maturity, but you cannot say you are truly mature without them. A second way to define fruit is motivation. This means fruit is not just the end result, it's also the motivation to do or want something. The fruit of exercising regularly and having a good diet is typically better health and a better physique. The fruit of you even wanting to work out (motivation) is typically a result of something you thought of, saw, or heard that you wanted. Think about purchases of food, clothes, a watch, cellphone, car, or house that you wanted. The fruit of what you had seen, felt, heard, or experienced led you (fruit that motivated you) to work for it, and then eventually you purchased it (fruit). Remember, fruit has two sides. Use both to your advantage.

Maturity is living with God's love in your heart toward others. This is not about getting everyone to like you or letting people get away with their responsibilities. It is about respecting and treating an individual as a real person with dignity. Ever met or worked with someone who was mean to you for seemingly no reason? Especially when you have been decent or good to them? It can be difficult to respond in a respectable way, but you can do it. The goal is 1 Corinthians 13:4-8. It may seem like a high bar to reach, but with Christ you can do it.

Faithfulness is a mark of maturity. Faithfulness is the way to promotion. Check out Matthew 25:21 and 25:23. Matthew 25:14-28 is the story of three people who were given money and had the responsibility to make more money with it. Basically, the master told them to get a return on his investment. It was their job to take what they had been given and do something to increase it. In the end, two did, but one did not. Notice what was said to the two who were able to increase what they were given (verses 21 and 23): "Well done, good and faithful servant!" The word faithful here means one who is trustworthy, shows themselves faithful in the transaction of business, the execution of commands, or the discharge of official duties; one who can be relied on.[603] Now that's maturity. A faithful person is consistent. So the question here is: do you think you are being faithful with the things God has given you responsibility for? Are you leading people well? Have you increased your investments? Have you taken good care of your responsibilities on and off the job?

Are you faithful to be and do what you are purposed or called to? If you have a family, you are supposed to be more faithful to your spouse and children than you are to your friends or watching your favorite program or sporting event. Some of you know more stats and figures about the players on your favorite sports team than your spouse's likes and dislikes. Mature people overcome their character flaws and focus on what's important. Without maturing, you may become or stay toxic, and you will not endure the things you need to work through as a leader. At least not well. Without maturity you make bad decisions. Without maturity you act like a child. Always remember, age has nothing to do with being mature.

Marriage: The main point I will make about marriage is a simple one. Married couples need to make their relationship a priority. After God, it is the most important relationship you will have. For instance, unless extreme short-term situations dictate otherwise, do you find yourself working a hundred hours a week but only spending five hours a week with your spouse? You are being faithful to, and prioritizing, the wrong thing. Do you really think a job is worth more than your health, marriage, or family? I hope not. Do not let less important side things become the main priorities. A good rule of thumb: God first, spouse and family second, and (depending on your profession) ministry or job third. Balance them properly. Seek to live an ordered, structured life. This does not mean a boring life. It means you have your priorities in the right order. Practicing the art of prioritization, order, and structure is an important skill you will need through life.

Methods: Do not live a hypocritical lifestyle. Properly represent God in what you do and how you do it. Present yourself well. The main thing to remember: people hear what you say and see what you do and notice a difference between the two. If there is a gap, they'll see it. You cannot speak about treating people well and then turn around and put down and scold people on a continual basis. Close the gap and decrease the separation between words and actions. I know it's easier said than done at times because our carnal (immature) nature wants its way. For those of us who are tempted with being carnal far too often, we are being given an important message: do not say one thing and do something else completely different.

Read Titus 1:16. The apostle was explaining to Titus that there are people who try to represent themselves one way, but their actions clearly say another. Again, identify and remove the division. In a practical sense, you should not be working for one company while following the rules, codes, and regulations from another. Think about it: imagine working as a partner at a boutique law firm while following the dictates of the small burger joint you worked at when you were in high school. The goal is to be whole, not divided. Again, stop saying one thing and living by another.

As leaders we need to stop denying Christ by the ungodly things we do. If you are an emerging leader, then work hard to be a great one. Stop with the personal excuses. As I wrote before, God wants us rigidly righteous and walking in absolute integrity. If you fail, repent and get back on the plan and path God has for you. Stop making excuses and finding ways to give yourself a pass and thus denying Christ with your actions. Don't stop at who you are now; aim for the better person you could be. To reiterate: bad methods do not justify a good end. A person makes himself or herself look like a hypocrite with such nonsense.

Manners: In a movie I saw once, one of the main characters said, "Manners maketh man." I believe that was his way of saying a person's manners separate them from the animals and other lower life forms. Manners are what make a man a gentleman and a woman a lady. Simply put, your behavior, etiquette, protocols, ways and means, conduct, and methods separate you from others and keep you from being one of the lower beasts that trudges its way through life. People with bad manners are a bear to be around. Examples of bad manners can run the gamut from being rude or unkind to things such as scolding people unnecessarily, telling a person's private business to others, and a host of other actions. Bad manners, according to Dr. Hamon's account, are poor examples of Christ.[604] Let's back that up by looking at Titus 1:7-9. It says that leaders should not be arrogant, quick-tempered (lack self-control), drunkard, violent, or greedy.

Leading the good and godly way, people are to be hospitable, love good things, be self-controlled, upright, devout, and disciplined. If you are not these things, you have some things to work toward. We are to stop speaking evil of others, avoid needless arguing and fighting, be gentle, and show perfect courtesy toward all people.[605] The leaders that God wants are supposed to be different from the world. We are not supposed to act like, treat people like, nor think like, everyone else in the world. Love is to be the mandate of how we interact with others. Again, review 1 Corinthians 13. Set the example by not using profanity, vulgarity, being cruel, or using harsh language.

Money: What people will do for it is sickening. People will sell out themselves, their family, and their community for it. People will lie, cheat, steal, kill, and die for it. Many put their morals aside entirely to get the seemingly almighty dollar. Trust me, it's not almighty. The lust for things and the power that riches and wealth bring a person can be a strong motivator. Especially for those who don't have good morals or personal standards established on good character. Make a note of this: truly, the love of money is at the root of all sorts of evil and wickedness, and those who have given themselves up for it go astray (go off course in life, or stray from where they should be going) and torture their soul with sorrows (including personal griefs and pains).[606]

Money is not evil, and there is no problem with you having and using it. Currency is amoral. The things people can do with money, and to get it, can be nothing short of hideous. Money works as an amplifier. Just as a musician playing an electronic instrument uses an amplifier to make their sound louder, so is money to a man or woman. It often amplifies what's on the inside. If you are irresponsible, greedy, and spend your money on nonsensical things, you'll probably be the same when you have more money. If you are generous, kind, and responsible with limited finances, it's more probable you will be the same way when you have more money at your disposal. You can find this principle in Luke 16:10. It's not wrong to be wealthy; it is wrong to do wicked things with the wealth. Remember, leaders have followers. What example are you setting for others? What spirit or mindset is influencing you when you earn, spend, and otherwise interact with money?

Be careful of your desires; money may amplify your means and the opportunities you have to fulfill them. Drugs, crime, and indiscretions are fueled and fed with finances. On the flip side, so are things like supporting family and other sound personal life and business practices. Don't be fooled: just because you have lots of money does not mean you have the stamp of approval of God's blessing. Life is more than just accumulating things. People are the truest and most preeminent of all riches.[607]

If you find yourself jealous of people or overtaken with a greedy, selfish heart, remember you can fight this tendency by being generous. Giving, which includes giving away money, can help turn your heart in the right direction.[608] Give to help. Give to be a blessing to someone. Give to give, unselfishly.

Morality: People should be moral. That goes for everyone, and especially those in leadership roles. Many have ruined their businesses and relationships due to immorality manifested in various forms. Morality is not about pushing religion but about how you respect yourself and other people. It's about holding a standard. In a way, morality makes it easier for people to trust you.

As people in God's image, we are to put an end to the wickedness of our bad thinking and patterns of behavior that manifest in things like illicit sexual intercourse, lustful living, impure motives, inordinate affections, wicked and destructive thinking, desiring what is off limits through lustful cravings, and greedy desires to gain more.[609] Doing these things can lead others to admire, and desire, the wrong things. Far too many people sell out their souls on the table of greed, lust, and cravings for things like power, fame, influence, sex, money, and complete control. Leaders must stop their desire to tear down another person's good name, use nasty and obscene speech, and just plain filthy communication.[610] Things like these and others make you immoral, untrustworthy, hard to befriend, and hard to follow.

Motive: Let's talk about the *why* of your life. In important areas, what motivates you to do what you do? What is your *why*? What are the main motives that drive your behavior? What is your internal compass or North Star? Is it self-preservation wrapped up in me, my, myself, and I? Is it all about you, all roads lead to you, and conversations must start and make their final destination around you? What a horrible way to live. I recommend you live your life by love. Love gives, love helps. Without it, you are nothing.[611]

Remember, leadership is a social enterprise, one based on *people.* Part of your leadership mandate includes serving others. Stop being so full of your own self. This shows up in things like envy, arrogance, rudeness, and being irritable and resentful of others.[612] Acting in genuine love and demonstrating a walk of love should not seem strange. It can look like a lot of things. For example, being patient and kind to others is a good representation of love.[613] Being a leader means you are called to live and demonstrate the love walk. Leaders represent more than themselves.

All these preventive measures should be supported by spiritual disciplines. I covered several of these in my book *Leadership in the Age of Narcissism.* Once again, I recommend studying these disciplines and applying them to your leadership.

NOTES

Sixteen

SELF-CARE? SOUL CARE?

Yes to both. Self-care: do you know what it is, and more importantly, do you practice it? Here are a couple of definitions. Self-care is the use of a range of activities with the ultimate goal of keeping you functioning well.[614] Another definition: self-care is a process of using practices that promote your personal holistic health and well-being.[615] Self-care has nothing to do with masculinity or femininity. It's about demonstrating care for yourself. People get entirely accustomed to performing routine maintenance on their car or residential HVAC system, but won't do a thing to promote their mental or physical well-being.

Soul care is different but closely related to self-care. Both can work in close tandem with one another.[616] Soul care is about learning to live our life with God.[617] It is about nourishing and nurturing our soul as a shared work between ourselves and the Holy Spirit.[618] It is for everyone, not just for those who feel weak or consider themselves more spiritual than others.[619] And just like self-care, there is biblical precedent for soul care.[620] Soul care is more about spiritual disciplines (reading Scriptures, worship, and praying to God, etc.).[621] Continue reading and observe how they can intermingle with one another.

Self-care and soul care are important. I believe not taking care of yourself can influence toxic behavior and your responses to people and situations. Think about it. How have you responded physically and mentally when you experienced long, consistent periods of stress? What has been your response to situations and people? Do you agree the more difficulty you have with your character flaws, stressors, disappointments, and responsibilities, the more difficult you can be toward other people? When you are under more pressure, are you likely to put more pressure on others?

According to the Mayo Clinic, common effects of stress on the body include headaches, muscle tension or pain, chest pain, fatigue, change in sex drive, upset stomach, and problems sleeping.[622] The negative effects on your mood include anxiety, restlessness, lack of motivation and focus, feeling overwhelmed, irritability, anger, sadness, and depression.[623] The damaging effects on your behavior are overeating, undereating, angry outbursts, misuse of drugs or alcohol, tobacco use, social withdrawal, and less exercise.[624]

The pressures of life go both up and down the work organizational chart. Position and title do not prevent you from behaving badly and do not always make you immune to being treated poorly. If you are suffering the effects of a stressful season of life, imagine how those stressors are affecting your family, coworkers, and others you associate with. In plain terms, whatever is influencing you may be affecting and impacting others through you. Please be aware that if you are not in a good place physically and mentally, it can easily affect others.

If you deal with stress and the busyness of life, you should incorporate self-care practices into your routine just like a nutritionist might tell you to incorporate more water, fruit, and vegetables for a healthier diet. You are spirit, you have a soul, and you possess a body.[625] When are some of you going to realize that your soul needs ministry? It needs to be tended to. Your mental and emotional health must be worked on to help support a healthier state of being. The pressures and stressors include, but are not limited to, your occupation, mental burnout, traumatic experiences, exhaustion, academics, finances, relationships, and health issues.[626]

It's important to know that self-care is not an indulgence. Nor is it something especially extra, or overly nice, to do for yourself.[627] It should be seen as a regular part of your life. You do not have to be extravagant with self-care, but you must not ignore your need for a good hobby or mental break. Everyone needs healthy pressure release valves to alleviate the tension and stressors of life.

Your life has several facets. They include spiritual, physical, emotional, intellectual, occupational, financial, and social dimensions.[628] Take care of all the dimensions of your life, not just one or two of them. All are important. Self-care should be considered part of self-leadership. Multidimensional self-care is important and, when modeled correctly, can support a culture of well-being so others can see and also copy the behavior.[629]

There are several benefits to self-care.[630] Some are:

- You think more clearly and realistically.

- Practicing self-care in several areas of your life can help you recognize, reflect, and prioritize what is most important to you.

- Self-care helps leaders accomplish more because it helps them achieve peak performance by optimizing their skills.

- It becomes a culture-changer: by role modeling it, others see it is okay to take care of themselves.

BURNOUT

Living a busy and full life without caring for yourself can be compared to driving a car low on gas with overdue maintenance required and a low battery. There is no badge of honor in being a workaholic and constantly finding work to do without properly taking care of yourself. You have to take care of you, because if you do not, then your work, personal life, and the numerous responsibilities you have will all suffer. Avoid burnout. Burnout is hitting rock bottom in your attitude and perception toward your job and/or career.[631] Burnout is a state of sheer emotional, physical, and mental exhaustion caused by excessive and prolonged periods of stress.[632]

You may not be able to totally avoid stress, but do your best to avoid burnout. Being overly stressed or stressed for long periods of time easily leads to burnout. The negative effects of this kind of exhaustion can spill over into every area of life: home, work, and social life.[633]

There are physical, emotional, and behavioral symptoms. The physical signs are you feel tired and drained most of the time, you have lowered immunity, frequent illnesses, repeated headaches or muscle pain, and changes in your sleep habits or appetite.[634] The emotional symptoms are doubting yourself and feeling like you are failing; feeling helpless, hopeless, and defeated; feeling detached and alone; reduced motivation; an increasingly negative outlook; and overall decreased satisfaction and feeling of accomplishment.[635] Some behavioral signs are withdrawing from your responsibilities; isolating yourself from other people; procrastinating; coping with food, drugs, or alcohol; and taking out your frustrations on others.[636]

Eva Szigethy, M.D. and Ph.D., author of *Burnout: Strategies to Prevent and Overcome a Common—and Dangerous—Problem*, wrote that there are three stages to burnout.[637] Are you in any of these stages now?

Stage One: Mild symptoms
- Feeling mental fatigue at the end of the day
- Feeling unappreciated, frustrated, or tense
- Physical aches or pains
- The feeling you are falling behind in work
- Dreading going back to work the next day

Stage Two: Longer-lasting symptoms that are more challenging to reverse

- Disillusionment, disenchantment, and disappointment about the job

- Feeling bored, apathetic, or frustrated

- Feeling ruled by a schedule

- Psychological symptoms: irritable, aggressive, having anxiety, depression, substance abuse; suicidal thoughts

- Physical symptoms: tiredness, problems sleeping, changes in weight, gastrointestinal problems

Stage Three: Severe stage

- Chronic symptoms; if left untreated, these can devolve into psychiatric and physical health disorders (depression, heart attacks, peptic ulcers)

- Other expensive and severe personal consequences: substance dependence, shorter life expectancy, divorce, high job turnover, suicide

The hope is that you do not find yourself in any of these stages. If you do, you need to make immediate changes. You cannot continue to do your best, be your best, and fulfill all your obligations if you get burned out—especially stage three. Reprioritize yourself and your mental and physical well-being. One independent business consultant wrote that if a person is so stressed that they are losing their hair, there is no reason to continue doing the same work with all the same responsibilities.[638] Do you agree? Burnout is preventable, so use the defensive mechanisms of self-care.

Here are some practical ways to prevent burnout.[639]

- Learn and get better at self-reflection.

- Address your own needs.

- Adjust or reprioritize your goals and expectations for yourself.
- Analyze your typical weekly schedule and reduce or eliminate unnecessary items.
- Complete a periodic assessment and realignment of goals, skills, and work responsibilities.
- Exercise regularly.
- Eat a balanced, healthy diet.
- Get enough sleep.
- Include daily enjoyable activities (such as hobbies).
- Look for healthy support systems for the professional and personal sides of your life.
- Have dedicated family time.
- Meet with trusted people (coaches, mentors, consultants) to discuss setbacks, time management strategies, and other perceived barriers.

You can also do things like set strict boundaries so people are not expecting you to do excessive work after hours or when you have days off; take time off to relax and de-stress; and prioritize your self-care.[640] Work is important, but do not allow it to dominate your life so much that it is slowly killing you with frustration, anger, stress, anxiety, and mental heaviness that you cannot handle long-term. Do not let the pressures of this life drive you to become—or stay—toxic, the very thing we are seeking to avoid throughout this book.

Remember, self-care should have a place in your life but not *be* your life. Soul care is also important to your life, spiritually and physically. With soul care, practicing spiritual disciplines can yield many benefits and give your life real meaning. As a leader, your main focus is on other people, but you should take care of your other major responsibility: yourself.[641]

CHANGE YOUR MIND

One of the biggest and most often overlooked abilities you have at your disposal is to repent. I do not mean repent or repentance defined as remorseful or sorry for what you have done. Instead, what is meant is the fuller, biblical form of repentance, which means to change your mind.[642] Have you ever made a decision to do something and then changed your mind? Have you decided to buy something one minute and then decided not to make the purchase? Have you ever moved in one direction to get to a specific location and then decided to go somewhere else? That's a form of repenting.

In these instances you were going in one direction, doing one thing, thinking a certain way, then changed your mind to go in another direction, do something else, or think another way. The point is you can change. I hope you have seen some of your character weaknesses and flaws highlighted in the mirror of this book—all with the idea of leading to repentance. Changing your mind means changing your actions. To repent also means to turn around.[643] It has also been used as a military term to describe a soldier marching in one direction and then doing an about-face.

This book is written to bring you to genuine repentance and bring out the better leader in yourself. It's not meant to beat you down or point fingers, but to shine the light of exposure so you can deal with what needs to be dealt with. If you see things in yourself that need change, it is your job to list them, understand what you are doing wrong, and take practical steps to begin walking in a new direction. As a leader, your life will be full of moments of repentance. Just make sure when you change your mind you are walking in a better direction—away from toxicity.

GET COUNSELING OR THERAPY

The terms *counseling* and *therapy* are often used interchangeably, but there are differences.[644] Counseling is often focused on a specific issue for a limited amount of time.[645] Therapy can be more long-term and focuses on you as an individual, how you see yourself and the world, your thoughts, your behaviors, and the underlying patterns of why you do the things you do.[646] There are also differences in education, training, licenses, and treatment plans for these mental health professionals.[647]

Consider this side-by-side list explaining the differences between counseling and psychotherapy.[648]

Counseling	Psychotherapy
• Focuses on current problems and situations	• Focuses on chronic or recurring problems
• Concentrates on specific situations or behaviors	• Focuses on overall patterns; concentrates on the big picture
• Short-term therapy (a few weeks to six months)	• Long-term therapy (continuous or intermittent; likely, years)
• Focuses on action and behavior	• Focuses on feelings and experiences
• Talk therapy	• Therapy may include other tests (ex.: personality, intelligence) and other therapies (talk, cognitive behavioral, etc.)
• Provides guidance, support; educates to help others identify and find their own solutions to current problems	• Comprehensive focus on internal thoughts and feelings; leads to personal growth

Figure 9: The differences between counseling and psychotherapy

There is no shame in receiving counseling or therapy. I have often told people to get the help they need to sleep better or have a better life. Many, if not all of us, at one time or another need help. It is okay to need or want help. People may find themselves more motivated to get therapy when they're in a crisis or facing stressful life events.[649] Just like your cocktail of personal and toxic flaws are specific to your life, so too are your stressful life events, unique triggers, and life experiences.[650]

As you seek a counselor or therapist, make sure they have the education and training to address the area you need help in. Not all counselors and therapists focus on the same area. For example, counseling services can cover areas such as family problems, marital and relationship problems, issues with anger or low self-esteem, behavioral problems, addiction and substance abuse, grief, anxiety, and depression.[651]

You should consider getting therapy if you want assistance in these areas.[652]

- Managing your mental health

- Controlling your emotions

- You have a pattern of practicing unhealthy coping skills

- To increase your self-awareness or understand yourself better

- Dealing with major life events, changes, or to process traumatic events

- You want to be empowered to make the best decisions

- To change negative thinking patterns

- Showing symptoms of mental illness

- You are grieving[653]

It's okay to start therapy when you think you need a little extra help.[654] A therapist is like a personal trainer for your mind, so you can think of therapy as a form of healthcare, like going to the dentist or doctor.[655] Taking care of your mental health is important to your life. Get the support you need to enhance your ability to cope with stressors and handle challenges well. Get the help you need to untie yourself from a toxic lifestyle and way of thinking. Remember, both counselors and therapists are mental health professionals. Use them to achieve a better quality of life.

WHY PEOPLE DON'T GET HELP

I think it is important to cover why people don't proactively get the help they need. Many know about counseling and therapy but refuse to get assistance from these trained professionals. I can empathize and understand why, because the issues discussed are so private. But much of what people believe about therapy is rooted in the wrong way of thinking. Dr. Loren Soeiro provides several reasons why people refuse to talk to therapists.[656]

I'd rather talk to my friends. If they are trustworthy, yes, you should talk to your family and friends. In hard times, this kind of support is important. The main point: therapy cannot take the place of friendship and friendship cannot do the work of psychotherapy. A therapeutic relationship goes beyond friendship because it challenges you to gain valuable insights into yourself. Therapists are trained listeners who can help you find the source of your problems.

It costs too much. Even if insurance does not cover the full cost of psychotherapy, remember it is an investment in yourself. If affordable, an investment in therapy today can head off much costlier, life-affecting problems in the future.

I don't have the time. If the problems you are dealing with will not go away, finding a few hours to deal with them now might actually save you time, money, and misery in the end.

I saw a psychologist once and it did not help. (It amuses me when I hear people say they tried counseling for one or two sessions, but the problems they are facing have been in their life for many years. Do not expect two hours of therapy to dismantle decades of bad experiences, wrong thinking, and poor behavior.) Every psychologist is an individual, with a unique personality, so there's no reason to believe that a new therapist would work the same way as the old one.

What good is talking going to do? When it comes to difficult topics, it often helps to talk to someone you trust and knows you well. The working alliance you develop with your therapist is a platonic relationship. As you develop that relationship, permanent change becomes possible.

I feel weird talking to a stranger about my problems. It will not take long for you to feel that your therapist is no longer a stranger. Most therapists are skilled at making you feel comfortable quickly, and will not come across as a judgmental stranger. If you have a few sessions with a new therapist and don't feel comfortable, you can try being open about your concerns, or you can seek a different therapist. Therapy is a relationship that is both professional and personal, and the association you form with your psychologist is an important factor in the treatment.

Therapists don't say anything; they just sit there and judge you. Some therapists who do more listening than talking are not judging you—they are quietly working to empathically perceive your problems from your perspective. And if you do feel judged by your therapist, you should bring up those feelings. If (or when) in doubt, talk it out. Many therapists will tell you right away what's on their mind. They will offer practical advice or provide detailed feedback about the way they understand you and your problems.

Therapists do not really care about you, they do it for the money. Generally, people choose psychotherapy as a career because they care about people and want to help. How many rich therapists do you know?

I would not want to air my dirty laundry in public. Psychotherapy is confidential, and the material discussed in therapy sessions is protected by law. As long as you do not present a danger to anyone, what you talk about with your therapist will not leave the therapy room. Warning: stop trying to find a reason not to do something that's good for you, like exercise, getting a full night's sleep, or finding a therapist. If you are going through a stressful time, feel anxious, or are unsatisfied with yourself and your life, please don't talk yourself out of getting help or therapy.

Do not let fear stop you from going to get some mental and life help. Stop thinking, "Only crazy people go to therapy."[657] Crazy is an emotional label and not a scientific one.[658] People with all levels of difficulties go to psychotherapy.[659] Normalize getting help when you need it. Therapy is not a rich thing, race thing, or young thing. It's just a people thing.[660] So be open and get vulnerable in a safe space.

NOTES

NOTES

Seventeen

LEADERS' SELF-HELP

Much of this book has covered the different ways to identify toxic ways of thinking and behaving. You can now more easily identify things in your life, and in others, that need to change to bring about better leadership and followership. As you read in the previous chapter, counseling and therapy are helpful efforts and can aid you in managing your emotions and life better. You are also given several corrective ways of thinking and acting. Things to think about, become, and teach others.

In this chapter I will give you some pointed guidance on steps to take to change yourself.

I want you to live with two assumptions. First, to stop or slow bad leadership means you have to stop and slow bad followership.[661] They feed off one another like a self-eating organism. One provides support for the other.

Secondly, to stop or slow the tide of bad leaders, you cannot ignore or dismiss the problem.[662] You have to be proactive and intentional about it. Stop avoiding issues of poor headship. Most leaders will not change their ways unless they see the costs of leading badly and the benefits of leading well.[663] As leaders and followers, we need to be responsible for who we are and what we allow.

LEADERS' SELF-HELP LIST

To enhance the capacity to lead well, consider these ideas from Barbara Kellerman.[664] Which apply to you the most? Then, which apply to other people you believe are toxic?

Limit your time in leadership positions. That is right: limit your tenure. Some leaders, when they are in the lead role too long, tend to pick up bad habits and grow complacent, overreach, are not in tune with reality, and lose their moral footing. Focus on developing your character and living a life of integrity.

Share your power. Centralized power, or power kept by an elite few, is likely to be misused. Delegating and working with others becomes an important defense against power-hogging.

Do not believe your own press. Leadership is a social enterprise that involves other people. Leadership is not all about you as the leader. You are not in charge to be a ruler surrounded by minions to do your bidding. You are not in leadership to be a superstar.

Stay sober, stay grounded. "Stay sober" means to think clearly and not be drunk on the potential benefits of being in charge. "Stay grounded" refers to staying humble, relatable, touchable, and in tune with reality. As a leader you are not above the law, and the rules still apply to you. Your toxic and poisonous ways will affect other people. See the good and bad of what you are doing and how it impacts the organization. Be levelheaded.

Have checks and balances. Stated differently, compensate for your weaknesses. A military commander of a training unit told me leaders should hire what they lack. He knew he was not a detail-oriented person. Because of that he hired a secretary who was thorough so he would not miss out on important appointments and events. Surround yourself with the expertise you do not have in yourself. If you know you are weak in an area, have others around you who are stronger in that way.

Balance, balance, balance. Leaders who are balanced develop healthier organizations. For example, if you are married with children but choose to consistently work long hours with few days off, you are not balanced. This situation becomes toxic when you neglect to be there and support the family you have. This is not about making you mediocre, but making you balanced in word and action. What good is it to work so long, and so hard, to lose your family, friends, and health? Balance and boundaries are important.

Stay mission minded. Remember why the organization, ministry, or institution exists (to serve people, to make a product, etc.). It is not all about you.

Think about your health. Work to upkeep your mental and physical health. It's hard to perform well for yourself and others when you are unhealthy.

Develop a personal support system. Who are the trusted people around you who can hold you accountable? Personal (family, friends, mentors, and others) and paid (consultants, coaches, counselors, therapists). Who can pull you back in when you are out of line? Who can tell you what you need to hear and not what you want to hear? Bring in advisors who are strong and independent. Never allow yourself to be surrounded by yes men or yes women. Feckless, spineless, and gutless people should not be in your pool of advisors, cabinet members, or inner circle.

Know your hungers and control your appetites. It's easier to avoid your own problems and pitfalls when you are aware of your problem areas. Do you know your patterns? What are you prone to do when you are tired, hungry, lonely, under stress, and in other difficult situations? Do you know yourself well enough?

Reflect. Think about yourself. Know yourself. Why do you succeed or fail in certain areas? What are you good or bad at? Do you spend time thinking? What are your good and bad habits? Be intentional and proactive: *think*.

Establish a culture of openness where open communication is encouraged. Respectfully calling attention to things that are wrong, or being open to hearing new ideas, are good things. Be open to hear from those who disagree. They might have a better idea. You might learn how things you are doing are not productive or constructive, but destructive. Avoid the dreaded groupthink. This is being around people who have only your point of view. Full and frank discussions should be welcomed.

Being open to truthful conversation, feedback, and transparency will also open yourself to being told when you are out of line. Transparency can be defined as the level to which information flows openly in an organization among managers, employees, and stakeholders.[665] As leader, and as those being developed to be leaders, you should create an environment of candor.[666] Learn to be generous with information. Stop hoarding all your information power. Give at least some of it away. You should also model this kind of behavior in your home. Part of this communication process could also include admitting you made wrong decisions, and this can disarm your critics and even make fellow employees open up about their blunders.

Delegate authority and hold leaders accountable. Leaders who are in positions to hear and intervene in situations need to be empowered and held accountable to do their jobs. If there is toxic behavior going on, leaders in departments like human resources or equal employment opportunity need to know. Department heads, executives, and others need to have the legal right and authority to investigate and act on behalf of the complainant. Organizations with oversight boards need to use those boards to keep a close eye over the entire enterprise. In traditional organizations, the CEO answers to the board, not the other way around.

LEADERS, KEEP PRINCIPLES OVER PROCESSES

Before you finish this book, I would like to give leaders, and leaders in training, one more bit of advice. Live and lead with principles over process. Said another way: first principle, second process. Said a third way: first know your governing values or standards, then focus on what to do to accomplish them. For those in the faith-based areas of business and ministry, live and lead with theology over pragmatism. Restating: live by principles, by core biblical beliefs and doctrines, and let those be guidelines for what you practice. Not the other way around.

Stop looking at results to justify if you have been doing the right thing. That is not the best way to keep doing things. For example, leaders can do all kinds of things to get people to do their jobs or meet organizational goals. There have been leaders who have embarrassed their employees and coworkers in front of others for no reason, been maliciously critical, micromanaged, and been downright nasty and evil to fellow workers. Even with those cruel practices, some leaders are still able to be successful. The leaders often still get the job done.

Just because it worked is not a reason to keep doing it; such behavior is toxic. A leader can think: well, I said the wrong things, did the wrong things, did not do what I said I was going to do, cheated, lied, fudged numbers, and required employees to do things they should not have, but my department still made our quarterly goals! I will just keep doing what I am doing because it worked.

Wrong!

Just because you did not study all semester long and then crammed an entire course load of studying into two nights before a final exam, and you end up passing the test, does not mean you should keep studying that way. Just because you cheated on your spouse and they did not leave you when they found out (or they never found out) does not mean you should keep cheating. Just because you were able to talk yourself out of a bad situation with your charismatic skills several times does not mean you should keep doing bad things. Stop putting the process (or what you have practiced) above the right principles! Again, live by good principles, and your principles should drive your behavior, processes, practices, and activities.

In this book you have been shown and taught how to identify what is toxic. You read several examples of bad leaders and why their leadership sucked. Then you were advised what to do. You should live and lead with the correct North Star. You should live and lead with the best principles. You should set a high standard of how you treat others and do your best to have those standards duplicated in others. You live the standard for others to follow.

To those working in faith-based nonprofits, churches, and other ministries, put theology above pragmatism. Similar to what has been explained already, pragmatism is the belief that meaning, worth, or value is determined by the practical consequences.[667] It's the belief that if a technique, or the way you do something, works out the way you want it to, it must be good.[668] If it does not work out the way you want it to, it is bad.[669] That is *not* the way to make decisions.

The pragmatist analyzes beliefs based on what works, or he/she just looks for results.[670] The problem with pragmatism is it defines truth as what is useful, meaningful, and helpful.[671] Results do not define truth and the right way to do things; God does. God's Word is the foundation upon which you build your life, leadership, and organization. You follow His principles, and those principles, doctrines, and dogma drive everything else. Do not let results drive what you believe.

Doing it the other way around could have you doing things that are just not right or not in line with your principles. You could do a lot of things to get people to support your organization, but they may not be the right things. One writer said that hard-core pragmatism is wrongly influencing the church with things like pop psychology and other forms of entertainment to try to draw larger crowds.[672] Just because you have a large crowd does not mean you are teaching and leading the right way. This may be shocking, but just because you have a crowd (or followers) does not automatically mean success.

For pastors and church leaders, a large crowd also does not mean people are growing in their faith and becoming mature. In 2007, an article was written about Willow Creek Community Church in Illinois. Willow Creek was noted as one of the most influential churches in America.[673] The ministry, led by Pastor Bill Hybels, was a church driven by programs.[674] After a multiyear study on the organization was completed, Hybels realized he was leading the ministry the wrong way. Down the wrong path.

Hybels confessed that leadership had made a mistake.[675] He realized that when people became Christians, leaders should have started teaching those young believers to take responsibility to read their Bibles and commit to spiritual disciplines more aggressively on their own.[676] Willow Creek repented after spending thirty years creating and promoting a multi-million dollar organization driven by programs and measuring how often people participated in those programs.[677] Hybels repenting was the right thing to do. Unswervingly: be principle-driven, not results-driven.

Notice this portion of that article: "Spiritual growth doesn't happen best by becoming dependent on elaborate church programs but through the age-old spiritual practices of prayer, Bible reading, and relationships. And, ironically, these basic disciplines do not require multi-million dollar facilities and hundreds of staff to manage."[678]

Some of you need to stop confusing movement with progress. A treadmill is great for movement, but it literally will not get you anywhere. Willow Creek had great movement, but no real spiritual progress was being made in people's lives . . . at least not the way it should have been.

Leaders, values should drive processes and not the other way around. Keep them in the right order. Your theology should influence the way you live.[679] Biblical convictions should set your goals, not pragmatism.[680] To reiterate, your theology determines what you practice.[681] Do not accomplish only what is popular. Do what is right based on the right principles. Be principled more than pragmatic.

LEAD WITH EMPATHY

Have you seen the TV show *Undercover Boss*? It's a two-time Emmy Award-winning reality series that follows high-level executives as they go undercover within their organizations.[682] Each episode features a different leader giving up the comfort of their corner office to go on a hidden mission to examine the inner workings of their company.[683] Once an executive leaves their office and temporarily goes into a form of disguise, he or she observes and works in different positions. This includes working in the lower-level positions of the organization.

This serves a twofold purpose. On one side, the executive can find out if the person they are learning from and following is sticking to the rules and following the standard operating procedures and guidelines they are supposed to be following. On the other side, the leader gets a chance to learn about the personal lives of the people they are working with.

The leaders get to see the real issues people are going through. For some executives the experience of being an undercover employee is eye-opening. Each episode culminates with the boss revealing their identity, sometimes correcting, but more often rewarding employees in several ways such as updating company procedures and equipment, giving financial rewards, and perhaps other work opportunities. Quite often the employees are shocked and emotional. Many employees have received promotions, houses, cars, money for school, and assistance for their loved ones in need.

The executives are able to see work and life from another's perspective. They find out what other people are dealing with on and off the job. They learn why some procedures are not followed or if a certain aspect of the company is undermanned and/or underfunded. The leaders observe, listen, and learn.

Besides learning or relearning the inner workings of their company from an employee's standpoint, many have learned a word every leader needs in their arsenal: empathy. Empathy is putting yourself inside someone else's problem to understand them.[684] Empathy is a connector. It helps people feel seen and known for who they are.[685] Real empathy is radical humility, and this means: I don't know how you feel, but I'm here to listen.[686]

Professor Sherry Turkle came up with four empathy rules to help people with others at work or home. This empathic approach to leadership makes intimacy, honesty, innovation, and engagement happen.[687]

1. *Embrace not knowing.* Be open. It is the strategy of going into a situation *not knowing* that leaves you open to the truth. Be open to what you do not know and learn another person's viewpoint. Do not try to relate to others based on what you know. Stop, look, listen, and stay open because you don't necessarily know what someone else is thinking or feeling. It is not about what you think you know, it is what you are willing to learn that provides space for empathy.

2. *Embrace radical difference.* Empathy is not just about agreement and harmony, it accepts friction. To be empathetic, we must be willing to own the conflict, learn how to fight fair, and be fully involved in the situation, even when uncomfortable.

3. *Embrace commitment.* Empathy implies you will do the work to understand the place the person is coming from and also their problem. It's a standard, and a discipline, of basic respect. You have a hand in helping your neighbor make things better.

4. *Embrace community.* Empathy enlarges the people who offer it and binds them to others. Empathy cuts across the divisions in our lives. For example, the empathy you receive at work could

make you a better friend or parent. The empathy you receive at home could make you a better listener at work.

Actively using empathy and the humility that comes with it can be an ongoing weapon to fight against narcissistic, pompous, prideful, arrogant, and conceited ways of thinking. Intentionally humble yourself.[688] Empathy can help you understand there is another person on the other side of toxic, wicked, and undermining actions.

What do you plan to do with the information you were taught in this chapter? Take the time to lead yourself to a place of help, health, and true progress.

NOTES

NOTES

Eighteen

FOLLOWERS' SELF-HELP LIST

Followers play a significant part in the leadership ecosystem. Good followers are needed to fix the trail of bad leaders so many people and organizations are experiencing. When you are in the follower role/position, consider these opportunities (noted by Barbara Kellerman in her book, *Bad Leadership*).

- *Empower yourself.* Think right. Stop thinking that just because you are a follower you are not important and not powerful. Work gets done because of *you*. You have a voice. Leaders and department executives are important, but so are the other workers. Stop allowing yourself to fall under the age-old, top-down way of thinking. That those at the top are the only ones who are important and automatically more valuable than everybody else. You are important too.

- *Put your loyalty in the right places.* If you are following a polluted leader who is leading you and the organization down an illegal, immoral, and unethical path, realize that your loyalties may be misplaced. Stop supporting deliberate wickedness and hiding it under a "I just work here" mentality. With that attitude, you make yourself a bystander who stands around and lets corruption have its way.

- *Do not think like a drunk person.* What does this mean? Stop being intoxicated by people's talents, good looks, and charisma. Stop allowing yourself to be seduced by them. There are men and women who have all of that and are still terrible people. Leaders are not gods to be worshipped. They are human and can make mistakes like anyone else. I once listened to a woman confess to being in a sexual relationship with a married sports celebrity. She literally said that she was "a mere mortal" in the presence of this man's "greatness"; she knew he was married and cheating on his wife with her. She was seduced by the way she saw herself, and by the way she saw him, his money, and fame. Do not get drunk off other people's abilities. Think soberly.

- *Take a stand against that which is wrong.* For example, if there is blatant favoritism of some employees over others, if you repeatedly see corporate injustices such as the bribing of public officials, or the falsifying of information or financial records, then say something. Report it. Wrong is wrong. How many times have children been abused for years and the adults in the home who knew about it said nothing? To be good leaders and followers, you need to find the strength to stand for what is right, good, and appropriate. I am not talking about stonewalling your boss because you have personality conflicts. I'm referring to legitimate wrongdoings. Followers should be held accountable just like leaders should be held accountable.

As a follower, consider each bullet point as a personal question. Do you need to empower yourself? Are you placing your loyalty in the right places? Do you find yourself being seduced and intoxicated by people's gifts/giftings and ignore their character? Is there a significant issue occurring at your place of work you need to report or speak with leadership about? After you reflect and answer each question, the next chapter will provide more guidance leaders and followers should consider when dealing with bad leadership and a corrupt culture.

Nineteen

MORE OPTIONS WHEN DEALING WITH TOXIC LEADERSHIP

Here are additional options when dealing with toxic leaders and the entire leadership process. Several are adopted from Jean Lipman-Blumen in her book *The Allure of Toxic Leaders*. Some of the following may overlap with what has already been shared, but is still worth repeating.

Quit. Leave. Put in your two weeks' notice and go. Find another job. This move is not a coward's decision; it is a viable option to take seriously. If you are under so much toxic stress and pressure that it is negatively affecting your health, marriage, sleep patterns, your ability to be productive, and more, then it may be a wise move to find employment somewhere else. Preferably, find another job before you quit so there is no gap in income.

Whistleblower, blow your whistle. Whistleblowing is when a person reports another person's unethical behavior to a third party.[689] The term originated from English policemen who blew their whistle when they observed a crime happening, and it alerted other law enforcement officers and the general public.[690] The act of whistleblowing has at least four parts to it: (1) the person who is doing the telling, i.e., the whistleblower; (2) the complaint or wrongdoing being reported; (3) the organization, person, or group of people committing the wrongdoing; and (4) the party who receives the complaint of wrongdoing from the whistleblower.[691] Whistleblowing is not about small things or crying wolf. It is about serious, egregious (illegal, dishonest, immoral) acts being committed.[692] The whistleblowing act is not meant to harm the organization but to expose significant acts that may harm the organization.[693] Do not take whistleblowing carelessly because there may be consequences you have to deal with afterward.

If the leader is open to help, help them. I believe most situations should be addressed or confronted on the lowest level. A simple example: if someone is doing something that you think is offensive, like having inappropriate conversations or inappropriate touching, tell the person you are not comfortable hearing certain things or being touched. Be professional and direct. Likewise, if a leader does something that is wrong, tell them. You might be surprised: they may be open to the feedback and even apologize. I'm sure not everyone will respond that way, but it is worth a try. This is why holding people accountable to a standard is so important.

Policies, practices, procedures, limits. Have internal systems in place that limit leaders' authority. Here is where governing boards can play an important role. It is better to have a board (trustees, or directors) lead an institution to avoid the corruptive influence of concentrated power in the hands of one leader.[694] Another advantage of a governing board is better decisions are made when decided by a group, and its members can hold each other accountable.[695] The organization can set limits, for example, on how much leaders can spend, hire, fire, demote, promote, or make significant decisions by themselves.

Policies, practices, procedures, and limits should be taught and used to ensure leaders can only do so much by themselves until a limit is reached and a larger discussion, and approval, is given by an overseeing body. This is dependent on whatever works best for the organization. For instance, one company's board decided that once a budget is set, the CEO cannot spend a certain amount beyond that limit without having another board meeting and getting another round of approval. Some married couples have a joint financial account and funds cannot be withdrawn from that account until both signatures approve the transaction.

Another example is when firms establish a no-tolerance policy. Some behaviors should require immediate dismissal.[696] At your company, if a leader is reported for a flagrant act one time, investigate.[697] If appropriate, the offender can be given coaching or extended training if the person does not understand how their actions harm others.[698] Second, third, and fourth reports with no action taken sends the message that bad behavior can be concealed or ignored.[699] Companies need to take decisive action and terminate people who create toxic environments.[700]

If there are many toxic people in your family, company, ministry, or nonprofit, check your culture. Toxic, yet high-performing, bullies are a cancer on company culture.[701] One article referenced that in the U.S., toxic cultures cost companies about $50 billion per year.[702] Per year!

Leaders, stop putting up with bullies and other kinds of toxic leaders just because they deliver results. Stop reinforcing bad behavior with silence and tolerance. To those in charge of churches and faith-based nonprofits: stop inviting wicked clergy to speak at your meetings when you know they are not living up to a godly, biblical standard. Stop ignoring good values and avoiding the conflict to correct someone. Stop saying one thing and allowing another. Stop being hypocritical. Stop putting revenue before morals.[703] Leaving bad leaders in positions of power reveals the organization values profits over people.[704] These leaders bring in money but are wreaking havoc in people's lives. People are more important than money.

Here are some simple ideas to correct a contaminated culture: accept responsibility (acknowledge the problems and admit what is wrong); describe the negative impacts on the workplace; set boundaries; set guidelines for appropriate behavior.[705] Further, bring in an objective third party like a consultant, coach, or facilitator to help identify the root causes of the corrupt environment.[706] Then, when all the investigating and research is done, establish policies and hold everyone accountable to the standards.[707] If you have heard complaints, or are just not sure if your organization is toxic, then investigate and listen to others. Do a culture survey, use focus groups, and have one-on-one conversations with employees. Find out what happens to a complaint when an employee reports toxic behavior to the human resources department.[708] Staff members should feel confident when they submit a complaint that it will be taken seriously by the organization and investigated.

Pray. Ask God to help you change. Ask Him to help you in areas of your life that are weak, destructive, unhealed, and hurting. Do not allow pride to keep you from asking for help when you need it. Humble yourself and pray to the God who loves you. Spend some time looking up God's instruction on prayer.[709]

Up to this point, all this information should help you address the fault lines and deep cracks in your character and in other leaders. Do not try and be perfect, but look to be better. Do not settle for the "that's just the way I am" type of thinking. Do not settle for remaining toxic.

* * * * *

Spend some time thinking about what you have read. I mean *really* thinking about it. What about you needs to change? Which area will you address first, second, and third? From this chapter alone, what seems to be the most important thing for you to do?

NOTES

NOTES

SUMMING IT UP

I hope you have learned much. I hope your eyes have been opened to the other side of leadership. The dark side we all have seen in some form or another but seldom talk about. I hope there has been some light shined on the unpleasant inner areas of your life. The areas that need ministry, that need tending to. Like undergoing a comprehensive medical exam to make sure all major systems of the body are properly working, the information in this book has highlighted areas where you may be hurting and broken. Even worse, you may be hurting and breaking people by how you think, live, lead, and treat others.

This book is meant to be your personal whistleblower. It is telling *you* about *you*. It is your personal spotlight that is used on you before being used on anyone else. Exposure is often a good thing. Revelation is important for personal and professional growth. This developmental handbook will propel you forward, something like stepping on your car accelerator to help move you out of places you should avoid.

I would like to think that most leaders do not intend to be bad leaders. However, we can be blinded by our lusts and lose sight of what real leadership is supposed to be and look like. Being a leader should represent something. It should represent a standard others should aspire to. I encourage you to elevate, to come up in your mind. Come up in your standards; be a standard-bearer. Clear out any dirt and filth in your soul, your ways of thinking, and your ways of acting. Be the light. Be the great example people in charge are meant to be.

We've covered a lot of important information that, I hope, changes you. In chapters two and three we started off with the foundation of what this book is about. In today's times there will be difficult people to deal with. These are toxic people and toxic leaders. From there, chapter after chapter and page after page have been filled with information to motivate you to change—not just your actions, but more importantly your heart. We looked at various lusts and the high cost of leaders letting themselves or their constituents create a harsh work environment. Do not allow this anymore.

The main question is: what are you going to do with this information? What toxins do you have in you? What do you plan to do with them? How are you going to do things differently? How are you going to treat people better? How are you seeing things differently? Can you now evaluate people in a different way? How are you going to stop toxicity in your life and hold other leaders accountable for their poor—maybe even despicable—ways? Do you plan to change some things in your organization? What and how?

The time to change is *now*. The time to think and behave differently is now. Do not just want it or occasionally think about it. *Be* it. Do not waste any more time being the old you. Change the way you think. Step in to the new. As leaders, you are called to action and to call others to action. Act now, and decisively. Put the knowledge and wisdom you have learned into action and change your life.

Joseph Haroutunian, author and theologian, wrote: "Lust for power, like pride and contempt, is an aristocrat's vice . . . conquerors, kings and captains of industry, labor leaders, millionaires, bishops and bureaucrats. Almost all bosses are contaminated with it; so are one's rivals and superiors. . . . One must watch [these] men of power, and see to it that they do not turn into tyrants."[710] You have been given a road map. Stay away from the off limits and unsafe areas. This book has given you glasses to see and a filter to help you sift the good from the bad.

This book has provided many examples. Do not desire, and do, evil things like others have done; these have been written for your guidance and instruction.[711] Remember, as a leader the most prized asset is *people*—not things, not position, not money, not fame. Lead people with dignity, respect, and honor.

If you find yourself toxic, do all you can to detoxify yourself.

There is much talk in the leadership industry about motivating people and motivating followers. Leaders must first know what is motivating *them*. As leaders, be people-centered and not self-centered. Make an earnest effort to not allow the cracks in your character and wounds of your soul to bleed on the people you lead.

Leaders must deal with their trauma, not pass that trauma on. Get your eyes off of "glory" and all you think it could bring, and put your eyes on your character, on how God wants you to lead. As a leader, you are the example. Never settle to live and lead while being toxic. It is time for you to take action to justify who you really are. A leader called to live a high standard, raise up others to at least that standard, and accomplish goals. Use all this toxic intelligence that you have learned to end the reign of error. To end the reign of pain that others have to suffer with. Remove the toxicity in your leadership and in your sphere of authority and influence.

NOTES

For those of you who found this book informative,
please read another work by the author,
***Leadership in the Age of Narcissism:
God's Blueprint for Christian Leaders.***

ENDNOTES

[1] https://www.dallasobserver.com/news/the-reverend-freak-6406041, accessed May 7, 2022.

[2] Ibid.

[3] Ibid.

[4] Ibid.

[5] Ibid.

[6] Ibid.

[7] Hornbuckle, Renee F., *Suffering in Silence: Break the silence: Let the Suffering End . . . Let Healing Begin.* Jabez Books, 2012.

[8] Ibid.

[9] Ibid.

[10] Ibid.

[11] Ibid.

[12] https://www.cnbc.com/2018/03/09/pharma-bro-martin-shkreli-sentenced-to-7-years-in-prison.html#:~:text=Biotech%20and%20Pharma-;Pharma%20bro'%20Martin%20Shkreli%20sentenced%20to%207%20years%20in%20prison,%2C%20'This%20is%20my%20fault'&text=Convicted%20fraudster%20Martin%20Shkreli%20is,his%20former%20drug%20company%20Retrophin, accessed May 11, 2022.

[13] Ibid.

[14] https://www.npr.org/sections/thetwo-way/2018/03/09/592368883/martin-shkreli-sentenced-to-seven-years-for-securities-fraud, accessed May 11, 2022.

[15] Ibid.

[16] https://www.businessinsider.com/toxic-behaviors-parents-make-children-unhealthy-less-functional-adults, accessed May 12, 2022.

[17] https://thoughtcatalog.com/callie-byrnes/2018/04/20-people-tell-the-stories-of-the-worst-parents-they-ever-met-and-their-kids-who-never-had-a-chance/, accessed on May 12, 2022.

[18] Ibid.

[19] Ibid.

[20] https://www.theatlantic.com/family/archive/2018/10/crime-runs-family/573394/, accessed on May 12, 2022.

[21] Ibid.

[22] Ibid.

[23] Ibid.

[24] Merriam-Webster.com Dictionary, s.v. "in error," accessed January 17, 2023, https://www.merriam-webster.com/dictionary/in%20error.

[25] Romans 4:15.

[26] Kellerman, Barbara. *Bad Leadership: What It Is, How It Happens, Why It Matters*. Harvard Business Press, 2004, 13.

[27] Merriam-Webster.com Dictionary, s.v. "troubleshooter," accessed December 17, 2021, https://www.merriam-webster.com/dictionary/troubleshooter.

[28] McIntosh, Gary L., and D. Samuel Sr. *Overcoming the Dark Side of Leadership: How to Become an Effective Leader By Confronting Potential Failures*. Baker Books, 2007: 28.

[29] Ibid., 28.

[30] https://www.clickworker.com/ai-glossary/contextual-intelligence/#:~:-text=World%20of%20AI-,Contextual%20Intelligence%20%E2%80%93%20Short%20Explanation,where%20you%20live%20and%20work; https://www.cnbc.com/2021/03/10/harvard-psychologist-types-of-intelligence-where-do-you-score-highest-in.html; https://online.hbs.edu/blog/post/emotional-intelligence-in-leadership; https://hbr.org/2008/09/social-intelligence-and-the-biology-of-leadership; https://hbr.org/2004/10/cultural-intelligence; https://

www.verywellmind.com/gardners-theory-of-multiple-intelligences-2795161; https://www.niu.edu/citl/resources/guides/instructional-guide/gardners-theory-of-multiple-intelligences.shtml accessed on March 13, 2023.

[31] Kellerman, Barbara. "Leadership–It's a System, Not a Person!" Daedalus 145, no. 3 (2016): 83-94.

[32] Ibid.

[33] Bennis, Warren G. *On Becoming a Leader*. Basic Books, 2009.

[34] Ibid., 5.

[35] Ibid.

[36] https://hbr.org/2013/12/the-focused-leader accessed on January 17, 2023.

[37] Kellerman, Barbara. "Leadership–It's a System, Not a Person!" Daedalus 145, no. 3 (2016): 83-94.

[38] Ibid.

[39] Ibid., 91.

[40] Ibid., 92; Bennis, Warren G. *On Becoming a Leader*. Basic Books, 2009, 5-20.

[41] https://www.forbes.com/sites/karlmoore/2012/10/05/the-end-of-leadership-at-least-as-we-know-it/?sh=6d41bfd30788 accessed on December 28, 2022.

[42] Barbara Kellerman. "Leadership–It's a System, Not a Person!" Daedalus 2016; 145 (3): 83–94.

[43] Ibid.

[44] https://www.forbes.com/sites/karlmoore/2012/10/05/the-end-of-leadership-at-least-as-we-know-it/?sh=6d41bfd30788 accessed on December 28, 2022.

[45] Ibid.

[46] Clinton, Robert J. *1 and 2 Timothy Apostolic Leadership Picking Up the Mantle*, Clinton's Biblical Leadership Commentary Series 2006.

[47] Acts 9.

[48] Acts 23:6; Britannica, T. Editors of Encyclopaedia. "Pharisee." *Encyclopedia Britannica*, August 20, 2020. https://www.britannica.com/topic/Pharisee.

[49] Galatians 1:14; Acts 7:58-8:3; Acts 26:10-11.

[50] Acts 9:1-2.

[51] Dunnett, Walter, M. *New Testament Survey, Broadening Your Biblical Horizons*, Matthew-Revelation. Evangelical Training Association, 2003. 34.

[52] Yarbrough, Robert W. *The Letters to Timothy and Titus*. Wm. B. Eerdmans Publishing, 2018.

[53] Ibid., 60.

[54] 2 Timothy 1:2.

[55] Acts 16:1-5; Yarbrough, Robert W. *The Letters to Timothy and Titus*. Wm. B. Eerdmans Publishing, 2018.

[56] Yarbrough, Robert W. *The Letters to Timothy and Titus*. Wm. B. Eerdmans Publishing, 2018.

[57] Long, Thomas G. *1 & 2 Timothy and* Titus: A Theological Commentary on the Bible. Westminster John Knox Press, 2016.

[58] Ibid., 221.

[59] Ibid.

[60] Ibid., 222.

[61] Ibid., 223.

[62] Ibid.

[63] Ibid.

[64] Ibid.

[65] Johnson, Luke Timothy. "Letters to Paul's Delegates: 1 Timothy, 2 Timothy, Titus." (1996).

[66] Ibid., 83.

[67] Ibid.; 2 Timothy 3:5.

[68] Ibid., 86.

[69] Ibid.; 1 Corinthians 4:17.

[70] Chironna, Mark. Email communication with author. December 20, 2022; https://www.markchironna.com.

[71] Frederic Hudson. *The Adult Years: Mastering The Art of Self-Renewal*, San Francisco: Josey Bass, 1999. Chapter 5.

[72] Chironna, Mark. Email communication with author. December 20, 2022.

[73] Ibid.

[74] Ibid.; https://www.youtube.com/watch?v=TXUxqV39rWI accessed on December 29, 2022; https://jameshollis.net/hollisBooks.html.

[75] Ibid.

[76] Ibid.

[77] Reeves, Michael RE, and Hans Madueme, eds. *Adam, the Fall, and Original Sin: Theological, Biblical, and Scientific Perspectives*. Baker Academic, 2014.

[78] *Merriam-Webster.com Dictionary*, s.v. "sin," accessed May 8, 2021, https://www.merriam-webster.com/dictionary/sin.

[79] https://www.blueletterbible.org/lang/lexicon/lexicon.cfm?Strongs=H2403&t=ESV; https://www.blueletterbible.org/lang/lexicon/lexicon.cfm?Strongs=G266&t=ESV.

[80] Tillich, Paul. You are accepted. Charles Scribner's Sons, 1948.

[81] Ibid., Luke 15:17-24; Isaiah 59:2.

[82] Genesis 3; Reeves, Michael RE, and Hans Madueme, eds. Adam, the fall, and original sin: Theological, biblical, and scientific perspectives. Baker Academic, 2014.

[83] Tillich, Paul. You are accepted. Charles Scribner's Sons, 1948.

[84] Ibid., 2.

[85] Dunnett, Walter, M. *New Testament Survey, Broadening Your Biblical Horizons, Matthew-Revelation*. Evangelical Training Association, 2003. 76.

[86] Ibid.; Rensberger, David. *Abingdon New Testament Commentaries: 1, 2, & 3 John*. Abingdon Press, 2011.

[87] Ibid., 80.

[88] Ibid.

[89] Smith, D. Moody. *First, Second, and Third John: Interpretation: A Bible Commentary for Teaching and Preaching*. Westminster John Knox Press, 2012.

[90] Naselli, Andrew David. "Do Not Love the World: Breaking the Evil Enchantment of Worldliness (A Sermon on 1 John 2: 15–17)." *The Southern Baptist Journal of Theology* 22, no. 1 (2018): 111-125.

[91] Ibid., 114.

[92] Smith, D. Moody. *First, Second, and Third John: Interpretation: A Bible Commentary for Teaching and Preaching*. Westminster John Knox Press, 2012.

[93] Ibid., 66.

[94] Ibid.

[95] Yarbrough, Robert W. *1-3 John*. Baker Academic, 2008. 128.

[96] Ibid., 132, 134.

[97] Ibid.

[98] Rensberger, David. *Abingdon New Testament Commentaries: 1, 2, & 3 John*. Abingdon Press, 2011.

[99] Chironna, Mark. Email communication with author. December 20, 2022.

[100] Yarbrough, Robert W. *1-3 John*. Baker Academic, 2008. 133.

[101] Rensberger, David. *Abingdon New Testament Commentaries: 1, 2, & 3 John*. Abingdon Press, 2011.

[102] Yarbrough, Robert W. *1-3 John*. Baker Academic, 2008. 133.

[103] Ibid.

[104] Isaiah 5:15; Proverbs 6:17; Proverbs 21:4

[105] Chironna, Mark. Email communication with author. December 20, 2022.

[106] Numbers 15:39

[107] Yarbrough, Robert W. *1-3 John*. Baker Academic, 2008. 133.

[108] Ibid., 133.

[109] Ibid., 134.

[110] Rensberger, David. *Abingdon New Testament Commentaries: 1, 2, & 3 John*. Abingdon Press, 2011.

[111] *Merriam-Webster.com Dictionary*, s.v. "North Star," accessed May 8, 2021, https://www.merriam-webster.com/dictionary/North%20Star; https://solarsystem.nasa.gov/news/1944/what-is-the-north-star-and-how-do-you-find-it/.

[112] https://theweeklychallenger.com/the-north-star-a-symbol-of-inspiration-and-hope/.

[113] Tillich, Paul. *You are accepted*. Charles Scribner's Sons, 1948.

[114] Romans 1:7.

[115] Chironna, Mark. Email communication with author. December 20, 2022.

[116] Ibid.

[117] Ibid.

[118] Tillich, Paul. *The Shaking of the Foundations*. Wipf and Stock Publishers, 2012.

[119] https://www.npr.org/2017/10/30/559996276/the-trick-to-surviving-a-high-stakes-high-pressure-job-try-a-checklist, accessed October 16, 2022.

[120] Separation & Alienation (sin); Misdirected Passions, Misdirected Focus, and Ego Inflation – 1 John 2:16; Times of Difficulty – 2 Timothy 3:1-5.

[121] Ibid.

[122] Proverbs 3:5, 6.

[123] www.thesaurus.com/browse/toxic.

[124] *Merriam-Webster.com Dictionary*, s.v. "toxic," accessed May 15, 2021, https://www.merriam-webster.com/dictionary/toxic.

[125] Lipman-Blumen, Jean. *The Allure of Toxic Leaders: Why We Follow Destructive Bosses and Corrupt Politicians—And How We Can Survive Them.* New York: Oxford University Press, 2006.

[126] Ibid., 21, 22.

[127] Ibid., 22.

[128] Zamry, Mohd Nor, and Nur Syafinaz. *Corporate Governance and Its Determinants: A Study on Wells Fargo Scandal.* No. 93726. University Library of Munich, Germany, 2019.

[129] Triplett, Ashley. "Incentive-Based Compensation Arrangements: An Examination of the Wells Fargo Scandal and the Need for Reform in Financial Institutions." *University of Baltimore Law Review* 47, no. 2 (2018): 6.

[130] Ibid., 2.

[131] Ibid., 11.

[132] Gangel, Kenneth O. "Surviving Toxic Leaders: How to Work for Flawed People in Churches." *Schools and Christian Organizations* (Eugene, OR.: Wipf & Stock, 2008) 3 (2007).

[133] Shirkani, Jen. *Ego vs. EQ: How top leaders beat 8 ego traps with emotional intelligence.* Routledge, 2016.

[134] Ibid.

[135] https://www.huffpost.com/entry/why-cruel-leaders-get-all_b_7484588, acquired May 29, 2021.

[136] Ibid.

[137] Waller, James E. *Becoming Evil: How Ordinary People Commit Genocide and Mass Killing.* Oxford University Press, 2007.

[138] Ibid., 13.

[139] Ibid., 13.

[140] Dinham, Stephen, and Catherine Scott. "Responsive, demanding leadership." *Management Today* (2008): 32-35.

[141] Ibid., 19.

[142] Art Padilla, Robert Hogan, Robert B. Kaiser, "The toxic triangle: Destructive leaders, susceptible followers, and conducive environments," *The Leadership Quarterly*, Vol. 18, Issue 3, 2007, Pages 176-194, ISSN 1048-9843.

[143] Lipman-Blumen, Jean. *The Allure of Toxic Leaders: Why We Follow Destructive Bosses and Corrupt Politicians—And How We Can Survive Them.* New York: Oxford University Press, 2006.

[144] Padilla, Art, Robert Hogan, and Robert B. Kaiser. "The toxic triangle: Destructive leaders, susceptible followers, and conducive environments." *The Leadership Quarterly* Vol. 18, Issue 3 (2007): 176-194.

[145] Ibid.

[146] Conger, Jay A., and Rabindra N. Kanungo. *Charismatic Leadership in Organizations.* Sage Publications, 1998.

[147] Shamir, Boas, Robert J. House, and Michael B. Arthur. "The motivational effects of charismatic leadership: A self-concept based theory." *Organization Science* 4, no. 4 (1993): 577-594.

[148] Art Padilla, Robert Hogan, Robert B. Kaiser, "The toxic triangle: Destructive leaders, susceptible followers, and conducive environments," *The Leadership Quarterly*, Vol. 18, Issue 3, 2007, p. 180.

[149] House, Robert J., and Ram N. Aditya. "The social scientific study of leadership: Quo vadis?" *Journal of Management* 23, no. 3 (1997): 409-473.

[150] Ibid., 414.

[151] Campbell, W. Keith, Brian J. Hoffman, Stacy M. Campbell, and Gaia Marchisio. "Narcissism in organizational contexts." *Human Resource Management Review* 21, no. 4 (2011): 268-284.

[152] Ibid., 269.

[153] Ibid., 270.

[154] Ibid.

[155] Buffardi, Laura E., and W. Keith Campbell. "Narcissism and social networking web sites." *Personality and Social Psychology Bulletin* 34, no. 10 (2008): 1303-1314.

[156] Proverbs 16:18

[157] Art Padilla, Robert Hogan, Robert B. Kaiser, "The toxic triangle: Destructive leaders, susceptible followers, and conducive environments," *The Leadership Quarterly*, Vol. 18, Issue 3, 2007, Pages 182.

[158] Ibid.

[159] Kellerman, Barbara. "What every leader needs to know about followers." *Harvard Business Review 85*, no. 12 (2007): 84.

[160] Ibid., 1.

[161] Ibid., 2.

[162] Jiang, Zhou, and Xuan Jiang. "Core self-evaluation and life satisfaction: The person-environment fit perspective." *Personality and Individual Differences, 75* (2015): 68-73.

[163] Ibid.

[164] Art Padilla, Robert Hogan, Robert B. Kaiser, "The toxic triangle: Destructive leaders, susceptible followers, and conducive environments," *The Leadership Quarterly, Volume 18, Issue 3, 2007*, p. 183.

[165] Ibid., 183.

[166] Kellerman, Barbara. *Followership: How Followers are Creating Change and Changing Leaders.* Boston, MA: Harvard School Press, 2008.

[167] Hirschi, Andreas, and Daniel Spurk. "Ambitious employees: Why and when ambition relates to performance and organizational commitment." *Journal of Vocational Behavior, 127* (2021): 103576.

[168] Judge, Timothy A., and John D. Kammeyer-Mueller. "On the value of aiming high: The causes and consequences of ambition." *Journal of Applied Psychology 97*, no. 4 (2012): 758.

[169] Ibid., 759.

[170] Art Padilla, Robert Hogan, Robert B. Kaiser, "The Toxic Triangle: Destructive leaders, susceptible followers, and conducive environments," *The Leadership Quarterly*, Vol. 18, Issue 3, 2007, p. 184.

[171] Ibid.

[172] Philippians 2:3

[173] https://www.dictionary.com/browse/misery-loves-company.

[174] Art Padilla, Robert Hogan, Robert B. Kaiser, "The Toxic Triangle: Destructive leaders, Susceptible Followers, and Conducive Environments," *The Leadership Quarterly*, Vol. 18, Issue 3, 2007, p. 184.

[175] Conger, Jay A., and Rabindra N. Kanungo. "The empowerment process: Integrating theory and practice." *Academy of Management Review* 13, no. 3 (1988): 471-482; p. 645.

[176] Art Padilla, Robert Hogan, Robert B. Kaiser, "The Toxic Triangle: Destructive Leaders, Susceptible Followers, and Conducive Environments," *The Leadership Quarterly*, Vol. 18, Issue 3, 2007, p. 185.

[177] Ibid.

[178] Ibid.

[179] Ibid., 186.

[180] Lessing, John. "The checks and balances of good corporate governance." Enterprise Governance eJournal *1*, no. 1 (2009): 6914.

[181] Kellerman, Barbara. *Bad leadership: What It Is, How It Happens, Why It Matters*. Harvard Business Press, 2004.

[182] Reed, George E. "Toxic leadership." *Military Review 84*, no. 4 (2004): 67-71.

[183] Ibid., 67.

[184] Ibid.

[185] Ibid.

[186] Ibid., 69.

[187] Ibid.

[188] Ibid.

[189] Kellerman, Barbara. *Bad Leadership: What It Is, How It Happens, Why It Matters*. Harvard Business Press, 2004, 22.

[190] Ibid.

[191] Ibid.

[192] Lipman-Blumen, Jean. *The Allure of Toxic Leaders: Why We Follow Destructive Bosses and Corrupt Politicians—And How We Can Survive Them.* New York: Oxford University Press, 2006.

[193] Ibid.

[194] Ibid.

[195] Ibid.

[196] Ibid.

[197] Ibid.

[198] Ibid.

[199] https://www.psychologytoday.com/us/blog/cutting-edge-leadership/201910/why-do-people-follow-bad-leaders, accessed on November 6, 2022.

[200] Ibid.

[201] Ibid.

[202] Ibid.

[203] Lipman-Blumen, Jean. *The Allure of Toxic Leaders: Why We Follow Destructive Bosses and Corrupt Politicians—And How We Can Survive Them.* New York: Oxford University Press, 2006.

[204] Ibid.

[205] Ibid.

[206] Ibid.

[207] Kellerman, Barbara. *Bad Leadership: What It Is, How It Happens, Why It Matters.* Harvard Business Press, 2004, 22.

[208] Ibid.

[209] Ibid.

[210] Ibid.

[211] Lipman-Blumen, Jean. *The Allure of Toxic Leaders: Why We Follow Destructive Bosses and Corrupt Politicians—And How We Can Survive Them.* New York: Oxford University Press, 2006.

[212] Ibid.

[213] Ibid.

[214] Ibid.

[215] Ibid.

[216] Ibid.

[217] Ibid.

[218] https://hbr.org/2004/09/why-people-follow-the-leader-the-power-of-transference, accessed on January 6, 2022.

[219] Ibid.

[220] Ibid.

[221] Ibid.

[222] Ibid.

[223] Ibid., https://www.britannica.com/biography/Sigmund-Freud, accessed January 6, 2022.

[224] https://hbr.org/2004/09/why-people-follow-the-leader-the-power-of-transference accessed on January 6, 2022.

[225] Ibid.

[226] Ibid.

[227] Terrell, Robert Steven, and Katherine Rosenbusch. "How global leaders develop." *Journal of Management Development* (2013).

[228] Ashley, Greg C., and Roni Reiter-Palmon. "Self-awareness and the evolution of leaders: The need for a better measure of self-awareness." *Journal of Behavioral and Applied Management* 14, no. 1 (2012): 2-17.

[229] Ibid., 2.

[230] Eurich, Tasha. "What self-awareness really is (and how to cultivate it)." *Harvard Business Review* (2018).

[231] Ibid., 5.

[232] Ibid., 5.

[233] https://www.oxfordlearnersdictionaries.com/us/definition/english/critical-thinking?q=critical+thinking, accessed May 25, 2021.

[234] Tjan, Anthony K. "Ways to become more self-aware." *Harvard Business Review*, 5.

[235] Tasha Eurich, "Increase your self-awareness with one simple fix," TedxMileHigh published November, 2017, https://www.ted.com/talks/tasha_eurich_increase_your_self_awareness_with_one_simple_fix?language=en.

[236] Ibid.

[237] https://www.collinsdictionary.com/us/dictionary/english/psychometric-test, accessed May 26, 2021.

[238] https://indvstrvs.com/psychometric-tests/, accessed May 26, 2021.

[239] Eurich, Tasha. "What self-awareness really is (and how to cultivate it): HBR guide to your professional growth." *Harvard Business Review Press*. 2019.

[240] Ibid., 40.

[241] Scharmer, C. Otto. "Uncovering the blind spot of leadership." *Leader to Leader 2008*, no. 47 (2008): 52-59.

[242] Ibid., 53.

[243] Ibid.

[244] Ibid.

[245] Ibid., 54.

[246] Bazerman, Max H., and Ann E. Tenbrunsel. *Blind Spots*. Princeton University Press, 2011.

[247] https://www.investopedia.com/terms/e/enron.asp, accessed June 10, 2021.

[248] https://www.wsj.com/articles/SB1023409436545200. Assessed June 10, 2021.

[249] https://www.investopedia.com/terms/e/enron.asp, accessed June 10, 2021.

[250] Bazerman, Max H., and Ann E. Tenbrunsel. *Blind Spots*. Princeton University Press, 2011. 81.

[251] Bazerman, Max H., and Ann E. Tenbrunsel. *Blind Spots*. Princeton University Press, 2011. 1.

[252] Ibid.

[253] Ibid.

[254] Stevenson-Moessner, Jeanne, and Mary Lynn Dell. *The Elephant in the Church: What You Don't See Can Kill Your Ministry*. Abingdon Press, 2013.

[255] https://www.inc.com/marissa-levin/the-top-10-leadership-blind-spots-and-5-ways-to-tu.html accessed on May 18, 2022.

[256] Ibid.

[257] Williams, Kenneth R. "The cost of tolerating toxic behaviors in the Department of Defense workplace." *Military Review* 99, no. 4 (2019): 54.

[258] Ibid., 1.

[259] Ibid., 2.

[260] https://www.organisationalpsychology.nz/_content/Toxicity_in_the_workplace.pdf, accessed June 13, 2021.

[261] https://www.aspanet.org/ASPADocs/Annual%20Conference/2018/Papers/WilliamsKenneth.Pdf.

[262] *Merriam-Webster.com Dictionary*, s.v. "incivility," accessed June 14, 2021, https://www.merriam-webster.com/dictionary/incivility.

[263] Goleman, Daniel, Richard E. Boyatzis, Annie McKee, and Sydney Finkelstein. *HBR's 10 Must Reads on Emotional Intelligence (with featured article "What Makes a Leader?" by Daniel Goleman) (HBR's 10 Must Reads)*. Harvard Business Review Press, 2015.

[264] Ibid., 96.

[265] https://www.aspanet.org/ASPADocs/Annual%20Conference/2018/Papers/WilliamsKenneth.Pdf.

266 Dunham, Shea M., Shannon B. Dermer, and Jon Carlson, eds. *Poisonous Parenting: Toxic Relationships Between Parents and Their Adult Children.* Routledge, 2012.

267 Ibid., 1.

268 Ibid., 2.

269 Ibid., 3.

270 Ibid,. 6.

271 Romans 12:21

272 https://www.history.com/topics/british-history/robin-hood, accessed on May 29, 2022.

273 Hamon, Bill. *Prophets, Pitfalls, and Principles: God's Prophetic People Today.* Destiny Image, 1991, 84.

274 https://www.focusonthefamily.com/faith/whats-a-christian-worldview/, accessed May 2, 2021.

275 Phillips, W. Gary, William E. Brown, and John Stonestreet. *Making Sense of Your World: A Biblical Worldview.* Sheffield Publishing, 2009.

276 https://anntatlock.com/truth-in-culture/biblical-worldview/ accessed on March 15, 2023.

277 Ibid., 8.

278 Ibid.

279 Luke 6:45

280 Merriam-Webster.com Dictionary, s.v. "incongruous," accessed June 1, 2021, https://www.merriam-webster.com/dictionary/incongruous.

281 https://www.focusonthefamily.com/faith/whats-a-christian-worldview/, accessed May 2, 2021.

282 Ibid.

283 Romans 12:2

[284] https://www.focusonthefamily.com/faith/whats-a-christian-worldview/, accessed May 2, 2021.

[285] Ibid.

[286] Ibid.

[287] Colossians 2:8, New Living Translation

[288] Ibid.

[289] https://www.barna.com/research/only-half-of-protestant-pastors-have-a-biblical-worldview/ accessed December 20, 2021.

[290] Kouzes, James M. and Barry Z. Posner. *The Leadership Challenge*. Fifth ed. US: Jossey-Bass, 2012.

[291] https://www.blueletterbible.org/lang/lexicon/lexicon.cfm?Strongs=G2590&t=ESV.

[292] Yukl, Gary A. *Leadership in Organizations*. 5th ed. Upper Saddle River, N.J: Prentice Hall, 2002.

[293] Northouse, Peter Guy. *Leadership: Theory and Practice*. 6th ed. Thousand Oaks: SAGE, 2013.

[294] Ibid.

[295] Yukl, Gary A. "Leadership in organizations," Eighth ed., Upper Saddle River. (2013).

[296] Raven, Bertram H. "The Bases of Power and the Power/Interaction Model of Interpersonal Influence." *Analyses of Social Issues and Public Policy* 8, no. 1 (2008): 1-22.

[297] Bell, Chris M. and Justin Hughes-Jones. "Power, Self-Regulation and the Moralization of Behavior." Journal of Business Ethics 83, no. 3 (2008): 503-514.

[298] Hinkin, Timothy R. and Chester A. Schriesheim. "Development and Application of New Scales to Measure the French and Raven (1959) Bases of Social Power." Journal of Applied Psychology 74, no. 4 (1989): 561-567.

[299] https://www.mindtools.com/pages/article/newLDR_56.htm accessed May 7, 2022.

[300] Yukl, Gary A. *Leadership in Organizations*. 5th ed. Upper Saddle River, N.J: Prentice Hall, 2002.

[301] Ibid.

[302] Hinkin, Timothy R. and Chester A. Schriesheim. "Development and Application of New Scales to Measure the French and Raven (1959) Bases of Social Power." *Journal of Applied Psychology* 74, no. 4 (1989): 561-567.

[303] Armstrong, Michael. Armstrong's Handbook of Management and Leadership for HR: Developing Effective People Skills for Better Leadership and Management. Fourth ed. GB: Kogan Page Ltd, 2016.

[304] Kouzes, James M. and Barry Z. Posner. *The Leadership Challenge*. Fifth ed. US: Jossey-Bass, 2012.

[305] Ibid.

[306] Armstrong, Michael. *Armstrong's Handbook of Management and Leadership for HR: Developing Effective People Skills for Better Leadership and Management*. Fourth ed. GB: Kogan Page Ltd, 2016.

[307] Velsor, Ellen Van, Cynthia D. McCauley, and Marian N. Ruderman. *The Center for Creative Leadership Handbook of Leadership Development*. 3. Aufl.; 3rd ed. US: Jossey-Bass, 2010.

[308] Northouse, Peter Guy. *Leadership: Theory and Practice*. 6th ed. Thousand Oaks: SAGE, 2013.

[309] https://hbr.org/2007/12/what-every-leader-needs-to-know-about-followers, accessed May 7, 2022.

[310] Bodden, Rickardo. *Leadership in the Age of Narcissism: God's Blueprint for Christian Leaders*. Carpenter's Son Publishing, 2020.

[311] https://www.charismamag.com/spirit/spiritual-warfare/40936-these-perverse-spirits-might-be-why-you-can-t-get-free-from-lust.

[312] https://www.collinsdictionary.com/us/dictionary/english/lust, accessed August 12, 2021.

[313] *Merriam-Webster.com Dictionary*, s.v. "lust," accessed August 12, 2021, https://www.merriam-webster.com/dictionary/lust.

[314] https://dictionary.cambridge.org/us/dictionary/english/lust, accessed August 12, 2021.

[315] Kellerman, Barbara, and Todd L. Pittinsky. *Leaders Who Lust: Power, Money, Sex, Success, Legitimacy, Legacy*. Cambridge University Press, 2020.

[316] Ibid., 2.

[317] Ibid.

[318] Ibid.

[319] Haroutunian, Joseph. *Lust for Power: A Study of the Misuse of Power*. Wipf and Stock Publishers, 2011.

[320] Ibid., 4.

[321] Kellerman, Barbara, and Todd L. Pittinsky. *Leaders Who Lust: Power, Money, Sex, Success, Legitimacy, Legacy*. Cambridge University Press, 2020.

[322] Ibid., 14.

[323] Ibid.

[324] https://www.wired.com/2010/08/the-psychology-of-power/, accessed August 16, 2021.

[325] Ibid.

[326] Ibid.

[327] Ibid.

[328] https://www.britannica.com/topic/Chinese-Communist-Party, accessed 8/16/21.

[329] Ibid.

[330] Ibid.

[331] https://www.wsj.com/articles/xi-jinping-deng-xiaoping-dictatorship-ant-di-di-economy-communist-party-beijing-authoritarian-11628885076, accessed August 16, 2021.

[332] Ibid.

333 Ibid.

334 https://www.bloomberg.com/opinion/articles/2021-04-24/for-an-all-power-ful-dictator-putin-is-surprising-vulnerable, accessed August 16, 2021.

335 Ibid.

336 Dangreau, Francois. "How a leader turns to dictator: Analysis of Kaddafi's life through leadership theories." (2012).

337 Ibid, 47.

338 Ibid.

339 Ferris, Gerald & Zinko, Robert & Brouer, Robyn & Buckley, M. & Harvey, Michael. (2007). "Strategic bullying as a supplementary, balanced perspective on destructive leadership." *The Leadership Quarterly*. 18, 195-206. 10.1016/j.leaqua.2007.03.004.

340 Ibid.

341 Citation is Riggio, Ronald E., Ira Chaleff, and Jean Lipman-Blumen, eds. *The Art of Followership: How Great Followers Create Great Leaders and Organizations*, Vol. 146. John Wiley & Sons, 2008.

342 Ibid., 233.

343 Ibid., 224.

344 Hartman, Karen L. "Intertextuality and apologia: Rhetorical efficacy through shared values as illustrated through the firing of coach Bobby Knight." *Speaker & Gavel* 45, no. 1 (2008): 4.

345 Ibid.

346 Ferris, Gerald & Zinko, Robert & Brouer, Robyn & Buckley, M. & Harvey, Michael. (2007). "Strategic bullying as a supplementary, balanced perspective on destructive leadership." *The Leadership Quarterly*, 18. 195-206. 10.1016/j.leaqua.2007.03.004.

347 Kellerman, Barbara, and Todd L. Pittinsky. *Leaders Who Lust: Power, Money, Sex, Success, Legitimacy, Legacy*. Cambridge University Press, 2020.

[348] Seuntjens, Terri G., Marcel Zeelenberg, Seger M. Breugelmans, and Niels Van de Ven. "Defining greed." *British Journal of Psychology* 106, no. 3 (2015): 505-525.

[349] Kellerman, Barbara, and Todd L. Pittinsky. *Leaders Who Lust: Power, Money, Sex, Success, Legitimacy, Legacy.* Cambridge University Press, 2020.

[350] https://www.theatlantic.com/magazine/archive/1915/09/war-and-the-wealth-of-nations/555902/.

[351] Ibid.

[352] Ibid.

[353] https://www.forbes.com/sites/meghanbiro/2012/09/30/are-you-a-character-based-Leader/?sh=becce6519af3, accessed on April 27, 2022.

[354] 3 John 2

[355] Proverbs 4:23

[356] Kellerman, Barbara, and Todd L. Pittinsky. *Leaders Who Lust: Power, Money, Sex, Success, Legitimacy, Legacy.* Cambridge University Press, 2020.

[357] https://irle.berkeley.edu/what-really-caused-the-great-recession/, accessed August 20, 2021.

[358] Ibid.

[359] Ibid.

[360] Ibid.

[361] https://www.businessinsider.com/what-caused-the-great-recession.

[362] Kellerman, Barbara, and Todd L. Pittinsky. *Leaders Who Lust: Power, Money, Sex, Success, Legitimacy, Legacy.* Cambridge University Press, 2020.

[363] Ephesians 5:3-6

[364] https://www.nytimes.com/2020/02/24/nyregion/harvey-weinstein-verdict.html, accessedAugust 28, 2021.

[365] Ibid.

366 https://www.washingtonpost.com/arts-entertainment/2021/07/21/harvey-weinstein-los-angeles-sexual-assault-case/, accessed August 28, 2021.

367 https://www.cnn.com/2023/02/23/entertainment/harvey-weinstein-sentencing-los-angeles/index.html accessed March 28, 2023.

368 https://www.nytimes.com/2023/02/23/us/harvey-weinstein-sentence-los-angeles.html accessed March 28, 2023.

369 Ibid.

370 Ibid., 82.

371 Ibid.

372 Kellerman, Barbara, and Todd L. Pittinsky. *Leaders Who Lust: Power, Money, Sex, Success, Legitimacy, Legacy.* Cambridge University Press, 2020.

373 https://www.apa.org/topics/substance-use-abuse-addiction, accessed August 31, 2021.

374 https://www.medicalnewstoday.com/articles/porn-addiction#signs, accessed 31, 2021.

375 Ibid.

376 https://www.therecoveryvillage.com/process-addiction/porn-addiction/pornography-statistics/; https://www.prnewswire.com/news-releases/top-five-warning-signs-of-internet-pornography-addiction-280653822.html; https://www.mayoclinichealthsystem.org/hometown-health/speaking-of-health/does-society-have-a-sex-addiction-problem accessed April 8, 2023.

377 *Merriam-Webster.com Dictionary*, s.v. "pornography," accessed August 31, 2021, https://www.merriam-webster.com/dictionary/pornography.

378 https://www.medicalnewstoday.com/articles/porn-addiction#signs, accessed 31, 2021.

379 Ibid.

380 https://www.britannica.com/biography/Silvio-Berlusconi, accessed September 2, 2021.

381 https://www.forbes.com/profile/silvio-berlusconi/?sh=13fbdc113e8f, accessed September 2, 2021.

[382] Ibid.

[383] Ibid.

[384] https://www.britannica.com/biography/Silvio-Berlusconi, accessed September 2, 2021.

[385] Ibid.

[386] Ibid.

[387] Cosentino, Gabriele, and Waddick Doyle. *Silvio Berlusconi, One Man Brand.* na, 2010.

[388] Ibid., 233.

[389] Kellerman, Barbara, and Todd L. Pittinsky. *Leaders Who Lust: Power, Money, Sex, Success, Legitimacy, Legacy.* Cambridge University Press, 2020, p. 100.

[390] Ibid.

[391] Cosentino, Gabriele, and Waddick Doyle. *Silvio Berlusconi, One Man Brand.* na, 2010, p. 235.

[392] Ibid.

[393] Ibid., 237.

[394] https://www.forbes.com/sites/chasewithorn/2022/06/02/lebron-james-is-officially-a-billionaire/?sh=18994831453e, accessed on July 15, 2022.

[395] Ibid.

[396] https://www.nba.com/player/2544/lebron_james.

[397] http://www.espn.com/nba/history/leaders; https://www.nba.com/stats/alltime-leaders; https://www.nbcsports.com/bayarea/warriors/here-are-top-35-nba-scoring-leaders-all-time accessed March 13, 2023.

[398] https://www.magzter.com/stories/Lifestyle/SilverKris-magazine/Whatever-Success-I-Have-Had-Is-Never-Enough-I-Always-Want-More.

[399] Kellerman, Barbara, and Todd L. Pittinsky. *Leaders Who Lust: Power, Money, Sex, Success, Legitimacy, Legacy.* Cambridge University Press, 2020, p 173.

[400] Ibid., 140.

[401] https://archive.boston.com/globe/spotlight/abuse/archives/081392_porter.htm, accessed on May 14, 2022.

[402] Ibid.

[403] https://www.bishop-accountability.org/news2013/05_06/Porter-Timelinepdf, accessed on May 14, 2022.

[404] Shupe, Anson D., William A. Stacey, and Susan E. Darnell, eds. *Bad Pastors: Clergy Misconduct in Modern America*. NYU press, 2000.

[405] Ibid.

[406] Ibid., 2.

[407] Ibid.

[408] https://archive.boston.com/globe/spotlight/abuse/archives/120793_porter.htm, accessed on May 14, 2022.

[409] https://www.themuse.com/advice/the-worst-boss-i-ever-had-11-true-stories-thatll-make-you-Cringe, accessed on May 15, 2022.

[410] https://www.businessinsider.com/worlds-worst-bosses-2011-7#george-pullman-a-railroad-baron-people-are-pets-7, accessed on May 15, 2022.

[411] https://www.businessinsider.com/worlds-worst-bosses-2011-7#alex-campbell-ran-a-day-and-night-spa-branded-employees-with-mandatory-tattoos-10, accessed on May 15, 2022.

[412] https://nypost.com/2014/11/28/the-8-worst-bosses-of-all-time/, accessed on May 15, 2022.

[413] Ibid.

[414] Ibid.

[415] Ibid.

[416] https://www.merriam-webster.com/thesaurus/routinely accessed on January 19, 2023.

[417] Carsten, Melissa K., Mary Uhl-Bien, Bradley J. West, Jaime L. Patera, and Rob McGregor. "Exploring social constructions of followership: A qualitative study." *The Leadership Quarterly* 21, no. 3 (2010): 543-562.

[418] Ibid., 543.

[419] Kelley, Robert E. *In Praise of Followers*. Harvard Business Review Case Services, 1988.

[420] https://iveybusinessjournal.com/publication/followership-the-other-side-of-leadership/, accessed December 23, 2021.

[421] Ibid.

[422] Bjugstad, Kent, Elizabeth C. Thach, Karen J. Thompson, and Alan Morris. "A fresh look at followership: A model for matching followership and leadership styles." *Journal of Behavioral and Applied Management* 7, no. 3 (2006): 304-319.

[423] Kellerman, Barbara. *Followership: How Followers Are Creating Change and Changing Leaders*. Boston, MA: Harvard School Press, 2008.

[424] Kelley, Robert E. *In Praise of Followers*. Harvard Business Review Case Services, 1988.

[425] Ibid.

[426] Ibid.

[427] https://iveybusinessjournal.com/publication/followership-the-other-side-of-leadership/ accessed December 23, 2021.

[428] Kelley, Robert E. *In Praise of Followers*. Harvard Business Review Case Services, 1988.

[429] https://iveybusinessjournal.com/publication/followership-the-other-side-of-leadership/ accessed December 23, 2021. 307.

[430] https://www.researchgate.net/publication/252457195_A_Fresh_Look_at_Followership_A_Model_for_Matching_Followership_and_Leadership_Styles accessed October 20, 2022.

[431] Kelley, Robert E. *In Praise of Followers*. Harvard Business Review Case Services, 1988.

[432] Ibid.

[433] Ibid.

[434] Ibid.

[435] https://www.britannica.com/event/Watergate-Scandal accessed September 7, 2021.

[436] Ibid.

[437] https://www.history.com/topics/1970s/watergate accessed September 7, 2021.

[438] Ibid.

[439] Ibid.

[440] Ibid.

[441] Ibid.

[442] https://www.washingtonpost.com/wp-srv/politics/special/watergate/time-line.html. Accessed September 7, 2021.

[443] Scott, David Hunter, and Alistair Gray. "Applied Followership for Sustainable Competitive Advantage."

[444] Kellerman, Barbara. *Followership: How Followers Are Creating Change and Changing Leaders.* Boston, MA: Harvard School Press, 2008.

[445] https://www.npr.org/2020/12/15/945031391/poll-despite-record-turnout-80-million-americans-didnt-vote-heres-why accessed December 24, 2021.

[446] Ibid.

[447] Ibid.

[448] https://www.dictionary.com/browse/anti-semitism accessed December 24, 2021.

[449] https://www.reuters.com/article/factcheck-edmund-burke-quote/fact-check-edmund-burke-did- not-say-evil-triumphs-when-good-men-do-noth-ing-idUSL1N2PG accessed December 24, 2021.

[450] Kellerman, Barbara. *Followership: How Followers Are Creating Change and Changing Leaders.* Boston, MA: Harvard School Press, 2008.

[451] https://pmworldlibrary.net/wp-content/uploads/2014/02/pm-wj19-feb2014-suda-in-praise-of-followers-SecondEdition.pdf accessed December 24, 2021.

[452]https://www.ncbi.nlm.nih.gov/pmc/articles/PMC526313/#:~:text=Merck%20%26%20Co.,com pared%20with%20patients%20receiving%20placebo, accessed December 25, 2021.

[453] http://votf.org/node/1182 accessed December 25, 2021.

[454] Ibid.

[455] Ibid.

[456] https://pmworldlibrary.net/wp-content/uploads/2014/02/pm-wj19-feb2014-suda-in-praise-of-followers-SecondEdition.pdf accessed December 25, 2021.

[457] https://www.britannica.com/biography/Martin-Luther-King-Jr accessed December 25, 2021.

[458] Ibid.

[459] Ibid.

[460] https://kinginstitute.stanford.edu/encyclopedia accessed December 26, 2021.

[461] https://www.cmohs.org/medal accessed December 26, 2021.

[462] https://www.cmohs.org/recipients/john-a-chapman accessed December 26, 2021.

[463] Kellerman, Barbara. *Followership: How Followers Are Creating Change and Changing Leaders*. Boston, MA: Harvard School Press, 2008.

[464] Ibid.

[465] Kilburn, Brandon R. "Who Are We Leading? Identifying Effective Followers: A Review of Typologies." https://www.jwpress.com/Journals/IJABW/BackIssues/IJABW-Spring- 2010.pdf#page=16 accessed December 26, 2021.

[466] Oyetunji, Christianah O., "The Relationship between Followership Style and Job Performance in Botswana Private Universities." Published by Canadian Center of Science and Education. https://files.eric.ed.gov/fulltext/EJ1067183.pdf Accessed December 26, 2021.

[467] Ibid.

[468] Ibid.

[469] Ibid.

[470] Ibid.

[471] Ibid.

[472] Ibid.

[473] Ibid.

[474] https://hbr.org/1988/11/in-praise-of-followers accessed October 17, 2022.

[475] Kellerman, Barbara. Followership: *How Followers Are Creating Change and Changing Leaders*. Boston, MA: Harvard School Press, 2008.

[476] Zawawi, Azlyn; Kamarunzaman, Nur; Hussin, Zaliha; Campbell, J. "The Power of Followership: Leaders, Who Are You Leading?" 2012 IEEE Symposium on Humanities, Science and Engineering Research. https://www.academia.edu/26400463/The_power_of_followership_Leaders_who_are_you_leading.

[477] Oyetunji, Christianah O., "The Relationship between Followership Style and Job Performance in Botswana Private Universities." Published by Canadian Center of Science and Education. https://files.eric.ed.gov/fulltext/EJ1067183.pdf Accessed December 26, 2021.

[478] Ibid.

[479] Ibid.

[480] Ibid.

[481] Ibid.

[482] Ibid.

[483] Ibid.

[484] Zawawi, Azlyn; Kamarunzaman, Nur; Hussin, Zaliha; Campbell, J. "The Power of Followership: Leaders, Who Are You Leading?" 2012 IEEE Symposium on Humanities, Science and Engineering Research. https://www.academia.edu/26400463/The_power_of_followership_Leaders_who_are_you_leading.

[485] Oyetunji, Christianah O. "The Relationship between Followership Style and Job Performance in Botswana Private Universities." Published by Canadian Center of Science and Education. https://files.eric.ed.gov/fulltext/EJ1067183.pdf Accessed December 26, 2021.

[486] Ibid.

[487] Ibid.

[488] Ibid.

[489] Ibid.

[490] Ibid.

[491] Ibid.

[492] Ibid.

[493] Zawawi, Azlyn; Kamarunzaman, Nur; Hussin, Zaliha; Campbell, J. "The Power of Followership: Leaders, Who Are You Leading?" 2012 IEEE Symposium on Humanities, Science and Engineering Research. https://www.academia.edu/26400463/The_power_of_followership_Leaders_who_are_you_leading.

[494] Ibid.

[495] https://osipt.com/blog/wordpress/wp-content/uploads/2014/10/Curphy-Roelling-Followership.pdf accessed December 28, 2021.

[496] Ibid.

[497] Ibid.

[498] Ibid.

[499] Ibid.

[500] https://osipt.com/blog/wordpress/wp-content/uploads/2014/10/Curphy-Roelling-Followership.pdf accessed December 28, 2021.

[501] Ibid.

[502] https://writingexplained.org/idiom-dictionary/brown-noser accessed December 12, 2022.

[503] Ibid.

[504] Kellerman, Barbara. *Bad Leadership: What It Is, How It Happens, Why It Matters*. Harvard Business Press, 2004.

[505] Kellerman, Barbara. *Followership: How Followers Are Creating Change and Changing Leaders*. Boston, MA: Harvard School Press, 2008.

[506] Ibid., 230.

[507] Chaleff, Ira. *The Courageous Follower: Standing Up to and for Our Leaders*. Berrett-Koehler Publishers, 2009.

[508] Scott, David, Applied Followership for Sustainable Competitive Advantage. Dissertation, 2019.

[509] Scott, David, Applied Followership for Sustainable Competitive Advantage. Dissertation, 2019.

[510] Col. Phillip S. Meilinger, "The Ten Rules of Good Followership" (PDF).

[511] https://pmworldlibrary.net/wp-content/uploads/2014/02/pm-wj19-feb2014-suda-in-praise-of-followers-SecondEdition.pdf accessed December 24, 2021.

[512] Ibid.

[513] Ibid.

[514] Ibid.

[515] Ibid.

[516] Ibid.

[517] Ibid.

[518] Ibid.

[519] Ibid.

[520] https://www.verywellmind.com/what-is-toxic-masculinity-5075107 accessed January 10, 2022.

[521] Ibid.

522 https://www.shrm.org/hr-today/news/all-things-work/pages/how-toxic-masculinity-is-ruining-your-workplace-culture.aspx accessed May 3, 2022.

523 Ibid.

524 https://hbr.org/2018/11/how-masculinity-contests-undermine-organizations-and-what-to-do-about-it accessed January 10, 2022.

525 "Speaking of Psychology: How masculinity can hurt mental health" (Podcast) https://www.apa.org/news/podcasts/speaking-of-psychology/men-boys-health-disparities, accessed January 10, 2022.

526 Why I'm just trying to be "man enough." Justin Baldoni. Ted Talk https://www.youtube.com/watch?v=Cetg4gu0oQQ.

527 "Speaking of Psychology: How masculinity can hurt mental health" (Podcast) https://www.apa.org/news/podcasts/speaking-of-psychology/men-boys-health-disparities accessed January 10, 2022.

528 Ibid.

529 Why I'm just trying to be "man enough." Justin Baldoni. Ted Talk https://www.youtube.com/watch?v=Cetg4gu0oQQ.

530 Ibid.

531 Genesis 2:18

532 https://www.inc.com/matthew-jones/20-brutal-truths-no-one-wants-to-admit-about-themselves.html accessed January 12, 2022.

533 Why I'm just trying to be "man enough." Justin Baldoni. Ted Talk https://www.youtube.com/watch?v=Cetg4gu0oQQ.

534 Ibid.

535 Ibid.

536 Ibid.

537 https://www.britannica.com/event/American-civil-rights-movement accessed January 12, 2022.

[538] Chamberlain, Andrew. "Demystifying the Gender Pay Gap: Evidence from Glassdoor salary Data" (pdf) March 2016. https://www.classlawgroup.com/wp-content/uploads/2016/11/glassdoor-gender-pay-gap-study.pdf.

[539] Ibid.

[540] https://www.pewresearch.org/fact-tank/2021/05/25/gender-pay-gap-facts/ accessed January 13, 2022.

[541] Ibid.

[542] Ibid.

[543] https://www.weforum.org/press/2021/03/pandemic-pushes-back-gender-parity-by-a-generation-report-finds accessed January 12, 2022.

[544] Ibid.

[545] https://www.payscale.com/research-and-insights/gender-pay-gap/ accessed January 13, 2022.

[546] Ibid.

[547] Ibid.

[548] Ibid.

[549] https://www.aauw.org/issues/equity/motherhood/ accessed January 13, 2022; Correll, Shelley J., Stephen Benard, and In Paik. "Getting a Job: Is There a Motherhood Penalty? 1." *American Journal of Sociology* 112, no. 5 (2007): 1297-1339.

[550] https://hbr.org/2018/10/how-men-get-penalized-for-straying-from-masculine-norms accessed January 14, 2022.

[551] Ibid.

[552] Genesis 2:18

[553] https://hbr.org/2018/10/how-men-get-penalized-for-straying-from-masculine-norms accessed January 14, 2022.

[554] Ibid.

555 Merriam-Webster.com Dictionary, s.v. "empathy," accessed January 13, 2022, https://www.merriam-webster.com/dictionary/empathy.

556 https://hbr.org/2018/10/how-men-get-penalized-for-straying-from-masculine-norms accessed January 14, 2022.

557 Ibid.

558 Ibid.

559 Giles, Doug. *If Masculinity Is Toxic, Call Jesus Radioactive*. White Feather Press, 2020.

560 Wilson, Jason. *Battle Cry*. Nelson Books. 2021.

561 Ibid., 5.

562 https://www.dictionary.com/browse/trauma accessed January 31, 2022.

563 Wilson, Jason. *Battle Cry*. Nelson Books. 2021.

564 Ibid., 7.

565 Read the books of Genesis and Song of Solomon.

566 Merriam-Webster.com Dictionary, s.v. "equal opportunity employer," accessed May 4, 2022, https://www.merriam-webster.com/dictionary/equal%20opportunity%20employer.

567 https://kids.frontiersin.org/articles/10.3389/frym.2018.00015#:~:text=The%20patterns%20of%20Emotion%20that,%2C%20joy%2C%20nostalgia%2C%20relief%2C accesses February 2, 2022.

568 Wilson, Jason. *Battle Cry*. Nelson Books, 2021, 19.

569 Ibid., 23.

570 Ibid.

571 Farrar, Steve. King Me: What Every Son Wants and Needs From His Father. Moody Publishers, 2006.

572 Job 1:5; Joshua 24:15; 1 Timothy 5:8; Ephesians 5:28; https://www.collinsdictionary.com/us/dictionary/english-thesaurus/nurture accessed on February 5, 2022.

[573] https://www.psychologytoday.com/us/blog/sex-sexuality-and-romance/201908/toxic-femininity accessed January 15, 2022.

[574] Ibid.

[575] https://www.forbes.com/sites/drnancydoyle/2021/07/13/we-need-to-talk-about-toxic-femininity-at-work/?sh=5e03ec2c2769 accessed February 19, 2022.

[576] Ibid.

[577] Ibid.

[578] Patten, Tim. "Heroism and Gender." *New Male Studies* 6, no. 1 (2017).

[579] Gress, Carrie. *The Anti-Mary Exposed: Rescuing the Culture from Toxic Femininity*. TAN Books, 2019.

[580] Ibid., 10.

[581] Tooley, James. *The Miseducation of Women*. Rowman & Littlefield, 2003.

[582] Gress, Carrie. *The Anti-Mary Exposed: Rescuing the Culture from Toxic Femininity*. TAN Books, 2019, p. 13.

[583] The book of Genesis

[584] https://www.livehope.org/article/a-real-woman-defining-biblical-femininity/ accessed on February 10, 2022.

[585] Ibid.

[586] Ibid.

[587] https://www.britannica.com/science/human-reproductive-system/The-uterus accessed February 18, 2022.

[588] https://www.livehope.org/article/a-real-woman-defining-biblical-femininity/ accessed on February 10, 2022; Genesis 2:18-25.

[589] Malachi 3:2, 3

[590] Romans 9:19-21; Isaiah 64:8

[591] Deuteronomy 30:19, 20

[592] https://www.inc.com/dustin-mckissen/harvard-mbas-keep-going-to-prison-so-why-do-they-still-rule-the-world-.html accessed December 22, 2021.

[593] https://www.jumpstartmag.com/harvard-entrepreneurs-that-failed-spectacularly/.

[594] Ibid.

[595] https://www.nia.nih.gov/health/vitamins-and-minerals-older-adults, accessed June 18, 2021.

[596] Ibid.

[597] https://health.clevelandclinic.org/should-you-take-vitamins-for-eye-health/. Accessed June 18, 2021.

[598] Hamon, Bill. *Prophets, Pitfalls, and Principles: God's Prophetic People Today.* Vol. 3. Destiny Image Publishers, 1991.

[599] https://christianinternational.com/bill-hamons-story.

[600] Hamon, Bill. *Prophets, Pitfalls, and Principles: God's Prophetic People Today.* Vol. 3. Destiny Image Publishers, 1991.

[601] Romans 8:29

[602] James 1:5

[603] https://www.blueletterbible.org/lexicon/g4103/esv/mgnt/0-1/. Accessed 6/22/21.

[604] Hamon, Bill. *Prophets, Pitfalls, and Principles: God's Prophetic People Today.* Vol. 3. Destiny Image Publishers, 1991: 85.

[605] Titus 3:2

[606] 1 Timothy 6:10

[607] Luke 16:11

[608] https://www.christianity.com/wiki/christian-terms/what-is-greed-definition-and-bible-verses-about-greed.html.

[609] Colossians 3:5

[610] Colossians 3:8

611 1 Corinthians 13:2

612 1 Corinthians 13:4, 5

613 1 Corinthians 13:4

614 Barnett, Jeffrey E., and Natalie Cooper. "Creating a culture of self-care." American Psychological Association (2009): 16.

615 Bressi, Sara K., and Elizabeth R. Vaden. "Reconsidering self care." *Clinical Social Work Journal* 45, no. 1 (2017): 33-38.

616 https://www.thegospelcoalition.org/article/self-care-soul-care/ accessed November 15, 2022. https://renovare.org/articles/selfish-care-vs-soul-care accessed November 15, 2022.

617 https://renovare.org/articles/selfish-care-vs-soul-care accessed November 15, 2022.

618 https://prayer.asburyseminary.edu/what-is-soul-care/ accessed November 15, 2022.

619 https://www.christianitytoday.com/better-samaritan/2021/march/from-self-care-to-soul-care.html accessed November 15, 2022.

620 1 Kings 19; Deuteronomy 4:9, 6:5, 26:16; Psalm 19:7, 23:3, 35:9, 42:5-6, 127:2; Proverbs 4:23; Ephesians 5:18, 29; 1 Peter 2:24-25; Romans 12:2

621 https://renovare.org/articles/selfish-care-vs-soul-care accessed November 15, 2022.

622 https://www.mayoclinic.org/healthy-lifestyle/stress-management/in-depth/stress-symptoms/art-20050987 accessed March 25, 2022.

623 Ibid.

624 Ibid.

625 1 Thessalonians 5:23; James 2:26; Hebrews 4:12

626 https://www.apa.org/gradpsych/2011/03/matters accessed on February 22, 2022.

627 Barnett, Jeffrey E., and Natalie Cooper. "Creating a culture of self-care." American Psychological Association (2009): 17.

[628] Trimm, Cindy. *The Prosperous Soul: Your Journey to a Richer Life*. Destiny Image Publishers, 2015.

[629] https://www.forbes.com/sites/forbescoachescouncil/2021/06/28/why-multidimensional-self-care-is-essential-to-better-leadership/?sh=483bae835d56 accessed on March 28, 2022.

[630] Ibid.

[631] https://www.inc.com/larry-alton/are-you-on-verge-of-burning-out-7-warning-signs-to-look-for-and-how-to-cope.html accessed on March 28, 2022.

[632] https://www.helpguide.org/articles/stress/burnout-prevention-and-recovery.htm accessed on March 29, 2022.

[633] Ibid.

[634] Ibid.

[635] https://inside.ewu.edu/calelearning/psychological-skills/preventing-burnout/.

[636] Ibid.

[637] https://www.psychiatrictimes.com/view/burnout-strategies-prevent-and-overcome-commonand-dangerousproblem accessed March 29, 2022.

[638] https://www.inc.com/larry-alton/are-you-on-verge-of-burning-out-7-warning-signs-to-look-for-and-how-to-cope.html accessed on March 29, 2022.

[639] https://inside.ewu.edu/calelearning/psychological-skills/preventing-burnout/.

[640] https://www.inc.com/larry-alton/are-you-on-verge-of-burning-out-7-warning-signs-to-look-for-and-how-to-cope.html accessed on March 28, 2022.

[641] Mark 6:31

[642] https://www.christianity.com/jesus/following-jesus/repentance-faith-and-salvation/what-does-it-mean-to-repent.html accessed April, 6, 2022.

[643] Ibid.

644 https://mentalhealthmatch.com/articles/about-therapy-and-mental-health/what-is-the-difference-between-therapy-and-counseling#:~:text=Usually%2C%20counseling%20focuses%20on%20a,do%20the%20things%20you%20do accessed April 10, 2022.

645 Ibid.

646 Ibid.

647 healthline.com/health/counselor-vs-therapist#differences accessed on April 11, 2022.

648 https://www.verywellmind.com/counselor-or-psychotherapist-1067401 accessed on April 11, 2022.

649 https://www.healthline.com/health/mental-health/reasons-for-therapy-#There-are-lots-of-reasons-to-start-therapy,-and-all-of-them-are-equally-valid accessed April 10, 2022.

650 Ibid.

651 https://www.healthline.com/health/counselor-vs-therapist accessed on April 11, 2022.

652 https://www.verywellmind.com/how-to-know-when-it-s-time-to-see-a-therapist-5077040 accessed April 10, 2022.

653 https://www.forbes.com/sites/nomanazish/2019/09/20/10-sure-signs-you-need-to-see-a-therapist-and-how-to-find-the-right-one/?sh=366c6a1d501b accessed April 10, 2022.

654 https://www.healthline.com/health/mental-health/reasons-for-therapy-#Therapy-can-be-especially-beneficial-right-now accessed on April 11, 2022.

655 Ibid.

656 https://www.psychologytoday.com/us/blog/i-hear-you/201710/10-reasons-why-people-refuse-talk-therapists.

657 https://www.linkedin.com/pulse/why-people-dont-go-therapy-reasons-should-steven-j-hanley.

658 Ibid.

659 Ibid.

[660] https://www.menshealth.com/health/a27496158/ excuses-guys-make-not-going-to-therapy/.

[661] Kellerman, Barbara. *Bad Leadership: What It Is, How It Happens, Why It Matters*. Harvard Business Press, 2004, 232.

[662] Ibid.

[663] Ibid.

[664] Ibid., 233-235.

[665] https://hbr.org/2009/06/a-culture-of-candor accessed on April 25, 2022.

[666] Ibid.

[667] https://www.gty.org/library/questions/QA209/what-is-pragmatism-why-is-it-bad accessed on May 15, 2022.

[668] Ibid.

[669] Ibid.

[670] https://www.evidenceunseen.com/articles/truth/the-perils-of-pragmatism/ accessed May 15, 2022.

[671] https://www.gty.org/library/questions/QA209/what-is-pragmatism-why-is-it-bad accessed on May 15, 2022.

[672] Ibid.

[673] https://www.christianitytoday.com/pastors/2007/october-online-only/willow-creek-repents.html accessed on May 16, 2022.

[674] Ibid.

[675] Ibid.

[676] Ibid.

[677] Ibid.

[678] Ibid.

[679] https://www.smallgroups.com/articles/2012/danger-of-pragmatism.html accessed on May 16, 2022.

[680] Ibid.

[681] Ibid.

[682] https://www.cbs.com/shows/undercover_boss/ accessed March 30, 2022.

[683] Ibid.

[684] https://hbr.org/2022/02/empathy-rules Accessed on March 31, 2022.

[685] Ibid.

[686] Ibid.

[687] Ibid.

[688] Luke 22:24-27, John 13:4-15, 1 Peter 5:5-6

[689] Dungan, James, Adam Waytz, and Liane Young. "The psychology of whistleblowing." *Current Opinion in Psychology* 6 (2015): 129-133.

[690] Dasgupta, Siddhartha, and Ankit Kesharwani. "Whistleblowing: A survey of literature." *The IUP Journal of Corporate Governance* 9, no. 4 (2010): 57-7.

[691] Ibid.

[692] Ibid.

[693] Ibid.

[694] Keith, Kent M. *Servant Leadership in the Boardroom: Fulfilling the Public Trust*. Greenleaf Center for Servant Leadership, 2011, p. 18.

[695] Ibid.

[696] https://hbr.org/2022/04/leaders-stop-rewarding-toxic-rock-stars?ab=hero-main-text accessed April 21, 2022.

[697] Ibid.

[698] Ibid.

[699] Ibid.

[700] Ibid.

[701] https://hbr.org/2022/04/leaders-stop-rewarding-toxic-rock-stars#:~:text=-Most%20of%20us%20have%20known,harmful%20to%20women%20of%20color accessed on April 23, 2022.

[702] Ibid.

[703] https://www.forbes.com/sites/forbescoachescouncil/2021/03/03/14-mistakes-leaders-make-that-set-a-bad-example-for-team-members/?sh=7fa3b-99c791b accessed April 23, 2022.

[704] Ibid.

[705] https://www.forbes.com/sites/heidilynnekurter/2019/12/23/4-strategies-to-repair-a-toxic-culture-from-the-top-down/?sh=50cf03b540e0 accessed April 23, 2022.

[706] Ibid.

[707] Ibid.

[708] https://hbr.org/2022/04/leaders-stop-rewarding-toxic-rock-stars#:~:text=-Most%20of%20us%20have%20known,harmful%20to%20women%20of%20color accessed on April 23, 2022.

[709] 2 Chronicles 7:14; Jeremiah 33:3; James 5:13; Matthew 26:41; Psalm 17:6; Psalm 145:18; Proverbs 15:29; Matthew 6:9-13

[710] Haroutunian, Joseph. *Lust for Power: A Study of the Misuse of Power*. Wipf and Stock Publishers, 2011.

[711] 1 Corinthians 10:6-11

NOTES

NOTES

NOTES